Palgrave Studies in Accounting and Finance Practice

Series Editors

Vassili Joannidès de Lautour, GDF, Grenoble École de Management, Le Blanc, France

Danture Wickramasinghe, Adam Smith Business School, University of Glasgow, Glasgow, UK

Aude Deville, IAE de Nice, Université Côte d'Azur, Antibes, France

More information about this series at
https://link.springer.com/bookseries/16220

Ed Danter

Audit Defense

A Management Audit Readiness Guide

palgrave
macmillan

Ed Danter
Kean University
Leonia, NJ, USA

ISSN 2524-8251 ISSN 2524-826X (electronic)
Palgrave Studies in Accounting and Finance Practice
ISBN 978-3-030-92465-2 ISBN 978-3-030-92466-9 (eBook)
https://doi.org/10.1007/978-3-030-92466-9

This Palgrave Macmillan imprint is published by the registered company Springer Nature Switzerland AG
The registered company address is: Gewerbestrasse 11, 6330 Cham, Switzerland

Preface

I realized after spending nearly 45 years in corporate America and another 8 years teaching auditing at a local university that there was something missing and it was bothering me. I was troubled by an enigma that was puzzling and which I strongly believed needed to be addressed.

Let me use a metaphor to address my concern. Most of us are aware that there are sports teams (e.g. football) that have both offensive and defensive players and these teams will very likely have different coaches. The teams consist of athletes who specialize in either offensive or defensive tasks and different instruction is needed, dependent on their roles. There are some players, who play both positions, but that is not the general rule. My point is that the teams primarily have two different groups, each with their own coach and each instructed by their coaches on how best to play their positions to the best of their abilities. The reason for this focus on specialization is that both sides contribute their knowledge and skill toward achieving a winning team. It is the synergy of the two groups exercising their responsibilities to the highest level that enables them to be on the right track for victory. They both contribute, having been trained differently, but it is still one team. The same can be said of Corporate America when we examine the roles of internal auditors and audited personnel, frequently referred to as audit clients.

I believe, after having spent the majority of my professional career in audit-related functions either as an auditor or audit client and having taught audit classes, that audit education and preparation are slanted and mostly one sided. Internal audit (IA) personnel are schooled and educated either with formal classes or with on the job training. New auditors joining an IA department are frequently assigned to work with more experienced auditors, or lead auditors, for seasoning. This practice allows them to expand their learning of the audit process until they are ready, comfortable, knowledgeable, and able to assume the role of lead auditor. This is what I experienced when I became an internal auditor and what I observed as other newly assigned auditors were trained and prepared for their audit assignments.

Then, there is the other side—the education of audit clients. This group of managers and their staff will likely have their processes, procedures, and controls audited one day, if they haven't been audited already, especially if they are employed in a large corporation. When this occurs, they should have the knowledge and the confidence necessary to achieve successful audits.

However, I am skeptical since most of the managers being audited do not receive the same level of formal education as internal auditors—most clients are educated *during* and not *prior* to being audited. There is an expression that good judgment comes from experience and experience comes from bad judgment. Audit clients mostly learn as a result of being burnt and in many cases exercising bad judgment when being audited. Unfortunately, the flames are hot and they can quickly get out of control during an audit. The client, once subjected to an audit and faced with the consequences of a failed audit, will learn via trial and error. Sadly, the scars can be severe and may take a long time to heal, provided that they even will eventually heal.

Many managers not only suffer financial losses and promotional setbacks but some even lose their jobs because they are caught by surprise and are not ready for an audit—the preparation and education needed to be audit ready are lacking. The reason, too many times, is that there is not a level playing field. Internal auditors and audit clients are not equally groomed for success. And who suffers in the end? It is the company. Auditors and audit clients need to realize that they are on the same team and that as processes and controls are established, expanded and improved, it is the company that reaps the benefits.

The IA organization can and should identify issues, exposures, and risks. Their responsibility is to report concerns and make recommendations for remediation. This is what they are assigned to do and what they are compensated for. However, management and their staff being audited often posses a fear of the audit, feel intimidated by the auditors, and are scared. It can be detrimental to a company if the audit client, because he or she is afraid of failing an audit, hides or refrains from revealing necessary information. This additional information could even change the audit result and possibly question the reasonableness of suggestions made. Resources and time can be wasted in addressing audit report recommendations that are not necessarily cost justified or reasonable. Executive management can attempt to put corrective actions in place to mitigate or eliminate risks that in reality do not even exist. And of course, there is a possibility of other more significant issues that exist being ignored or overlooked.

It is unfortunate that auditors and audit client managers are frequently at odds with each other and are rivals even though they work for the same company. Both IA and management who are being audited should have similar objectives. They both should be striving to ensure the adequacy of procedures and controls and be able to attest to the fact that processing functions are working effectively. Both groups should be looking to increase profits and maintain the solvency of their company. They need to focus on eliminating or mitigating exposures that result in financial losses or potential fraudulent activities or that can be harmful or destructive to their company, in any way.

Their goals should focus on protecting the corporation and its executives from potential losses, whether intentional or unintentional, while validating that processes within the company are adequately measured, controlled, and their objectives effectively accomplished. Both the internal auditors and audit clients should strive to ensure that their company's stakeholders, stockholders, investors, and shareholders have a comfort level that the company is audit ready, from external as well as internal audits and that the entity is well controlled.

The corporation's IA staff and its audit clients are *on the same team*. The achievement of obtaining successful audits should be desirable by all. Unfortunately, to the detriment of many, management and their staffs fear internal auditors. And there is definitely a reason for this concern. A failed audit could result in financial reprisals, demotions, or being looked upon negatively by executive management, blocking future career advances.

IA has a job to find exposures and there is a natural proclivity by many auditors to garner evidence of existing or potential issues, but in so doing are intimidating and hostile toward audit clients. This is a dereliction of duty and limits their value to the enterprise that they serve. They can and should also strive to be true value add, which is needed. They should fulfill a consultant's role and establish meaningful recommendations for remediation and process improvement. An audit report should be a seminal work effort resulting in suggestions being proposed for improving controls, establishing more efficient processes, and minimizing risk.

Internal auditors have an extremely important role within a company—they are there for protection. They are the eyes and ears of executive management and the audit committee. On the other hand, audit clients are accountable for achieving and maintaining smooth and profitable operations that display well-controlled processes within their purview and it is essential that they be audit ready.

I am an advocate of a level playing field and I am aware of the gravitas of the situation when there is not a level playing field. Audit clients, as well as auditors, need to be educated in and knowledgeable of the audit process so they can protect the company. The IA department usually schools their audit staffs on how to conduct an audit and how to identify and report on issues and exposures. However, audit clients also need to be taught and need to be prepared on how to interface with auditors and need to make sure that the reports are beneficial and equitable and not unjustly cataclysmic. The auditor's job is to make executive management and the audit committee aware of process and control weaknesses, while audit clients need to ruminate thoughtfully on the outcome of the audits and make sure that they receive an audit report with issues that are valid and fairly reported. Audited management needs to validate that reports are not unjustly draconian and that the reports take into consideration management's challenges and risks.

It is one company with the two groups having responsibilities to corporate executives, audit committees, and stakeholders. There is a necessity that audit clients as well as IA be thoroughly educated so that management can be pro-active and prepare for audits to the extent where they, as well as the internal audit organization, can best serve the company.

Leonia, USA Ed Danter

Contents

1 Introduction: Objectives, Focus and Description of the Text 1

Part I Corporate Governance and the Audit Process

2 Responsibilities, Regulations, Control Frameworks 9
Responsibility of External Audit Firms 10
Enron 11
Adelphi 12
HealthSouth 13
ImClone 13
Tyco 14
WorldCom 14
Responsibilities of the PCAOB 16
Responsibilities of the Board of Directors (BOD) 16
Responsibilities of the Audit Committee 16
Responsibilities of Senior Management 18
Internal Auditor Responsibilities 18
Responsibilities of First Line Managers 21
COSO 23
COBIT 24
Summary 27
Guidance 28
Chapter 2 Exercises 28

Chapter 2 Questions 28
References 30

3 The Audit Beginning 31
Pre-Planning 32
Announcement Letter 33
Kickoff Meeting 35
Summary 37
Guidance 37
Chapter 3 Exercises 38
Chapter 3 Questions 39

4 Audit Fieldwork 43
Documentation Requests 44
The Interview 46
Fact Sheets 49
Status Meetings 51
Summary 52
Guidance 53
Chapter 4 Exercises 54
Chapter 4 Questions 54

5 Audit Conclusion 59
Audit Reports 59
Recommendation and Responses 61
Audit Report Sign-Off 63
Personal Experience 5.1 65
Summary 66
Guidance 67
Chapter 5 Exercises 68
Chapter 5 Questions 68

Part II Controls Overview

6 Types of Audits and Controls 73
Types of Audits 73
Control Importance 76
Control Benefits 79
Control Axioms 81
Control Principles 82

Preventive Controls 87
Deterrent Controls 88
Detective Controls 89
Reporting Controls 89
Corrective Controls 90
Recovery Controls 90
Summary 91
Guidance 92
Chapter 6 Exercises 92
Chapter 6 Questions 93
Reference 95

7 **Administration Controls** 97
Service Level Agreements 97
Table of Contents 103
SLA Introduction 103
Definitions and Abbreviations 103
Purpose 104
Contractual Parameters 104
Examples of Client Responsibilities 104
Examples of Service Provider Responsibilities 104
Service Level Priorities 105
KPIs and Metrics 105
Version Details and Document Change History 105
Document Approvals 106
Password Controls and User ID Administration 106
Request for Access 107
Password Guidelines 108
Summary 109
Guidance 111
Chapter 7 Exercises 111
Chapter 7 Questions 112
Reference 114

8 **Physical Controls** 115
Building Access 116
Personal Experience 8.1 117
Restricted Space Access 119

	Proprietary, Confidential, and Personal Information	123
	Personal Experience 8.2	125
	Summary	127
	Guidance	127
	Chapter 8 Exercises	128
	Chapter 8 Questions	128
	Reference	130
9	**System and Application Access Controls**	131
	System Access Controls	131
	Application Access	136
	System Security	139
	Summary	146
	Guidance	147
	Chapter 9 Exercise	148
	Chapter 9 Questions	148
	References	151
10	**Operational Controls**	153
	Change Management	154
	Library Control	156
	Code Migration	158
	Issues Management	162
	Business Recovery and Continuity	163
	Summary	165
	Guidelines	166
	Chapter 10 Exercises	167
	Chapter 10 Questions	168
	Reference	169
11	**Separation of Duties**	171
	Why Is SoD Important?	173
	What Is the Risk?	173
	Separation of Duties in IT	175
	IT Separation of Duties Matrix	181
	Accounting Separation of Duties	184
	Revenue	184
	Example I of Segregation of Duties Matrix for Revenue and Accounts Receivable	187

Example II—Segregation of Duties Matrix for Revenue and Accounts Receivable 188
Purchasing and Accounts Payable 188
Example I—Segregation of Duties Matrix for Purchasing and Accounts Payable 191
Example II—Segregation of Duties Matrix for Purchasing and Accounts Payable 192
Human Resources Separation of Duties 192
Payroll Separation of Duties Matrix 194
Inventory 195
Inventory Managment Separation of Duties 197
Financial Functions Separation of Duties 197
Personal Experience 11.1 200
Summary 201
Guidelines 202
Chapter 11 Exercises 203
Chapter 11 Questions 203
References 205

12 **Application Controls** 207
Application Controls 209
Project Management 210
Personal experience 12.1 212
Input/Output/Interface Controls 213
Editing and Auditing Data 215
Error Handling 215
Personal experience 12.2 216
Balancing/Database Reconciliation 217
Application Monitoring 219
Backup and Restart Procedures 222
Summary 223
Guidelines 224
Chapter 12 Exercises 225
Chapter 12 Questions 226

13 **Recent Challenges** 229
Spreadsheet Controls 229
Cloud Computing 233
Risks and Guidance 235
Outsourcing Controls 237

Health Insurance Portability and Accountability Act (HIPAA) 241
Summary 243
Guidelines 244
Chapter 13 Exercises 244
Chapter 13 Questions 245
Reference 246

Part III Pro-active Measures

14 Identification of Exposures and Issues 251
Processes, Procedures, and Control Documentation 252
Processes 254
Process Narratives 255
Process Flow Diagrams and Control Points 257
Narrative of Issues Management Flow Diagram with Control Points 258
Personal Experience 14.1 260
Procedures 260
Personal Experience 14.2 263
Self-Assessments 264
Peer Reviews 269
Previous Audits 270
Personal Experience 14.3 271
Summary 272
Guidelines 273
Chapter 14 Exercises 274
Chapter 14 Questions 275

15 Risk Management 279
Issues Management Process 281
Risk Assessment Process 283
Risk Assessment Owner 285
Risk Assessment Form 285
Risk Acceptance 288
Risk Revalidation 288
Summary 289

Guidelines 289
Chapter 15 Exercises 290
Chapter 15 Questions 291

16 Testing 293
Unit Testing 294
Integration Testing 295
Regression Testing 296
Systems Testing 296
User Acceptance Testing 296
Parallel Testing 296
Pilot Testing 297
Test Plans 297
Test Cases 298
Test Results 298
Summary 299
Guidelines 300
Chapter 16 Exercises 300
Chapter 16 Questions 301

Part IV Mock Audits

17 Preparation for Mock Audits 305
Auditor's Preparation (If You Are Assigned to This Role) 306
Audit Client's Preparation (If You Are Assigned to This Role) 306
Summary 307
Guidelines for the Mock Audit Preparation 308

18 Mock Audit Fieldwork 309
Writing Announcement Letters 309
Kickoff Meeting 314
Conducting Interviews 315
First A/R Interview 326
Second A/R Interview 328
First IT Billing System Interview 335
Second IT Billing System Interview 337

Writing Fact Sheets 338
Summary 340
Guidelines 341

19 Writing and Presenting Mock Audit Reports 343
Audit Report Format 344
Examples of Audit Reports 346
Presenting the Audit Report 350
The Auditor's Role 350
The Audit Client's Role 351
Summary 352
Guidelines 352

Conclusion 353

Index 355

List of Figures

Chart 2.1	Corporate governance overview	10
Fig. 3.1	Overview of the audit process	32
Fig. 7.1	Access request	107
Fig. 9.1	Mainframe system	133
Fig. 12.1	Balancing records between programs	218
Fig. 12.2	Balancing records bypassed	218
Fig. 12.3	Balancing records exploded	219
Fig. 12.4	Database reconciliation	219
Fig. 14.1	Processes, procedures, and control documentation	253
Fig. 14.2	Process issues management frequency: monthly	258
Fig. 14.3	Self-assessment	268

List of Tables

Table 4.1	An example of a request log	46
Table 7.1	Service Level Agreement Table of Contents	103
Table 7.2	Severity level priorities	105
Table 7.3	KPIs and metrics	105
Table 7.4	Document details and change history	106
Table 7.5	Document approvals	106

List of Exhibits

Exhibit 2.1	Corporate audit hierarchy	11
Exhibit 2.2	Enron scandal headline	12
Exhibit 2.3	HealthSouth scandal headline	13
Exhibit 2.4	Tyco scandal headline	14
Exhibit 2.5	WorldCom scandal headline	15
Exhibit 11.1	IT SoD Matrix	181
Exhibit 11.2	First Revenue and A/R SoD Matrix	187
Exhibit 11.3	Second Revenue and A/R SoD Matrix	188
Exhibit 11.4	First Purchasing and A/P SoD Matrix	191
Exhibit 11.5	Second Purchasing and A/P SoD Matrix	192
Exhibit 11.6	Payroll SoD Matrix	194
Exhibit 11.7	Inventory Management SoD Matrix	197
Exhibit 12.1	Realtionship between Owners and IT	209
Exhibit 15.1	Risk management process	282
Exhibit 15.2	Example of a process issues log	283
Exhibit 15.3	Example of a risk assessment form	287
Exhibit 16.1	Testing sequence	294
Exhibit 16.2	Unit testing flow	295
Exhibit 16.3	Integration test flow	295
Exhibit 18.1	Example I (Financial statement audit)	310
Exhibit 18.2	Example II (another financial statement audit)	311
Exhibit 18.3	Example III (information systems audit)	313
Exhibit 18.4	Interview question format	318
Exhibit 18.5	Example one—auditing the accounts receivable process (version 1)	320

Exhibit 18.6	Example two—auditing the accounts receivable process (version 2)	323
Exhibit 18.7	Example three—audit of the billing system (version 1)	329
Exhibit 18.8	Example four—audit of the billing system (version 2)	332
Exhibit 18.9	Example of a fact sheet for Change Management	339
Exhibit 18.10	Example of a fact sheet for Completeness of Cash Receipts	340
Exhibit 19.1	Example of financial statement audit report	346
Exhibit 19.2	Example of information system audit report	348

CHAPTER 1

Introduction: Objectives, Focus and Description of the Text

This textbook should be used primarily to educate audit clients, not auditors. There are numerous audit classes and audit textbooks that are geared toward instructing the auditor on how to perform their audit functions but very few classes where the purpose is to alleviate the fear of the audit and to help the audit client achieve audit readiness and defend themselves against audits. The objective of this textbook is to educate accounting, information technology, finance, and non-financial business students who are, or could become, future managers or key staff personnel during their careers. The textbook should be available to all business graduate students, not just future accountants where one generally finds the offering of auditing classes.

The aim of the textbook is to prime and adequately position current and future managers in achieving successful audits. They will probably, one day, be audit clients, exposed to audits, and they will need to be prepared.

This textbook should be used in audit classes for all business students. It is designed to educate prospective audit clients. It covers many topics within its chapters, reinforced by quizzes and exercises that should be

Supplementary Information The online version contains supplementary material available at (https://doi.org/10.1007/978-3-030-92466-9_1).

E. Danter, *Audit Defense*, Palgrave Studies in Accounting and Finance Practice, https://doi.org/10.1007/978-3-030-92466-9_1

utilized in preparing future managers and staff to be audit ready. By using this textbook, students will obtain or supplement their fundamental audit process knowledge. The textbook describes essential steps needed in preparing for and achieving successful audit results. It provides recognition in anticipation of an auditor's inquiries and expectations. It supplies and reinforces measures that an audit client needs to take in interacting with auditors, summarizing what they should say and what they should not say that could be detrimental and perilous.

Focus of this textbook and class structure is centered on the Mock Audit. In my opinion, there is no better way to introduce students to the challenges of an audit than to have them role-play as both auditors and audit clients. Participating in simulated audits where they engage in audits performing both roles should give them a perspective that is difficult, if not impossible, to acquire from just reading and discussing topics in a textbook. This approach might be unique but I found it to be well received, challenging, and energizing for students over the years.

Since more and more processes are automated in today's world, non-IT personnel are becoming more and more dependent on their IT organizations. As a result, more and more process audits overlap or are super imposed on top of Information Technology Audits. The two worlds of business process owners and IT professionals are intertwined and cannot be easily separated. All process owners and future audit clients are in a better position to be audit ready if they work closely with their IT organizations—they need to walk comfortably across that bridge as the two communities are challenged and brought closer together by audits. This textbook indicates that a synergistic and collaborative effort should exist between these two organizations to achieve successful audits. Moreover, there are many who believe that in today's world, the CPA profession is both an accounting and technology profession.

Unlike other textbooks and courses, the objective is not to prepare the accounting student to just pass the CPA exam but to enable all prospective audit clients to achieve successful audits. It will be an ancillary benefit if it helps the accounting student pass the CPA exam, but its benefit exceeds this one challenge.

The audience should not be restricted only to accounting students but should be available to any graduate business student who might someday be in a managerial position within a company. If the material in this textbook is not suitable to fit into an existing academic course, then thought should be given to possibly establishing a new course—perhaps one titled "Audit Readiness."

Many of the topics covered in this book should help management in preparing for either an Information System Audit, Financial Statement Audit, or any process-based audit. Non-financial and non-IT managers will also benefit by the education provided. Any corporate manager can be audited, whether purchasing managers, real estate managers, HR managers, supply chain mangers, inventory managers, etc. They all need to be audit ready and this education is a first step toward achieving that goal.

The textbook should be used as a vehicle to instruct future audit clients on what to expect from the time an audit is announced until the final audit report is written, signed and distributed. This involves educating students on the audit process; enhancing their knowledge of controls; gaining insight into pro-active activities in preparation for audits; providing insight on how to effectively interface with auditors; instructing students on knowing when to challenge auditors; teaching future audit clients on how to review audit findings and final audit reports; and making them aware of when to sign off on audit reports. Their jobs and reputations could very well be jeopardized as a result of a failed audit and they need to be advised of steps to take in order to achieve success. They need to reduce fear that they might have had before and during the audit when interfacing with auditors. And as equally important, they need to eliminate any illusions they might have about controls. They should realize that the only thing worse than the absence of control is having the illusion of control. If you believe that all functions and procedures are controlled and effectively being processed, you won't have an incentive to initiate corrective actions to establish and/or to even enhance or improve processes and controls—passing an audit will be a difficult, uphill struggle. When an audit is announced, audit clients need to have the prescience of possible audit failure and should take appropriate actions that hopefully result in success.

If you have already been exposed to audits or are a prospective audit client, this textbook can give you the knowledge and confidence needed to achieve a favorable audit report. By adhering to the principles outlined, you will be in a better position to participate on a level playing field.

This textbook should reduce fear of an audit and improve the likelihood of achieving audit success. However, it will not guarantee that you will pass audits. It is not a panacea—it's a significant step that you can take to help achieve audit readiness. It provides guidance that, if adopted, should be a bulwark against failed audits.

The book is divided into four sections with multiple chapters within each section. **Section I** focuses on the audit process ensuring that students are familiar with audit steps that are generally followed by auditors. It hones in on how audit clients should interact with auditors, from the receipt of the audit announcement letter until audit report sign-off. During this section, students are informed on what to say and what not to say when being interviewed or questioned by auditors. They are guided through the process of reviewing audit reports and impugning the veracity of the reports. **Section II** zeroes in on corporate governance hierarchy and accountability and responsibilities of both internal and external organizations. In addition, it focuses on the controls that should be established by audit clients for either financial statement audits or information system audits, stressing the importance of avoiding the illusion of control. The controls also apply to audits that are non-financial or non-IT related. Many of the controls are founded on common sense and fundamental control concepts that are applicable to effective execution and governance of *any* business process. It goes into detail on the controls that an audit client should be aware of and what controls they should implement, no matter what processes they are managing. It also talks about future challenges that we are faced with as our environment and technology keep expanding. **Section III** is directed toward education on how audit clients can be compliant and audit ready. It provides pro-active measures that can be established to reduce fear of an audit, while improving chances for a satisfactory audit. Further, it addresses risk assessments and testing activities. **Section IV**, which is somewhat a unique approach, describes how to stage and conduct mock audits by simulating audits—students role playing as both auditors and audit clients. Sections I, II, and III are pre-requisites before mock audits are conducted. The intent of role playing during a mock audit is for students to become cognizant of audit procedures and challenges and to be made aware of what they will be up against. They should be in a better position to defend themselves and respond to audit challenges once the audit process and pro-active measures are known. Classes should devote much of their allocated time to the mock audit, which, if done right, cannot only be instrumental in obtaining audit success but can be one of the most enjoyable as well as challenging segments of the course.

Please note that bold, larger, and italicized words and phrases are used throughout the textbook for emphasis, indicating that more attention needs to be focused on its importance.

Imbedded within the text, I have added personal experiences that I have encountered during my years in audit or in supporting audit clients. I hope they will enlighten the reader as to the gravity of not having a well-controlled environment and will put the seriousness of control shortcomings into a proper perspective.

Accounting, finance, and other business or management students, who are or who will soon be entering Corporate America, should be offered and take advantage of audit readiness education courses. Audit clients receiving adequate education will gain confidence and reduce their fear of audits while enhancing and improving their procedures and controls. This will not only further their opportunity regarding their own audit success and future careers but will be of greater value to their companies as well.

Additionally, audit committees as well as chief audit executives will benefit from knowing that there is a level audit field when everyone receives audit training. Internal auditors will be in a position to effectively conduct their reviews and process managers, as well as their staffs, will be in a better position to skillfully engage in audits. Everyone benefits, as the audits should be more robust and confrontational, resulting in more reasonable recommendations for improvement that will best serve their corporations and will be true value add.

Current and future management plays an important role in audit successes and in ensuring that corporations can achieve well-controlled processes and procedures. The futures of these men and women and survival of the corporations they work for could be at stake without adequate processes, procedures, and controls, reinforced by audit readiness schooling.

PART I

Corporate Governance and the Audit Process

The wish to acquire more is admittedly a very natural and common thing; and when men succeed in this they are always praised rather than condemned. But when they lack the ability to do so and yet want to acquire more at all costs, they deserve condemnation for their mistakes.—Niccolo Machiavelli

Today, corporate America is on shaky ground. The public's reaction is difficult to measure. Stock market performance is volatile and unpredictable, and there are countless instances of financial disappointment and loss. Corporations at risk must redeem creditability, pass external audits, and demonstrate strong effective controls to the satisfaction of government. They must also be able to stand up to public scrutiny.

The repercussions of fraudulent and inappropriate accounting and control practices can be widespread. The company's stockholders, creditors, and employees may suffer job loss and diminished retirement savings. Depositors in financial institutions and accountants may be subject to investigations. Attorneys, insurers who write officers' liability policies and experience large claims, customers who depend on the company's products, merger companies who may enter into partnership based on erroneous finances, and even companies whose reputations can be tarnished by association may all be affected. It is critical that corporations regain a sense of ethical and honest behavior and return to basic effective corporate governance.

It is critical to realize that corporate governance is a two-way street. There are roles that management plays in protecting the corporation and its executives from potential losses, whether intentional or unintentional and in assuring profit growth. The other element is that internal audit also plays an essential role. They are positioned to protect shareholders, stockholders, investors, and stakeholders. Both organizations play a meaningful role in corporate governance and have a stake in assuring that processes within a company are well controlled, adequately measured, and effectively executed. This will benefit companies, aid them in complying with regulations, and position them to be in a better position to pass external audits. The end goal of both organizations should be the same, to have well-controlled processes, procedures, and controls.

CHAPTER 2

Responsibilities, Regulations, Control Frameworks

In modern business, it is not the crook who is to be feared most, it is the honest man who doesn't know what he is doing.—William Wordsworth

A spotlight on corporate governance needs to be positioned to ensure that there exists effective and controlled processing, designed to reduce the possibility of fraud and erroneous activities. The intensity is brighter today than it ever was and it is growing stronger every day. The origin of this increased emphasis stems primarily from numerous corporate scandals that surfaced in our country at the turn of the twenty-first century. I am not saying that there was not a need for strong corporate governance earlier than the turn of this century, but incidents appeared to have exploded and have become more outrageous and egregious over the last 20 years. Corporate executives became more brazen with many individuals taking advantage of non-existent or weak government regulations that were not being effectively enforced. As a result, federal regulations were strengthened (e.g. Sarbanes Oxley) and audits have become much more demanding, diligent, and rigorous.

As a potential audit client, you need to understand the following pie chart that accents corporate governance. From this chapter, you should be able to recognize the role that you will play and the importance of passing audits (Chart 2.1).

E. Danter, *Audit Defense*, Palgrave Studies in Accounting and Finance Practice, https://doi.org/10.1007/978-3-030-92466-9_2

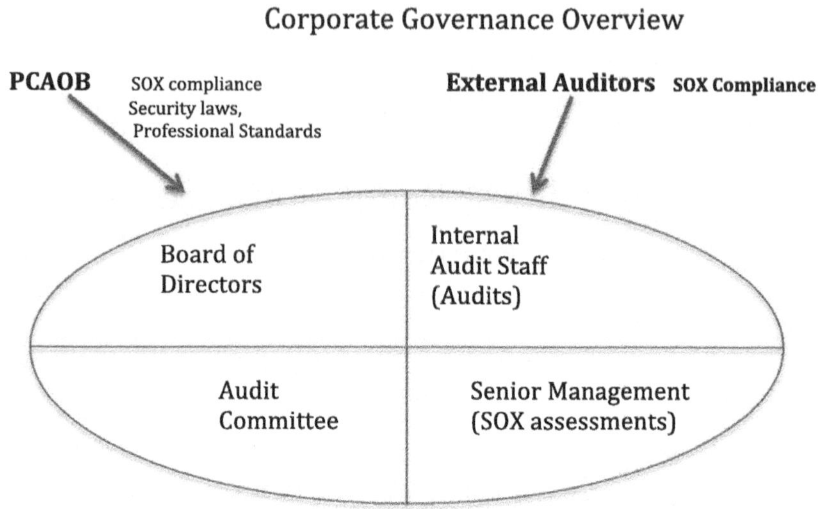

Chart 2.1 Corporate governance overview

Effective Corporate Governance is needed more than ever. We need to examine the roles of various entities in achieving this objective (Exhibit 2.1).

Responsibility of External Audit Firms

As a potential audit client, you should be aware of and familiar with the most significant US federal securities legislation imposed on business since the New Deal went into effect as a result of the great depression. The legislation is Sarbanes Oxley (SOX).

SOX legislature was developed primarily to ensure that accountability for compliance to SOX regulations and requirements was oversight responsibility of external auditors or independent accounting firms.

This legislation came into existence as a result of corporate financial scandals that mostly occurred at the turn of this century (e.g. Enron. WorldCom, Tyco, HealthSouth). These financial scandals not only had a significant impact on these and other corporations but financially ruined many investors and stockholders. They were responsible for many executives being incarcerated and/or financially penalized and it also led to

Exhibit 2.1 Corporate audit hierarchy

the disappearance of one of the major accounting firms in our country, Arthur Anderson.

Highlights of these financial scandals were:

Enron

- Enron was formed in 1885 by Kenneth Lay after merging Houston Natural Gas and InterNorth.
- Enron was the seventh largest company in our nation.
- Jeff Skilling, the CEO, developed a staff of executives that through the use of accounting loopholes, special purpose entities and poor financial planning, hid billions in debt from failed deals and projects.
- The CFO, Andrew Fastow, and other executives not only misled Enron's board of directors and audit committee on high risk accounting practices but also pressured their external auditor, Arthur Anderson, to ignore the issues.
- Shareholders lost nearly $11 billion by the end of November 2001.
- Enron's nontransparent financial statements did not clearly depict its operations and finances with shareholders and analysts.

- Fastow and other executives created complex financing structures and deals so bewildering that few people could understand them.
- Enron filed for bankruptcy on December 2, 2001, under Chapter 11.
- The US Justice Department in January of 2002 launched a criminal investigation into the epic fall of Houston's Enron Corporation.
- Executives were indicted for various charges and sentenced to prison.

The following is a headline from the Houston Chronicle on August 16, 2011 (Exhibit 2.2).

Enron collapse

Criminal investigation of Enron collapse opened
DAVID IVANOVICH, Copyright 2002 Houston Chronicle Washington Bureau
Jan. 9, 2002Updated: Aug. 16, 2011 9:05 p.m.
WASHINGTON -- The U.S. Justice Department acknowledged Wednesday it has launched a criminal investigation into the epic fall of Houston's EnronCorp.

Exhibit 2.2 Enron scandal headline

Adelphi

- In March 2002, Adelphi, the nation's fifth largest cable company, revealed that the Rigas family, which had founded the company, had borrowed more than $2 billion under an arrangement with Adelphi that made the family and the company responsible for each other's debt.
- In a four month trial, the prosecution called witnesses who testified to the Rigas family's lavish spending.
- John Rigas, the founder, and Timothy Rigas, his son, were each convicted of one count of conspiracy, 15 accounts of security fraud, and 2 counts of bank fraud; John was sentenced to jail for 15 years and his son received a 20-year sentence.
- Prosecutors stated that the family treated the company like their own ATM machine.

HealthSouth

- HealthSouth Corporation, in the first years in the twenty-first century, was the nation's largest owner and operator of rehabilitative hospitals.
- HealthSouth was involved in a corporate accounting scandal where the CEO, Richard Scrushy, was accused of directing company employees to falsely report grossly exaggerated company earnings in order to meet stockholder expectations.
- Richard Scrushy was indicted in November 2003, on 85 counts alleging by federal prosecutors that he was the mastermind of an enormous corporate fraud scheme that allowed him to personally pocket more than a quarter-billion dollars,

The following is a headline from Las Vegas Sun—November 4, 2003 (Exhibit 2.3).

> ExCEO of HealthSouth indicted on fraud charges
>
> Jay Reeves
>
> Tuesday, Nov. 4, 2003 | 11:16 a.m.
>
> BIRMINGHAM, Ala. -- Former HealthSouth Corp. head Richard Scrushy was indicted on 85 counts alleging he was the mastermind of an enormous corporate fraud scheme that allowed him to personally pocket more than a quarter-billion dollars, federal prosecutors said today.

Exhibit 2.3 HealthSouth scandal headline

ImClone

- On August 8, 2002, former ImClone Systems CEO, Sam Waksal, was arrested on securities fraud charges.
- He was indicted on charges relating to inside trading.
- There were charges of obstruction of justice and bank fraud against Waksal in addition to previous fraud and perjury charges.
- Prosecutors said that Waksal tried to sell ImClone stock after he learned the Food and Drug Administration was going to consider ImClone's application for a cancer drug.

Tyco

- Shareholders were not informed of $170 million in loans that were taken by Tyco's CEO, CFO, and chief legal officer. Many of the loans were taken interest free and later written off as benefits and were not approved by Tyco's compensation committee.
- The former CEO, Dennis Kozlowski, was accused of using company funds to purchase $18 million for an apartment in Manhattan.
- Kozlowski used company loans for the funds allowing him to avoid income taxes. He was also accused of fraudulently transporting $13 million worth of art to Tyco headquarters in New Hampshire to avoid more than $1 million in New York taxes.
- Tyco was also involved in a practice known as spring-loading, a financial manipulation in which the pre-acquisition earnings of the acquired company are underreported so as to give the merged company an artificial boost.
- Most members of the company's board of directors benefitted as a result of Tyco's practices.

The following is a SEC headline (Exhibit 2.4).

SEC Brings Settled Charges Against Tyco International Ltd. Alleging Billion Dollar Accounting Fraud
Company Agrees to Injunction and Payment of $50 Million Penalty

Exhibit 2.4 Tyco scandal headline

WorldCom

- WorldCom, which was the nation's second-largest long-distance telephone carrier, confessed that it had overstated cash flow by more than $3.8 billion during the last five quarters in what appeared to be among the largest cases ever of accounting fraud. The company improperly reported $3.8 billion in expenses as capital investments.
- An internal audit discovered that $3.3 billion in profits were improperly recorded on its books from 1999 to the first quarter of 2002.

- The suspicion is that WorldCom deliberately inflated its reserves to be able to dip into them to boost profits in order to meet profit projections.
- WorldCom's CEO, John Sidgmore, blamed the company's former CFO and former controller, and the two were fired and arrested, handcuffed in front of TV cameras. They were charged with securities fraud, conspiracy, and other charges.

WorldCom joined a growing list of companies struck by accounting scandals, led by Enron Corporation that shook public faith in business and Wall Street and created a flood of shareholder lawsuits.

The following is a headline from the New York Times (Exhibit 2.5).

WorldCom admits huge fraud in its accounting / Survival of MCI long distance at risk in $3.8 billion disclosure
Simon Romero and Alex Berenson, New York Times
June 26, 2002Updated: July 9, 2018 10:08 p.m.
WorldCom, the nation's second-largest long-distance telephone carrier, said Tuesday night that it had overstated its cash flow by more than $3.8 billion during the last five quarters in what appears to be among the largest cases ever of accounting fraud.

Exhibit 2.5 WorldCom scandal headline

SOX is used as a basis of corporate governance, not only in the United States but in the EU, Japan, China, and many other countries—it is the foundation of global audit focus and corporate global compliance. The EU's European Court of Auditors (EU's external auditors) audits systems and controls across the EU. EU also has an organization called Internal Audit Services (IAS) that has responsibility for internal audits. In addition, Australia conducts audits using SOX as a basis as does Japan. The Japanese have developed a Sarbanes type requirement for internal control over financial reporting for their public companies. Japan's version of Sarbanes Oxley is incorporated in its Financial Instruments and Exchange (FIE) and is called J-SOX. The scandals cited above, as well as other corporate scandals, were the impetus for direct or indirect worldwide-related Sarbanes Oxley legislature and corporate governance.

Responsibilities of the PCAOB

SOX also created a nonprofit corporation, called the Public Company Accounting Oversight Board (PCAOB), to oversee and regulate all auditing practices that relate to publicly traded companies.

The PCAOB has responsibilities to register public accounting firms (the external auditors) that prepare audit reports; to establish auditing, quality, control, ethics, independence, and other standards; to conduct inspection of accounting firms; and to enforce compliance with SOX, professional standards, and securities laws relating to the preparation and issuance of audit reports.

Responsibilities of the Board of Directors (BOD)

A corporation's board of directors establishes various committees to oversee its corporate policies and finances. These committees are responsible for corporate governance to ensure that the company is financially sound and profitable, follows laws and regulations, and provides adequate protection for its employees and shareholders. The BOD selects numerous committees from its members to sit on these committees. Examples are the: Finance Committee, Marketing Committee, Product Committee, Promotions and Sales Committee, Public Relations Committee, Ethics Committee, and last, where our attention is focused on, the Audit Committee. At least one member of the audit committee must have a financial background and of course they are independent, meaning that the CEO, CFO, or any other executive in the corporation who sits on the BOD cannot be a member of the audit committee. The members of the audit committee must be independent members of the board to avoid conflict of interests. Remember that independence is needed to regulate the activities of a company's top executives. There have been numerous scandals that have occurred and noted above where CEOs and CFOs have been involved—as a result, independence of the Audit Committee is of paramount importance.

Responsibilities of the Audit Committee

SOX defines the audit committee as a committee of directors that oversees the financial and accounting processes. All members of the audit committee must be excluded from being an affiliated person of the company and from accepting compensation for consulting, advisory, or other company activities except for director's fees. Internal auditors report to the audit committee and the audit committee also serves as a liaison between management and the outside auditor. They have numerous functions related to corporate governance. Some of the more important responsibilities are:

- *Appointing, compensating, and supervising the company's outside auditor.*
  They hire the outside audit firm and will replace them if not satisfied with their performance or if they are engaged in unethical practices. They should review their activities, ensuring that they are complying with contractual commitments. They will recommend rotation of external audit firms when appropriate.

- *Accounting for the accuracy of financial reporting.*
  The audit committee should review the accuracy of financial statements when released.

- *Appointing and directing a Chief Audit Executive (CAE) to oversee the audit infrastructure.*
  In some companies, this individual can be referred as the Director of Internal Audit.

- *Reviewing audit reports.*
  There are many audit reports that are not reviewed by the audit committee, especially if they are satisfactory reports. The committee might only review unsatisfactory audits. They decide on which reports they will review.

- *Meeting periodically with internal and external auditor management.*
  These meetings will take place when deemed necessary. The audit committee usually keeps informed of the planned audit activities of internal and external audit organizations.

- *Ensuring compliance with legal and regulatory laws.*
  The audit committees should ensure SOX compliance as well as concurrence with other federal, state, and local laws pertaining

to audits. This would include global conformity with legal and regulatory laws in other countries for global enterprises.

Responsibilities of Senior Management

SOX created new corporate governance guidelines that affect how companies manage themselves. These guidelines include placing more responsibility on senior executives to improve the quality of their company's financial disclosures and reports. When SOX uses the term corporate senior management, they are referring to CEOs and CFOs.

The two main sections of SOX are sections 302 and 404. Section 302 requires senior management to certify that adequate internal controls are in place. Section 404 requires senior management to annually address the effectiveness of the controls and that a company's external auditors can attest to management's assessment of its internal controls, including information technology control.

Internal Auditor Responsibilities

The internal audit staff, to maintain their independence, reports to the audit committee. This is a SOX requirement. There can be many internal audit groups within a company, depending on the size of the corporation, and one of them can be a group of auditors who possibly will audit your department.

If and when you are audited, it would be beneficial if you knew as much about your opposition as possible. Metaphorically speaking, think of an audit being similar to a chess game in one very important respect, knowing the strengths and weaknesses of your opponent and anticipating their next move could improve your chances of success.

The depth of audit staffs will vary depending on the size of your company. Usually, the greater the number of company employees, the larger the size of the audit staff. This is not always true as there are also dependencies on resources, growth forecasts, or the number of internal auditors can even be industry related. For example, very large internal auditing staffs are found in the banking industry as a result of the numerous audits that are required to be performed as a result of state and/or federal requirements and regulations. The level of focus on corporate governance in any financial institution can be overwhelming. The number of auditors that you can face can be staggering and the lengths of the audit duration can exceed what you would think would be an acceptable or a desirable time period. Don't be intimidated or discouraged. This textbook and course should reduce your stress and mitigate your fear of the audit, resulting in being audit ready.

There are managers within the internal audit department but you probably will not be directly engaging with them on a daily basis. There might be many audit managers in situations where the company is very large and they will probably report to a company executive who has the title of Chief Audit Executive (CAE) or Internal Audit Director. The audit manager will designate a lead auditor who will be the auditor in charge for your audit. This is the person who you will interface with on a daily basis. There will be other auditors on the audit team and the number will vary and be applicable to the size, importance, and scope of the audit.

Some companies will employ college graduates and train them to be auditors. Other companies will take experienced personnel from within the company and move them into auditor positions after they have gained knowledge of and have acquired experience working and becoming familiar with a company's policies and procedures. There are pros and cons depending on whether you will be audited by a newly hired college graduate or by a seasoned auditor. First, let's look at their responsibilities that they are expected to discharge. They are in a position to serve as the eyes and ears for the executives of the company. The CAE, under the auspices of the audit committee, has overall responsibility for audit governance leadership and oversees the internal audit organization.

Responsibilities of the Internal Audit Department are:

- Review, evaluate, and report on the adequacy and effective application of controls.
- Identify issues/exposures and recommend control improvements and stress importance to improve overall control posture.
- Advise management when an issue is closed and if recommendations as a result of an audit are complied with.
- Determine the extent of compliance with business processes, ethical standards, federal laws, and regulations.
- Assess the reliability and accuracy of data developed and reported within the company.
- Determine the protection of assets from possible loss.

Now that you are aware of the responsibilities of the internal auditor, who would you fear most or who would you rather have audit you, the recent college grad or seasoned employee? Don't worry. This is not your choice. You do not have any say in the background of the auditors that you face, but you should know what challenges that you would be up against with either individual auditing you.

The seasoned employee will probably be more of a challenge to you in one sense as they have greater knowledge and experience with the functions your department performs on a day-to-day basis. They will know where to look for the exposures, know where the bodies are buried, and have a wider understanding of your process, procedures, and controls. On the other hand, they will most likely be more receptive to the explanations you bring forward for discussion on your challenges. They should be in a better position to know what recommendations make sense by having greater business acumen than the recent grad because of their history, experience, and service within the company.

For example, let us assume that you are the purchasing manager in your company and you are being audited. One of the auditors is a former purchasing manager and he is familiar with the processes and procedures that your department follows. As a result, he knows what controls should be in place and knows what evidence to check in order to verify that they were effectively being executed. This auditor can be a risk that you were hoping to avoid but you had no choice. On the other hand, since he has experience with the purchasing process and its controls, he might be more receptive to listening to your challenges and accepting your explanations as to why things are not exactly in line with an audit checklist.

The recent college grad could be a plus because of your experience with your process and knowledge of company functions and procedures that the recent college grad will not have. It might be easier to convince them that your process, procedures, and controls are well defined and executed effectively during an interview discussion. They might be auditors and working in the company for less than a year and you might have been in your position for 10 or 15 years or even longer, or you might be able to rely on your staff members who have even more experience than you. With significant more experience among yourself and your staff than a recent college graduate, you should have an edge in explanations and acceptances.

However, you need to be careful with a recent grad because they might be difficult to reason with and you might receive recommendations that do not make sense. This is not an uncommon occurrence. You will have to respond to these recommendations, regardless, wasting a significant amount of time and resource. The other drawback is that since they are just starting out on their careers, they might try to make a name for themselves by taking hard unreasonable positions.

There are no guarantees which auditor you will fare better with, just be prepared and have your procedures and controls documented and able to demonstrate their effectiveness. This is essential, regardless of who is auditing you, recent college hire, or experienced auditor with extensive corporate process knowledge.

Responsibilities of First Line Managers

You will play a significant role in corporate governance when and if you embark on a managerial career. Your responsibilities as a first line manager will not only rely on your having established processes, procedures, and controls that are effectively being executed, but if and when audited, you will need to be able to demonstrate and convince auditors that execution of your process is being closely monitored.

When we talk about corporate governance, we need to ensure that there is accountability for the accuracy of a company's financial statements and adequacy of their internal controls. There is a strong reliance on the PCAOB as well as internal audit departments and external audit firms for timely and thorough review. However, it is important to realize that the establishment of effective internal controls and their compelling execution that will lead to successful audits is not the responsibility of the PCAOB or internal/external audit organizations but of management. It is incumbent on first line management (audit clients) and their key staff to understand the audit process, control expectations, and recognize how and when to establish effective and exemplary controls. This is what good corporate governance is all about. It is not just about detecting and identifying exposures and issues that exist but it also centers on preventing misstatements in financial statements and operational and system shortcomings from occurring. There should be effective controls in place to prevent delayed or lost revenue, loss of resources, damaged customer satisfaction, other business losses, or even fraud. It is up to management and their staffs to understand what controls are needed and how they can validate that they are in place and adequately being executed before issues arise.

This will be a huge step in assuring comprehensive and strong corporate governance resulting in satisfactory audits and in meeting or even exceeding reviewers' expectations.

The bedrock then of corporate governance, resulting in positive results, is not just the quality of internal audits conducted by reliable reviewers and organizations, but stems from the preparation for audits. Management needs to avoid the illusion of control and be audit ready. This will benefit corporations, executive management, audit committees, board of directors as well as investors, shareholders, and other stakeholders.

Case Study on Illusion of Control

Now image yourself as the manager of a payroll system who has just received an announcement letter for an internal audit that is to begin one month from the date of the letter. You have been the manager for only 6 months and have never been audited before. Your executive asks you if you are audit ready and if you think your department will pass the audit. You ask your staff, many of who have worked in the payroll department for many years, if they are prepared. They want to make a good impression and tell you that they are ready. You, in turn, want your manager to feel that he made the right choice in your promotion—you do not want to be embarrassed by telling him that you are not audit ready. After all, you were told by your staff that they were ready, so you relay the comfort level and message that you have received up the line to your executive who then tells the CEO and CFO that you are ready for the forthcoming audit. You are nervous and apprehensive but feel reassured by your department personnel that you will have a satisfactory audit. The audit takes place and it is a *disaster*. What a surprise. There are many issues and exposures cited in the audit report and your career is now in jeopardy. You suffered from what is called *an illusion of control*. The only thing worse than no control is the illusion of control. You thought that all of your procedures and controls were established and working effectively, because that is what you were made to believe, so not being aware of any issues, you did not bother to put any corrective actions in place. After all, why fix something, if it isn't broken. If you knew that there were inadequate procedures containing an absence of controls or ineffective controls, you could have addressed the problems and you should have adhered to the words of former President Ronald Reagan when he used the Russian proverb, "Trust but Verify".

We will be discussing controls that should be in place in subsequent chapters in the textbook. Pro-active measures that you can take to verify that controls are established and that they are effectively being executed will be described later.

Because of the dependence of business and financial reporting and accuracy of information system processing, it is imperative that audit clients understand requirements for compliance and the ramifications of noncompliance as well.

It is important to realize that you, as a process manager, are the first line of defense in protecting your executives from unsatisfactory audits, whether they are internal or external audits. If you take pro-active steps (we will detail them in a later chapter) to be audit ready, then it should position your department to be in a more advantageous posture to have a successful audit. Realize again that if you pass internal audits it will improve odds for passing external audits.

We need to be aware that the achievement of audit readiness is dependent on strong education. You can't fix problems if you don't know what you are looking for. We need to be cognizant of the fact that education of audit clients is just as important and essential as the education of any internal audit staff.

COSO

COSO, which stands for the Committee of Sponsoring Organizations, is a voluntary private sector organization dedicated to improving the quality of financial reporting through business ethics, effective internal controls, and corporate governance. It was founded in 1985 by the National Committee on Fraudulent Financial Reporting, the chairman of the Commission was James Treadway, and the National Commission is sometimes referred to as the Treadway Commission. The COSO control framework is recommended by SOX and is recognized as the standard framework to be adopted by public companies. There are 5 components under the COSO framework. They are:

- Control Environment
  - Demonstrate commitment to integrity and ethical values
  - Ensure that board exercises oversight responsibility
  - Establish structures, reporting lines, authorities, and responsibilities
  - Demonstrate commitment to a competent workforce

    - Hold people accountable

- Information and Communication
    - Use relevant, quality information to support the internal control function
    - Communicate internal control information internally
    - Communicate internal control information externally

- Control Activities
    - Select and develop control activities that mitigate risks
    - Select and develop technology controls
    - Deploy control activities through policies and procedures

- Monitoring
    - Perform ongoing or periodic evaluations of internal controls (or a combination of the two)
    - Communicate internal control deficiencies
    - Risk assessment

- Specify appropriate objectives
    - Identify and analyze risks
    - Evaluate fraud risks
    - Identify and analyze changes that could significantly affect internal controls

The COSO components outlined above will have more meaning and significance when the details on controls are discussed later in subsequent chapters.

COBIT

COSO and COBIT (Control Objectives for Information and Related Technology) although not inseparable are closely related. COBIT was established by the Information Systems Audit and Control Association (ISACA) to produce a high level and detailed set of control objectives for

IT management. COSO references COBIT as a good pro-active source for IT governance.

As a non-IT audit client, you should be familiar with COBIT objectives since the process that you will own most likely will be automated, to some extent, and you will be heavily dependent on information technology. As process owners, auditors will hold you accountable for being aware of IT governance. Even though you will be relying on IT for their services, the accountability will rest on your shoulders. You will not have IT expertise or direct authority for IT processes, procedures, and controls but although the responsibility lies with IT management for having effective governance, the accountability to know how their processes are managed and governed rests with you. They are a service organization for you. And like most service organizations, if they are not performing their tasks and responsibilities proficiently and ineffectively monitoring their processes and controls, it could be detrimental with regard to your expectations and needs.

For example, if you own a house and you have a leaky roof, your wife might ask you to get the roof repaired. You hire a contractor to do the work and he comes with his staff to replace the existing roof. Two weeks later, there is a heavy rain and the roof is leaking again. The contractor returns and he tells you that he will fix the roof, but it will cost you more than you originally paid him. He blames the problem and additional cost on a very heavy unforeseen downpour, freak of nature, that the new roof was not designed to handle. He will need to purchase additional material that was not originally planned. Realize that your wife will hold you accountable for the problem and not the contractor. She will yell at you, not the contractor. She asked you to get it fixed and you hired the contractor based on a recommendation from a neighbor. The contractor was responsible for the quality of the work but not accountable for the poor job from your wife's point of view. The contractor performed a service for you, and according to your wife, you should have reviewed his warranty and should have been inspecting his work as the project progressed to see if was satisfactory. So where was the governance? If the quality of the work was not what was expected, and by the way, the work took twice as long as was originally estimated and the cost exceeded your budget, you should have fired him and hired another contractor. You are accountable for the situation that evolved and not the contractor.

The same will hold true if you are a non-IT manager being audited and you use IT as a service organization. Audit will hold you accountable even though IT is responsible. They can easily include IT in an expanded audit scope and if they find issues with IT controls, can advise you of their concerns but the auditors will hold you accountable.

When we discuss different types of audits in the next chapter, we will focus more on IT audits. It is important to realize that IT management can be the process owner of IT functions. In this situation, the IT manager can be a direct recipient of an audit or you, as the manager of an accounting process within a company, can be the direct client of an audit with IT being an auxiliary component of the original scope. Accountability will be directed toward the process owner or the manager who is being audited.

COBIT helps organizations meet business challenges in the areas of regulatory compliance, risk management, and aligning IT strategy with organizational goals. COBIT 5, the latest iteration of the framework, was released in 2012.

COBIT 5 is based on five principles that are essential for the effective management and governance of enterprise IT:

- Principle 1: Meeting stakeholder needs
- Principle 2: Covering the enterprise end to end
- Principle 3: Applying a single integrated framework
- Principle 4: Enabling a holistic approach
- Principle 5: Separating governance from management

These five principles enable an organization to build a holistic framework for the governance and management of IT that is built on seven "enablers":

1. People, policies and frameworks
2. Processes
3. Organizational structures
4. Culture, ethics, and behavior
5. Information
6. Services, infrastructure, and applications
7. People, skills, and competencies

Summary

Effective corporate governance requires the fulfillment of responsibilities of internal audit organizations, external auditing firms, the board of directors, audit committees, and senior executives within the corporation. It is incumbent on all of these groups to abide by federal regulations and laws and to restore faith as well as to protect the company, its stockholders, and other stakeholders from any investments they might have or plan to have in the company.

As a result of the scandals in the beginning of the twenty-first century, Congress established and easily passed the Sarbanes Oxley Act, which places accountability on the CEOs and CFOs for the accuracy of their financial statements and to impose greater restrictions on them, designed to discourage them from fraudulent activities. They also imposed heavy penalties on them if they were not in compliance.

The two sections of Sarbanes Oxley that are the most important are sections 302 and 404. Section 302 requires certification by top executives as to the accuracy of their financial statements and effectiveness of their internal controls, and sections 404 requires an audit by an independent outside auditing firm to attest to the accuracy of the financial statements and controls.

Sarbanes Oxley recommends COSO as the standard framework for financial controls for public companies. There are five components of COSO which are: (1) control environment, (2) information and communication, (3) control activities, (4) monitoring, and (5) risk assessment.

COBIT established control objectives as an information technology managerial framework to help businesses design, organize, and implement strategies around information management and governance. There are five principles and seven enablers.

The primary responsibility to establish and monitor corporate governance will lie with first line process owners or managers even though executive management, CEOs, and CFOs will have ultimate accountability for the accuracy of the company's financial statements, as per SOX.

Guidance

1. Familiarize yourself with Sarbanes Oxley control requirements, especially sections 302 and 404.
2. If you are an IT manager, familiarize yourself with COBIT framework and control objectives.
3. Familiarize yourself with COSO components and controls.

Chapter 2 Exercises

1. You are a information technology manager of the billing systems in your company. You have never been audited before. However, you are now made aware that you are going to be audited next month. Your director asks you if you believe that you will pass the audit. What do you tell him and why?
2. Is there anything wrong with a CEO of a company being a member of the audit committee? If yes, what is the issue?
3. Explain the difference between COBIT and COSO.

Chapter 2 Questions

Select the best answer for each of the questions below:

1. What organization has responsibility to establish auditing standards?

   A. the SEC
   B. each state
   C. the PCAOB
   D. the COSO organization

2. COSO produced a high level and detailed set of control objectives for IT management.

   A. true
   B. false

3. The Chief Audit Executive (CAE) is appointed by:

   A. the CEO
   B. the CFO

C. the BOD
D. the Audit Committee

4. If you are a payroll manager who is being audited and rely on IT processing payroll checks, then you need not worry about being blamed if payments are frequently in error and late. You can just inform the auditors that IT does your payroll processing and that they are accountable for the accuracy and timeliness of the payments.

   A. true
   B. false

5. As an internal auditor, you will be responsible to:

   A. establish controls
   B. review, evaluate, and report on the effectiveness of controls
   C. certify the adequacy of controls by ensuring that they comply with Sarbanes Oxley
   D. establish auditing standards

6. The accounting scandals at the beginning of the twenty-first century led to the disappearance of which one of the following accounting firms?

   A. Deloitte
   B. PWC
   C. Arthur Young
   D. Arthur Anderson

7. The legislature used as a basis for accounting corporate governance is:

   A. New Deal
   B. Dodd Frank
   C. SOX
   D. SEC

8. Which organization, per federal regulations, is required to attest to management's assessment of its internal controls?

   A. SEC
   B. external auditors
   C. internal auditors

D. audit committee

9. First line managers play a minimal role during an audit. It is senior management who is involved in the day-to-day interface with the auditors.

   A. true
   B. false

10. The lead auditor during an audit is also referred to as:

    A. auditor number one
    B. the executive auditor
    C. the auditor manager's representative
    D. the auditor in charge

References

Simplilearn, July 15, 2021, "Understanding What Is COBIT and COBIT Framework". https://www.simplilearn.com/what-is-cobit-significance-and-framework-rar309-article.

Weaver Assurance, December 30, 2013, "COSO Framework's 17 Principles of Effective Internal Controls". https://weaver.com/blog/coso-frameworks-17-principles-effective-internal-control.

CHAPTER 3

The Audit Beginning

To quote Plato. “The beginning is the most important part of the work”.

All audits should begin by pre-planning conducted by the auditors, followed by an announcement letter sent out as an early warning in most cases, and subsequently with the commencement of a kickoff meeting.

Most audits follow a common process—there is a general thread. There is a similar path of audit steps that is adhered to throughout most audits from audit announcement until the final audit report is written and distributed. This is true for a company’s internal as well as external audits conducted by outside accounting firms. It is essential that all audit clients are at least familiar with the internal audit process that is adhered to by the internal audit (IA) organization at their enterprise. Once they are well informed with the internal audit process, it also should help in understanding the audit process of external audit firms (Fig. 3.1).

E. Danter, *Audit Defense*, Palgrave Studies in Accounting and Finance Practice, https://doi.org/10.1007/978-3-030-92466-9_3

Pre- Planning
Announcement Letter
Kickoff Meeting
Documentation Requests
Interviews
Fact Sheets
Status Meetings
Audit Reports
Recommendations and Responses
The Sign-off

Fig. 3.1 Overview of the audit process

Pre-Planning

by Vlada Karpovick

Before the audit begins, the auditors will conduct a pre-planning session. They will decide on the process or processes within their companies that they would like to audit, with the possibility that more than one audit will be conducted by IA at the same time. There is a rotation of processes within the company to be audited, adhering to a schedule that is established by the audit committee and chief audit executive/audit director. More critical functions (e.g. payroll, accounts payable, accounts receivables, new information systems being developed that are having major issues in meeting requirements, processes that recently failed audits with major exposures, processes where fraud previously occurred) are prime candidates for audits. As a process owner, you and your manager might be able to anticipate where the next audit will take place and when you can anticipate being an audit client before an announcement letter arrives. If you feel that you will be audited, you need to be ready. Pro-active measures that you can take will be discussed later in this textbook that will help you prepare for the audit.

Announcement Letter

The auditor's modus operandi begins with an announcement letter. Typically, the lead auditor sends this letter. This individual, who is also referred to as the auditor-in-charge, sends the announcement letter to the audit client who owns the process being audited or to his or her executive. The lead auditor is the auditor who is literally in charge of the audit. They are responsible for managing the audit from the initial stage until the audit is completed. They receive guidance and instruction from their manager but they are responsible for the day-to-day activities, interfaces, and communications with the audit client manager and their staff.

The announcement letter is frequently sent out between 4 and 6 weeks before the audit actually commences. Sometimes, there is a shorter time period before the start date of the audit, and sometimes there is a longer length of time—there is no hard rule. However, your enterprise might have established an audit announcement time line that is used as a guideline. The purpose of the announcement letter is a professional courtesy that allows the audit client sufficient time to make whatever arrangements are needed for having resources available to respond to the audit and to arrange for the necessary logistics. There might be vacations scheduled that need to be changed or business urgencies that need to be addressed before the audit scheduled start date, resulting in a short delay that the audit client asks for, hopefully agreed to by the auditors. The one exception to the advanced notice for an audit being sent to the audit client is a "surprise audit." As an example, a surprise audit can occur when internal audit or an executive within the company is perhaps suspicious of a potential or actual fraud and does not want the audit client manager or their staff to have time to hide, destroy, modify any incriminating documentation, or create any new documentation. A surprise audit can occur at any time, with very little or no warning.

The announcement letter, which could be an email or hard copy, usually contains the following:

- Indication of the process to be audited
- The scope of the audit or the process functions that will be reviewed
- Names of the auditors participating
- Stating when the audit is to begin
- The planned end date of the audit
- The period of time that the process being audited will cover (e.g. six months, one year)
- A reference to a kickoff meeting that indicates when the audit will actually commence
- The location as to where the audit will take place
- Any initial requests for documentation
- A request for the name of an audit interface (this could be a staff member and not necessarily the manager), who the lead auditor will directly communicate with on logistics and requests for documentation, interviews, status meetings, etc.

The audit client's manager and the audit manager should be copied on the announcement letter.

Now suppose you are the manager of the process being audited and you receive the announcement letter. Once you get over your initial jitters, you should take the following actions:

- Determine if there are any other business priorities that might interfere with the announced audit start date. These activities might be a merger scheduled when the audit is scheduled to take place, an ongoing federal investigation taking place, ongoing litigations, a new product announcement, etc.
- Verify if your key staff personnel or other supporting individuals for the audit will be available at the time of the audit (e.g. retirements,

personal tragedies, hospitalizations, honeymoons, engaged in other business priorities as indicated above).

- Respond to the audit announcement letter as soon as possible either accepting the date of the kickoff meeting or suggesting a postponement with a later date proposed. Explain your rationale, which should be both reasonable and compelling. If you suggest a postponement, with a good reason, the lead auditor and his or her manager might accept it.

Kickoff Meeting

Once you agreed to the original date of the kickoff meeting as reflected in the announcement letter, or you suggested a new start date that was consented to by the lead auditor due to unusual circumstances, you need to take the following actions prior to the kickoff meeting and the audit commencement:

- Have someone pull any documentation that was requested and have it available to be handed over at the kickoff meeting or send it to the lead auditor before the kickoff meeting.
- Designate an audit interface to receive and monitor all audit requests.
- Meet with your staff to determine if they are audit ready and ask them for the reason(s) why they feel that they are or are not ready. Take pro-active measures for audit readiness that will be discussed in a later chapter.
- If there are problems in being audit ready, determine if there are actions that can be taken to address the concerns before the audit starts.
- Make sure that all of your staff will be in attendance throughout the audit and if not, that there are backup personnel ready to step in.

At the kickoff meeting:

- Be ready to present the mission of your department.
- Document and be able to discuss the functions of your department on a high level.

- Have an organization chart that explains the roles and responsibilities of each of your team members and supporting departments.
- Assign someone on your staff to take notes during the kickoff meeting.

You should also be aware of what the audit organization will most likely want to discuss and what they will present at the kickoff meeting. The following are topics that are frequently discussed in the meeting:

- A brief overview of the audit organization
- The names of the auditors who will be conducting the audit (this list of names is not firm and can change at the discretion of the lead auditor as auditors are added or subtracted)
- The mission of the audit staff
- The audit reporting structure
- The protocol of the audit
- The audit process that will be followed
- An expectation on turnaround time on requests made (this usually is 24 or 48 hours)
- A status meeting schedule.

The decision as to which auditors will be in attendance at the kickoff meeting is decided by the lead auditor and his or her manager. It usually consists of the lead auditor and the other participating auditors along with the audit manager. You, as the audit client, will decide who should be present at the kickoff meeting who would be supporting you during the audit.

I suggest that in addition to being present yourself that you have key members of your staff who will likely be needed to partake in the audit, present in the meeting as well. Your manager or executive management should also be in attendance so that he or she knows the plans and expectations related to the audit. You can also invite other department managers and members of their staffs who will play an important role in the audit by supplying information and detail that only they can provide (e.g. IT manager, HR manager). You need to put everyone, who is or might be needed to support you in the audit, on a ready status and the best way to do this is to invite them to the kickoff meeting.

Note: The kickoff meeting will take place at a location at your site that you decide and you should ensure that the logistics are addressed for the kickoff meeting such as, office space, overhead projector, screen, storage bins, whiteboard, and enough seating. Since this is the auditors' meeting, ask them what they will need and determine how you can accommodate them, within reason. For example, you might be asked by the auditor in charge for an individual office for each auditor. This could be a problem if you do not have the space and some of the auditors might have to double up or they might have to work in a bullpen setting.

Summary

The audit process begins with a pre-planning session by the internal audit staff where they decide what to audit next and how to conduct the audit. This decision is based on what the critical processes are within a company; where executive management believes their biggest exposures might be; and where the company will benefit most from an ensuing audit.

Once a decision is made as to what process or processes will be audited (there can be multiple audits conducted at the same time by different audit staffs), an announcement letter will be sent by the lead auditor to the process owner who becomes the audit client. The announcement letter will indicate the planned starting date for the audit and the scope of the audit. The audit client's manager and the audit manager are copied on the letter. The announcement letter will indicate that the audit will start with a kickoff meeting. The lead auditor, audit manager, and the auditors who will be participating in the audit will be present at the kickoff meeting. The audit client will have his or her key staff members attending the meeting along with his or her manager. They can also invite other personnel who they feel could play a significant role in this audit based on the scope indicted in the announcement letter.

Guidance

1. If you receive an announcement letter from the auditors informing you that an audit will start shortly, meet with your staff and ask them if they are audit ready.
2. Decide if the audit start date is acceptable for your organization and that there is no reason why it needs to be delayed. If it needs to be delayed, then request that the audit be postponed along with the reason why it should be rescheduled.
3. Find out from your staff why they believe that they are or not audit ready.

4. Look at the announcement letter and supply the auditors with whatever documentation they would like to see prior to the kickoff meeting.
5. Ask your staff to make sure that they have all other documentation that they believe will be needed once the audit starts and review it with you.
6. Make sure that your key staff will be available during the audit. If they will not be available, then ask whether there is backup and if the backup personnel will be available during the audit.
7. Meet with your executive manager and review audit preparation and ready status with them.
8. Ensure that you have any risk assessments readily available that might be valuable during the audit.
9. Look at all previous audit findings and ensure that appropriate remediation has taken place or that plans to address any exposures, if not completed, are in progress.
10. Discuss the audit with other departments that might play a role in the audit and ask appropriate managers to attend the kickoff meeting.
11. Assign someone on your staff to be an audit interface who will work closely with the auditors and who will document audit requests and responses.
12. Gather presentation material that you will need for a kickoff meeting (e.g. organization charts) and review their currency—update the organization chart, if necessary.
13. Make sure that all personnel who no longer have a business need (e.g. personnel who have left the company or changed departments) have had their access removed from your data and files. This could lead to serious issues and signal a "red" flag to the auditors if not accomplished, so stay ahead of potential problems in this area. This issue is a common exposure identified in many audit reports.

Chapter 3 Exercises

As an audit client, explain what you would do in the following situations:

1. You are the Accounts Receivable manager and you have never been audited before. You receive an announcement letter about an upcoming audit where the lead auditor informed you that the audit is scheduled to start in three weeks. What do you do?
2. Who would you invite to the kickoff meeting?
3. The announcement letter asked you to supply initial documentation that you have already supplied. The lead auditor wants you to work with him or her after the kickoff meeting on scheduling interview sessions for the auditors. You have three members of your department who are responsible for exercising the functions that the auditors want to review. These employees have been working in your department for 6 months but have never been audited before. What precautions do you take?

Chapter 3 Questions

Assuming that you are the audit client. Please select the best answer:

1. Which of the following is true?

   A. You will receive the audit announcement letter directly after the kickoff meeting
   B. You must agree with the date the auditors want the audit to commence. You have no choice
   C. Responses to audit documentation must be supplied within 24 hours
   D. You should review prior audit issues pertaining to a previous audit for the process scheduled to be audited again and any actions that were taken for closure or actions that are in progress

2. Who should you invite to attend the audit kickoff meeting?

   A. Your key staff personnel
   B. Your manager
   C. The IT manager supporting your process
   D. All of the above

3. Who manages the kickoff meeting is responsible for asking that it be held and asks for presentations to be ready?

   A. The lead auditor

B. The audit client
C. The audit manager
D. The audit client's manager

4. As an audit client, which of the following should you prepare to bring to an audit kickoff meeting?

   A. Your organization chart identifying who is in your department and their functions
   B. The audit process
   C. An expectation of the turnaround time on audit requests
   D. All of the above

5. If you are dependent on any other department for service to support the process you will be audited on (e.g. IT, Human Resources), you should:

   A. Let them know about the audit and that you might need them
   B. Invite them to the kickoff meeting
   C. Ask them if they believe that they will be ready if and when questions are asked
   D. All of the above

6. If you are an audit client, you will always receive an announcement letter before an audit, usually 4 to 6 weeks before the audit starts.

   A. true
   B. false

7. An announcement letter for an audit will usually be sent to the audit client by:

   A. The audit manager
   B. The lead auditor
   C. The audit committee
   D. Any of the above

8. The scope will usually not be in the announcement letter. It will be decided in the kickoff meeting.

   A. true
   B. false

9. If you receive an audit announcement letter, which of the following actions should you take:

   A. Decide who will be your audit interface to work directly with the auditors
   B. Meet with your staff to determine if they will be audit ready
   C. Make sure all of your key staff will be in attendance throughout the audit, and if not, ensure that there is backup
   D. All of the above

10. Which of these statements is true?

   A. You cannot invite anyone to the kickoff meeting other than individuals from your department
   B. You should have someone take notes at the kickoff meeting
   C. You will probably not bring anything to the kickoff meeting, since it is the auditors meeting and you are there just to listen and understand
   D. All of the above are true

D. [illegible]
E. All of [illegible]

10. Which [illegible]

[illegible]

CHAPTER 4

Audit Fieldwork

> Facts are stubborn things; and whatever may be our wishes, our inclination, or the dictates of our passion, they cannot alter the state of facts and evidence.—John Adams

The auditors will conduct fieldwork to help them determine if your processes and procedures are effectively executed and well controlled. The fieldwork will include reviewing documentation, conducting interviews, writing fact sheets, and having periodic status meetings.

E. Danter, *Audit Defense*, Palgrave Studies in Accounting and Finance Practice, https://doi.org/10.1007/978-3-030-92466-9_4

Documentation Requests

created by Sora Shimazaki

During the kickoff meeting, there might be requests by the auditors for additional documentation that was not requested in the announcement letter. Your audit interface should ensure that all requests for documentation, either requested in the announcement letter or the kickoff meeting, are logged into a file that he or she maintains. The logging should indicate what the documentation was that was requested, who made the request, when it was requested, the name of the individual who will be assigned to provide it, to whom it was provided to, and when it was provided.

The auditors will be reviewing documentation either before the kickoff meeting, if it was supplied early, during or after the kickoff meeting. During the audit, the auditors will make a significant number of requests that they will most likely ask to be turned around within 24–48 hours. If there are any reasons why requests can't be complied with within the expected time frame, then the auditors need to be made aware of the reason, as soon as possible. There may be extenuating circumstances that will need to be explained. Frequent reasons for delaying turnaround are: (1) the absence of key personnel who are subject matter experts, (2) the urgency of addressing/resolving business issues that supersede audit requests, or (3) the documentation requested is off site and will take longer than 24 or 48 hours to retrieve.

It is advisable that you inform the lead auditor if there is a delay or postponement in complying with any request by the date requested and the reason for the delay. The auditors will generally accept a delay as long as there is a reasonable explanation for the setback.

Once the auditors finish reviewing the initial documentation, they will probably ask for additional records, files, notes, etc., to augment what was already given to them. Again, the audit interface needs to log all of these requests with status as the audit proceeds. There will probably be numerous requests for documentation throughout the audit, potentially dozens of requests from each auditor, and it is critical that all requests and responses be closely monitored and controlled. If you do not do this, you can be heading into trouble. There can be accusations that specific documentation that was requested was never supplied, or it was supplied late. It is important to note that to maintain control, all documentation should be sent back to the lead auditor who should be the one who requests all documentation. If requests come from other individual auditors, and they might, it should be noted who sent the request but the response should still go back to the lead auditor. Have all requests put into emails or text and then store the emails or texts in the request file. This will be your audit trail. Realize the importance of this audit trail and record all requests made and responses as there could be scores of requests from each auditor engaged in this audit. I cannot emphasis this enough—it is a key control that should be established to avoid an ugly situation, delays, and accusations. Another thing to keep in mind is that you need to make a copy of all documentation given to the auditors and keep the original for yourself. Unfortunately, there are times when the information that is given to auditors is lost or you are told that it was never received. You want to prevent this from occurring, if possible, or at least to be able to follow the trail from request to response.

The log that your audit interface is keeping captures and maintains a record not only of requests for documentation, but of any requests that might be made to arrange for interviews with key personnel or to hold status meetings.

Keep in mind that once all the material is reviewed, the auditor(s) still might have additional questions and they might want to arrange interviews with specific individuals to discuss the procedures that are followed and to ask them about their controls (Table 4.1).

Table 4.1 An example of a request log

Request	*Received from*	*Date received*	*Assigned to*	*Date forwarded*	*Forwarded to*
Last three months of reconciliation reports	Mary Snell	Sept 18, 2020	Jim Galo	Sept 19, 2020	Bob Grant
August error reports for entire month	Hilliary Cleave	Sept 18, 2020	Eric Small	Sept 20, 2020	Bob Grant
List of customers for audit period	Adam Long	Sept 22, 2020	Hannah Jabowski	Sept 21, 2020	Lillian Wolk (Bob Grant on vacation)
Documented balancing procedure	Bob Grant	Sept 25, 2020	Jacob Rich	Sept 25, 2020	Lillian Wolk
Set up meeting to discuss separation of duties	Bob Grant	Sept 26, 2020	Eric Small	Sept 26, 2020	Bob Grant
List of late payments made in October	Bob Grant	Nov 3, 2020	Becky Wright	Nov 8, 2020	Bob Grant

The Interview

created by Alex Green

The interview(s) is a key element in the audit. If the auditors want to have an interview with the audit client or their staff, they should make the request through the lead auditor who will then notify the audit interface in the client's department so that they can schedule the interview with the appropriate individual. It is during the interview that the auditor will review the material provided and discuss the procedures and controls that the interviewee follows. The auditor compares the answers that they receive to the documentation, looking for any discrepancies. If the auditor finds any issues or has any concerns, he or she will make note of them and probably identify them as exposures—these exposures could make their way to the audit report. You should be aware that an auditor could ask the same requests to more than one staff member to see if they follow the same procedure. Because of the importance of the audit interviews, and there can be many interviews from various auditors, the audit client needs to take rigorous and diligent measures.

During the interview, the audit client manager needs to pay particular attention in taking the following precautions:

If a staff person is requested to be in attendance in an interview by an auditor, the manager, whenever it is possible, should attend the interview and provide whatever support they can. This is especially true with an individual who is a member of his or her staff who has never been audited before. They will probably be intimidated by an experienced auditor and should not be left alone—this is a danger zone. If the manager is not available to sit with his staff person, then they should try to postpone the interview to a later date when the manager would be available or have one or more experienced senior staff personnel, sit in the interview for support.

It is important that the manager assigns one of his or her staff to take copious notes during the interview. The individual being interviewed may be too nervous to take detailed notes; however, note taking is critical. Every question that the auditor asks and the answer received should be documented. It is important because the responses to the auditor's questions could result in disagreements as to what was or what was not said. Please realize that the answers could result in an auditor having concern(s), resulting in assumed exposures that could very easily wind up in the final audit report.

Anyone being interviewed should be advised never to lie to an auditor. This could result in serious consequences, not only in unsatisfactory audit reports but in demotions, other disciplinary actions, and even dismissal. If information is requested and the answer is not known, the answer should not be guessed or fabricated. This frequently happens because the individual being interviewed does not want to look bad. Once you lie to an auditor and it is discovered, the auditor will not have any faith in whatever you tell them from that point on. If the answer is not known, then the answer should be "I don't know, but I will get back to you with that information as soon as possible."

The manager should advise the individual being interviewed to stay away from giving opinions and to adhere strictly to the facts—the audit report will have findings that should be based on *facts*.

There is a golden rule that is usually followed during an interview or whenever an auditor asks for information. And that is to give the auditor only what they ask for, whether it is documentation or an answer to a question during an interview. Audit clients are advised never to give more than what is asked for. They should restrict their responses to only what is asked and not offer any more information. By supplying more than what is asked for, they can be opening up the proverbial can of worms. For example, if asked for a list of people who have access to your accounts receivable database, then give the auditor a current list, provided that it has been updated. Do not give the auditor a list of individuals who had access for the entire year. There might be two individuals who perhaps had access for three months after they left the company and did not have their access revoked on a timely basis. The auditors could discover this if they dig deep enough. Just give the auditor what he or she asked for, nothing more as it can get you into trouble. In the scenario above, the auditors did not need to know how long the two individuals had access to the accounts receivable database after they left the company. There is one exception to this rule. If supplying more information will help you, then and only then should you give the auditor more than what he or she requested. For example, if asked for a specific reconciliation report for the current month and you don't have it but you have all of the previous months for the entire year, where there were no problems, then ask the auditor if they would want to see them. Your potential exposure could disappear from the audit report or at least, it can be mitigated. It is better if the auditor writes that one reconciliation report was missing for the year rather than saying that there were no reconciliation reports available when asked. Again, the reconciliations that were not asked for should only be given to the auditors if there were no problems.

A suggestion is that a manager should request that his or her employee asks the auditor at the end of the interview if the auditor has any concerns or issues in what they have or have not seen or heard. Have the individual who is taking notes document the auditor's response, whether there is a concern or not. This can then be used in status meetings with the auditor to get clarification before the final report is written. If the auditor states that there is no issue, it would be difficult for him or her to claim that there was an exposure later on.

Fact Sheets

After reviewing documentation and conducting interviews, auditors will usually write fact sheets where they identify any concerns that they might have.

Realize, however, that this is not always true. There are times when you may not see any fact sheets. Different audit organizations and reviewers could have different procedures that they follow and you may not see any.

However, there are numerous IA organizations, external accounting firms, and federal agencies that will generate fact sheets when conducting audits, so be prepared. In many companies, these fact sheets may also be referred to as finding sheets. These fact/findings sheets are extremely important—they are an interim step between the gathering of documentation and interviewing personnel before generating final audit reports. Questions stemming from documentation reviewed or interviews held that are not answered to the auditor's satisfaction will probably result in issues appearing in the audit report but will probably be stated in the fact sheets first. It is imperative for audit client managers and their staff to read these documents very, very carefully. They need to agree with the facts stated and protect themselves not only against potential statements that are not factual but comments that can also be misleading. The audit reports can be slanted one way or the other based upon the findings revealed. Fact sheets will frequently include percentages and numbers relating to the issues stated. As we will observe below, percentages and numbers can influence the perspective that the reader will have on the size and significance of the finding and the reader's perspective. You should suggest to the auditor, if they have not already done so, that they add percentages and numbers, when appropriate and where it will be beneficial.

Audit clients need to ensure that these finding sheets contain only facts and not opinions. Auditors' opinions will be disclosed in the final audit reports and are based on the facts. Hence, the importance of validating and determining that the fact sheets are valid and not misleading is crucial. One can hardly overstate the significance of carefully reviewing these findings as they can affect your future. You must inform any auditor if you are in agreement with his or her findings as they appear in their fact sheets. Failure to do so can lead to a serious problem.

Findings, as worded, will probably cycle back and forth between auditor and audit client with revisions and suggested changes made, until agreement is reached. Here is an example of an audit finding: "*213 million of accounts receivable revenue was recorded during the six month audit period from January through June. Message errors that were generated from the system during this time period were not resolved in a timely fashion. This resulted in delays of recording revenue during this period and delayed collection.*" This statement as worded might have been accurate, but it was misleading. The findings did not state how many error messages were generated during this time period, what the error messages were, the percentage of errors corrected timely, nor if there was delay in correction.

All of this additional information was important and should have been included. It's true that there were error messages, but additional wording should have been added to help the reader understand the impact of the problem. Let's assume that there were nineteen error messages generated during this time period. Eleven were warning messages that were not really application error messages and did not prevent records from being processed. They had to do with potential space problems as the number of records being processed increased. The message read "disk space approaching capacity, investigate future potential capacity concerns." Were these processing problems? No, they were not. Of the other eight that were valid processing error messages, we determined that six were corrected within the service level agreement of 24 hours and two, for five thousand dollars in combined revenue, were delayed by an additional 24 hours. They were tracked, recorded, and resolved as soon as the subject matter expert, who was engaged in resolving system outages when the errors were recorded, was available to work on them. If this finding, as originally worded, appeared in a final report, many executives would have been misled as to the seriousness and breadth of the problem.

Status Meetings

by Christina Morillo

As mentioned earlier, it is usually during the kickoff meeting when the schedule for status meetings is discussed. The auditors and audit clients should agree on the frequency for these status meetings in the meeting. It could be decided that they be held weekly, bi-weekly, or whatever other time period was agreed upon. There can also be status meetings held sooner than an established schedule, when necessary. This can be required if there are red flags that cannot wait for the regularly scheduled status meeting to take place. An example might occur when a fraud or strong possibility of a fraud is discovered.

At the status meeting, issues are discussed as well as perhaps the number of requests made and the number of requests still outstanding. Potential findings can also be discussed along with any significant issue that will increase the duration of the audit. Scope sometimes increases if the auditors want to expand the functions being audited. This can occur if there is something that is suspicious and warrants additional investigation. Issues of cooperation or unprofessional behavior on the part of the auditors or audit client might arise where escalation and discussion with executive management might be necessary for awareness and resolution.

The lead auditor and all the auditors should be present at the meeting. The audit manager can also be in attendance. The audit client manager will decide who attends from his or her organization. It is typical that the client manager, lead staff personnel, and sometimes the audit client's manager be in attendance at the status meetings. This depends on the seriousness of the issues discussed and perhaps requests from the auditors on who should be in attendance. The status meetings could be thought of as early warnings of things to come before the final report is written.

It is important that the managers being audited have someone on their staff assigned to take notes. They should record the date and time of the audit status meeting, who was in attendance, and the issues and status of the items discussed. It is also routine to discuss and record future plans regarding audit duration, names of new auditors if they were added to the audit team, any cooperation problems, etc.

Summary

The auditors can, if they choose, ask for initial documentation in the announcement letter. This request will be supplemented by additional requests during or after the kickoff meeting. There can be a very large number of requests, as each auditor will be submitting requests. Because of the sheer volume of requests that might be made, it is important that there are tight controls on what was asked, who asked for it, and when the documentation that was requested was supplied to the auditor. All requests and responses should be logged and followed up on. Otherwise, the audit can easily get out of control. This control is the responsibility of one individual on the audit client's staff referred to as the audit interface. All requests should come from the lead auditor and returned to the lead auditor. Usually, after the kickoff meeting and after the auditor's review of the documentation, there will be requests for interviews to further understand the procedures and controls that are exercised. It is during the interview sessions that the auditors, after digging deeper into the procedures and controls, will possibly have issues/concerns. It is customary that they indicate the issues in finding sheets, sometimes called fact sheets, and present these findings to the audit client. The fact/findings sheets will state each function that was reviewed where any issues were found. The auditors should describe their expectations for each function and their observations as far as what they found. They will also include recommendations for improvement. During the kickoff meeting, there is usually agreement reached as to how frequently status meetings are to be held to review the status of the audit. This usually includes a discussion of progress of the audit to-date, problems or issues identified so far, and plans for coming days. The status meetings are held throughout the audit process. They are usually held at least once a week but can be less frequent.

Guidance

1. If you are a process manger and audit client, do not allow inexperienced staff to sit with auditors alone during an interview.
2. Inform your staff to never lie to an auditor during an interview.
3. Assign a staff member to take notes (a scribe) during the interview.
4. If an answer is not known to a question that an auditor asks, tell your staff not to guess—tell the auditor that you will get back to the auditor with an answer.
5. When possible, search for any documentation that you have before an audit, but do not establish processes or controls after an audit is announced and mislead the auditor that you had it before the audit was announced. This could result in disciplinary action.
6. Have your managers read all fact sheets, when presented to you, very carefully and instruct them not to sign unless the facts are accurate.
7. You and your staff should read all fact sheets very carefully to ensure that they are not misleading before you sign off.
8. Ask auditors to add additional factual statements into fact sheets if they were not initially included but will help you.
9. Have as many key staff read the fact sheets, as possible, and agree to the facts before you sign off.
10. Realize that once you sign off that you are in agreement to any fact sheet, the exposures cited will most likely appear in the final audit report.
11. If you feel that you cannot sign off on a fact sheet, notify your executive of your reluctance and advise them not to sign the final audit report (we will discuss this again later). You need to make sure that your reasons are justifiable and that you can convincingly explain any objection that you have to your executive.

Chapter 4 Exercises

As an audit client explain what you would do in the following situations:

1. You receive finding sheets that cite exposures that the auditors found. The exposures cited are not substantiated and laced with opinions. The auditor claims that controls are missing but he does not take into consideration secondary controls that exist. What action do you take?
2. During a status meeting with the auditors, they state to you that not all of their requests have been responded to. You ask them for specifics and are told that for 14 requests in the last week that the auditors made, they never received responses to five of them. What action do you take?
3. You receive numerous fact sheets during the audit. The findings are all factual but some of the exposures stated are misleading since secondary controls exist that mitigate the risk and were not asked for by the auditor. You are concerned that what is written can be moved directly into the final audit report and can be misleading to the executives. What action do you take at this time to convince the lead auditor to be fair?

Chapter 4 Questions

Assuming that you are the audit client. Please select the best answer:

1. There are a vast number of audit interviews scheduled. What action should you take before the interviews?

   A. Ensure that the Chief Audit Executive (CAE) is present at all the interviews.
   B. Assign a member of your staff who is at the interview to take notes.
   C. Ensure that your entire staff is present at each interview.
   D. Instruct the staff member being interviewed that if they do not know the answer to the question asked that they take their best guess to reassure the auditor that they know what they are doing.

2. You receive an unusual number of documentation requests from the auditors, more than you or your staff were able to respond to within the requested 24 to 48 hour period. What do you do?

   A. You complain to your manager and ask them to escalate the problem.
   B. You ask the lead auditor that because of the huge volume and other daily functions you have, if the timeline on some of the requests can be extended.
   C. You ask the lead auditor if she can give you more time in responding to all requests beyond the initially requested 24 or 48 hours.
   D. You tell the lead auditor that you can't effectively handle all the requests. You tell her that there are too many, that she is unreasonable, and that they should reduce the number of requests.

3. The auditors have asked you to arrange an interview to discuss monthly reconciliations. The individual who is responsible for the reconciliations is a recent addition to your staff who has never been audited before. The action you take is to:

   A. Tell your new employee to do the best that they can and take their best guess in answering questions if they are not sure.
   B. Ask the lead auditor if you could sit in on the interview.
   C. Ask your entire staff to sit in on the interview to support the new hire.
   D. Advise your new employee to listen carefully, as they will be sitting alone, but to take notes during the meeting so you can review them later.

4. You receive a fact sheet from the lead auditor that is misleading. It states that there is an inadequate separation of duties that you do not believe to be true. What action do you take?

   A. Escalate your concern to the audit manager.
   B. Escalate your concern to your manager.
   C. Ask the lead auditor to be more specific where he or she feels that there is a separation of duties issue.
   D. Sign off on the fact sheet and wait to discuss it in a status meeting.

5. You receive a fact sheet and you agree with the facts, but the fact sheets do not inform the reader of secondary controls that the auditor never asked you about. What do you do?

   A. Escalate your concern to the audit committee.
   B. Sign off anyway on the fact sheet after you voice your concern with the auditor.
   C. Ignore the fact sheet and let the auditor know that you will not signing-off.
   D. Ask the auditor to revise the fact sheet with added comments and to include the secondary controls.

6. Auditors will sometimes ask the same question to more than one individual in the department that they are auditing. The reason for this would be to determine if:

   A. Both individuals are doing the same work and there is a possibility of a separation of duties concern.
   B. To see if the procedural documentation is clearly understood.
   C. To see which of the individuals, or if both, are following the documented procedures.
   D. Any or all of the above.

7. If you are the audit client and the auditor is interviewing you, you never supply more information that what is asked as it could open up areas for further questions that could lead to trouble.

   A. true
   B. false

8. At the end of an interview, one of the best things that you can do is:

   A. To ask the auditor if he or she has any concerns
   B. To ask the auditor if he or she has any concerns and ask the person taking notes to indicate the questions and response in their notes
   C. To ask the auditor who they would like to interview next
   D. None of the above

9. During a weekly status meeting, the lead auditor accuses you and your staff of not responding to thirty percent of documentation requests that were due and are still open. What do you do?

A. You accuse the lead auditor of being in error
B. You disagree and voice your objections to the audit manager
C. You tell the lead auditor that this is a surprise to you and you were told that all requests for documentation were supplied
D. You look at your request log to verify if what the auditor is accusing you is true and if not, then tell him, according to your log, who the documentation was sent to

10. During one of the status meetings, the lead auditor advises you that the scope of the audit is being expanded from what you were originally told. What action do you take?

A. You accuse the auditor of scope creep and tell him that it is not fair
B. You escalate your concern to your manager (who is not at the status meeting) and ask him if you can stop the audit
C. You ask the lead auditor if you can speak to her manager about the scope creep (her manager is not at the status meeting)
D. You understand that the auditors can extend the scope of the audit, if there is good reason, and ask the lead auditor for an explanation.

CHAPTER 5

Audit Conclusion

The things that hurt, instruct.—Benjamin Franklin

At the conclusion of an audit, audit reports should lead to improvement. Although they are the auditors' reports, they are distributed for the benefit of the company. The report is distributed to executive audit management, as well as audit client executives and other company executives who have a vested interest. This depends on the extent and seriousness of the issues. The more significant the exposures, the broader the audience with unsatisfactory audit reports possibly being distributed to the audit committee.

Corrective actions are recommended and should be implemented, when reviewed, and accepted by all parties. Control exposures should be closed and the likelihood of future problems minimized, if not eliminated.

Audit Reports

The audit report is to use the proverb, "when the rubber meets the road." This is the culmination of reviewing all documentation, conducting interviews, writing fact sheets, and having status meetings. The areas just mentioned are considered "fieldwork." The report itself does not just state the facts but also opinions. Auditors should cover the five "Cs," outlined below, in their reports. This is what you should be expecting auditors to highlight in their reports:

E. Danter, *Audit Defense*, Palgrave Studies in Accounting and Finance Practice, https://doi.org/10.1007/978-3-030-92466-9_5

- Criteria (identifying what procedures and controls should be in place for the process being audited)
- Condition (stating the current control state that they observed)
- Cause (indicating the reason for any exposure)
- Consequences (concluding what the effects of the exposures are)
- Corrective actions (making recommendations for control improvement).

You should anticipate that the audit report will cover the above elements and follow the format below or something very close.

- Salutation: This indicates who the recipient of the audit report is, usually the process owner; name of organization that was audited; and indication of who sent the audit report, usually the lead auditor.
- Introduction: The introduction describes the process or processes that were audited, what the purpose of the audit was, when the audit started, when it was completed, names of auditors who participated, etc.
- Scope: It states the functions within the process that were audited and the period of time that the audit covered (from when to when).
- Executive Summary: This is the overall opinion that the audit staff has reached. It is a summary of major issues and written so that executives who do not choose to read all the detail in the report can understand the overall control posture of the environment that was audited. The executive summary should be able to stand alone and identify all of the salient conclusions with a summary of supporting information for each area reviewed. It should describe the major functions in the audit where exposures were identified. Executives might decide to read the details of the report if they wish and have the time. However, they should be able to determine if the audit is satisfactory or not, know where exposures exist, and what are the ramifications of the weaknesses cited just by reading the executive summary.
- Details: The fact sheets (findings sheets) that were previously discussed should be moved, almost verbatim, into the detail section of the audit report, once agreement is reached. This will eliminate or minimize any surprises. The audit clients should be aware of what exposures, if any, will appear in the final report. If done correctly,

each function that was reviewed and had an issue should have a detail finding. If no issues were found with a particular function, the auditor should state that there were no exposures in this area. If he or she has not indicated this in the report, you should ask them to include a positive statement to this effect. Each function appearing in the final report, again these are issues, should have a description of the purpose of the function, observations on what exposures were found, what the concern or risk is with the exposure(s) cited, and recommendation(s) as what could be done to address the issue. The recommendations are the auditors' recommendations and do not have to be agreed to by the audit client, although it would be advisable for the auditor to discuss the recommendations with the audit client and their staff before they appear in the final report. If they do not make sense, time can be wasted. This will be explained when discussing the recommendations in more detail when focusing on responses.

- Favorable comments: The auditors should include procedures that are well documented, effectively working and well controlled within a process. As an audit client, you should be given credit for what is working well. If the praise is not apparent when the report is written, then you should ask the lead auditor to do so. It is the auditor's report so they may or may not agree. At the very least, you should ask that credit be given when deserved. You have nothing to lose by asking and can benefit if credit is given.
- The audit manager and the audit client's manager should be copied on the report. The common practice is to copy everyone on the report who was copied on the announcement letter.

Recommendation and Responses

The audit report as noted above can contain many recommendations, especially if it is an unsatisfactory audit. These recommendations are a result of audit findings. The recommendations do not have to be agreed to by the audit client, as I stated before, but they should be discussed to see if they make sense. The auditor's responsibility is to make the most valuable recommendation that he or she can compose to address any exposures in the functions audited. An auditor with years of business experience and business acumen is in a better position to understand the business impacts that might result if the exposures are not adequately addressed than an auditor with far less years of experience.

However, as the audit client manager, you are likely to have more years of experience in the process and functions that are being audited than the auditor has. You are in an excellent position to determine if the recommendation(s) are reasonable and justified. If they do not make any sense, the auditor has wasted a lot of time since every recommendation will require a response. There is usually a request in the audit report that you respond to every recommendation within a specific time period. This time can be two weeks, a month, or whatever the auditor thinks is acceptable. Your responsibility, as the audit client, is to indicate in your audit response if you accept or reject the recommendation.

If you accept the recommendation, it is incumbent on you to respond with a target date as to when you will have corrective action implemented. Your response should, if possible, describe the corrective action that is planned. Sometimes further analysis and review by various parties are needed before a corrective action is finalized. If this is true, then address this in your response. If the corrective action is known, your response should include the name of the individual, or more likely the title of the individual who will be responsible for the corrective action and the target date for implementation. The auditor will then have the option, if they choose, of tracking your corrective action until it is implemented.

If you reject the recommendation, you need to have a valid business reason that is usually reviewed by and agreed to by your manager. The auditor will probably accept the rejection if the reason for the rejection is logical and makes sense and is documented. For example, the recommendation might be rejected because the cost of eliminating the exposure or the cost of mitigating the issue might be more costly than the potential loss. You may not have the funds or resources to implement the recommended action. You need to convince the auditor of your conclusion. It would help your cause to obtain documented agreement by your manager to the rationale for rejection. Your rejection will carry more weight if he or she decides to reject the recommendation as well. Another action that would be beneficial would be if you could demonstrate that a risk assessment took place and was accepted by your manager before the final decision was made (the risk assessment process will be discussed later in more detail). The auditor will probably look favorably at your reason for rejection if you have a documented risk assessment with executive approval.

Another point is that if you are planning to respond to the recommendation but need more time than the auditor has given you, you should ask for an extension and explain the reason for the request. You might need more time than allotted to you for a thorough analysis since you might not be able to respond within the initial time requested. One way or another, you should respond to the auditor and let him or her know what your plans are as to when you will have the analysis completed and response ready of either acceptance with a corrective action plan or the possibility of rejection.

It is likely that every recommendation will be closely tracked not only by the audit staff but by your management team as well. It is your responsibility to closely evaluate the practicality of every recommendation in the audit report and if the recommendation(s) does not make sense, for whatever reason, you need to explain the rationale for rejection. In most cases, you will have more experience to judge the common sense of the recommendation made and its value than the auditor will have. Time should not be wasted. It is hopeful that every recommendation will be reviewed with you before it appears in print to improve its odds of being of value. However, unfortunately, this is not what will always happen. Both your team and the auditors work for the same company and the end result or response to the recommendation should be what is best for the company. Auditors should not be looking to generate as many recommendations as possible in the anticipation that their value add will be enhanced and you should not accept every recommendation, since some recommendations will just not have much merit and will result in unnecessary resource wastefulness.

Audit Report Sign-Off

The lead auditor should supply you with a copy of a draft of the audit report once it is completed with details and recommendations. This is a courtesy and an attempt to get your approval, if possible, with the content. Be careful—you need to ensure that the issues and exposures cited in the fact sheets are fairly represented in the audit report. The auditor does not have a literary license to change the facts that were stated and that you concurred with. Review the draft of the audit report very thoroughly, ensuring that the facts are stated correctly and that the report agrees with the facts in the findings sheets, previously reviewed. Surprises should not surface now.

Next, the final report should be presented to your executive manager. The executive manager will be asked to sign off on the report but should do so only if he or she feels that the report is accurate. The executive will be held accountable for all unsatisfactory audit reports and their future could be at stake with perhaps punitive steps enforced. The executive needs to be sure that the report is accurate, truly, and fairly stated and not erroneous or misleading. Your executive will most likely ask you if you read the report and if you agree with the report before they sign. They will probably ask you to opine as to whether the issues in the report, assuming that there are numerous exposures, are verifiable and factual.

The opinion is the auditor's but the facts are not. If auditors did their job equitably and professionally, the facts in the report should be valid and previously substantiated as to their veracity, before the report is distributed. There should be very few instances when reports are not signed but if it is not signed off when presented, then there needs to be a very good reason, one that can stand up under scrutiny. This rationale should be documented and reviewed by all levels of management.

Again, read the final audit report very carefully and compare it to the fact sheets that hopefully were reviewed with you. There should be no surprises. Whatever issues were identified in the fact sheets should be reflected in the final report. If there weren't any fact sheets previously written but issues were stated in the final audit report, your review of the final report will be much more difficult. It will result in significantly more time being consumed since you will have little to compare it to. When reading the final report, you need to be cognizant of any liberties that were possibly taken by the auditors. Unfortunately, this might occur. Look for erroneous or hyperbolic statements and issues stated that did not appear in the fact sheets nor revealed or discussed during the interviews. You should be in a position to provide sound advice based upon your review if and when your executive asks you if they should sign off. You can either recommend that they sign off or not to sign off. You should inform your executive that there will be an expected tidal wave of calls and emails exerting pressure on them to sign, asking them to explain any justification if they chose not to sign. This pressure can come from divisional executives within your company as well as from the audit manager and the chief audit executive. A lot depends on how carefully and thoroughly you and your staff read the fact sheets and subsequent final report. The importance of your responsibility can't be overstated here. This is the conclusion and end result of the audit so be very, very careful and take your time—careers could be at stake. I can't stress enough that hopefully there will be no surprises to the facts stated as all issues and concerns should have been previously discussed and identified. Unfortunately, this is not always true.

The following is a personal experience that I encountered after my mandatory, more than three-year audit term ended and I was asked to help manage an internal audit for the director at one of our outsourcing accounts.

After I left audit, I took a position with the business controls department as an interface between audit clients and the auditors. Executive management thought that because of my audit experience, knowing how the audit process works, that I could be of value in achieving successful results. My responsibility was to work with the audit clients, help them to prepare for audits, and assist their management and key staffs in working through the audit. I was there to recommend what they should say or not say and how to communicate with the auditors. I was there to give advice and counsel but not to directly interfere with the audit. My objective was to help them, if and when possible, to achieve satisfactory audits.

Personal Experience 5.1

My company was responsible for supplying IT service to a customer. I was sent to the customer's site to assist our director when an audit was announced. The director asked me to review the audit scope, to review documentation to see if it would satisfy auditors' requests, to attend interviews, to review fact sheets, to examine audit findings, and to review the final audit report. I focused on these activities during the audit fieldwork and was surprised and disappointed with the result when the director called me to review the audit report with her. The auditor had taken excessive liberties. It was an unsatisfactory audit with an opinion that was not substantiated by the facts. The report was laced with exaggerations and misleading statements. It was more opinionated than factual. What really upset me was that the auditor never brought some of these facts up or revealed her concerns before, not during the interviews or any fact sheets (of which there were none). In my opinion, it was an unfair audit report that instead of being a value add, appeared to be a vehicle to possibly further the auditor's own career. When the director asked me if she should sign, I recommended that she should not. I had never recommended this action before, but I believed that I had little choice this time. I told the director that if she did not sign that there would be a tsunami of pressure, which there was. First, the auditor was livid that the director had refused to sign. I sat in a meeting with the two of them and supported the rationale and recommend again, this time in front of the auditor, that the report not be signed. I said that it was not factual and misleading and the auditor disagreed vehemently. We were at a stalemate. The next moves were predictable. The director informed me that the audit manager and chief audit executive exerted pressure on her to sign and her vice president and other of our company's executives quizzed her on why she was refusing to sign. She asked me again if she should sign. I advised her that once she agreed to and signed off on the unsat audit it would not only be an unfair negative mark on her career but that she and her staff would need to spend an inordinate amount of time in establishing corrective action plans, that were not needed, and then monitoring them until closure. Not only would her department be spending a lot of time in addressing unfounded issues, but additionally, the unnecessary actions would be tracked by many of her executives. As difficult as it was, she had faith in what I told her. She stood her ground, did not sign, and documented her reasoning. The audit report was eventually released, but it was released and distributed without her signature.

Summary

The auditors will have completed their fieldwork once the fact sheets are agreed to, documentation supplied, and all the interviews held. They will then huddle together and write an audit report where they will summarize and review what they examined and what they found. The beginning of the audit report will have an introduction identifying pertinent information such as when the audit took place, who the auditors were, and the scope of the audit. The introduction is usually followed by an executive summary that identifies the issues and can usually stand by itself. Many executives will read just the executive summary and will not read the details in the audit report. However, the details are included in the report after the executive summary and can be read by anyone who wants to read the details. The details are usually a copy and paste from the fact sheets. The auditors will probably ask that the audit client respond to each recommendation by a specific date. The recommendations are the auditors and the audit clients do not have to comply with the suggestions made. However, they will need to respond back to the lead auditor and let them know if they accept the recommendations or not. If they accept a recommendation, they should indicate when they plan to have a corrective action established. If they reject the recommendation, the audit client should have a good reason documented as to why the recommendation is not going to be accepted after thorough analysis, usually documented in a risk assessment. The auditors will then take the audit report to the audit client's executive for final sign-off before distribution.

Guidance

1. Read the recommendations in the final audit report very carefully. They are the auditor's recommendations and you may not agree with them. Notify the auditor, if you don't.
2. Respond to the recommendations only after you have time to consult with your team. Let the auditor know if you need more time to respond then the response time frame that is requested in the report.
3. If you do not want to accept a recommendation, document a valid reason for not agreeing, and discuss the rationale for rejection with the auditor.
4. Review your objection for not agreeing with the recommendation with your manager and get their concurrence.
5. If you accept a recommendation, indicate a target date as to when any cited exposure will be eliminated or mitigated.
6. Log any plans for remediation in an issues log and track any action until implementation, indicating a closure date.
7. Reread any findings or fact sheets that were previously reviewed by you and compare the facts to the final report. If you believe that your executive manager should not sign the final audit report, make sure that you have a valid reason (e.g. the audit report not being factual or misleading).

Chapter 5 Exercises

As an audit client, explain what you would do in the following situations:

1. A draft of the final audit report is given to you. You realize that some of the recommendations make little sense and the auditor has asked for correction actions to be completed within 30 days. What do you do?
2. You go into the final audit meeting with your director and the audit lead. The audit report indicates serious control exposures and the audit report is unsatisfactory. You have not signed off on the fact sheets because you did not think it was fairly representative of your controls. However, the exposures were moved from the fact sheets to the final audit report. The audit lead asks your director to sign off on the report. What do you do?

Chapter 5 Questions

Assuming that you are the audit client. Please select the correct answer:

1. The recommendations in an audit report belong to:

   A. The audit staff
   B. You, the audit client
   C. You, the audit client, and audit staff
   D. The audit committee

2. Which of the following is true when you receive the audit report?

   A. When audit recommendations appear in the final report, you must accept them.
   B. When you accept the recommendations, you must have actions completed by the date the auditor requested.
   C. You do not have to accept all recommendations.
   D. Recommendations in the final audit report are open ended as far as the request as to when you should respond.

3. The audit report can be distributed:

   A. Only after your director signs
   B. Only after the audit committee signs

C. Only after both your director and the audit committee sign
D. Even without your director's or executive management's signature

4. You are the audit client and when you receive the audit report, there are recommendations that you are requested to respond to within 30 days. Your department is going through a major reorganization and there is a lot of uncertainty now about the direction ahead. What do you do?

   A. You establish a new response date of 60 days from the date the report was received.
   B. You explain the situation to your director and ask your director to escalate to the audit committee.
   C. You explain the situation to the lead auditor and ask for a delay in responding.
   D. You can do any of the above.

5. If you read a draft of the final audit report and you agree with the facts but not all of the recommendations.

   A. You let the lead auditor know that you will refuse to accept the report until the recommendations are changed to your preference.
   B. You inform the auditor of the changes to the recommendations that you would like to see and if he or she refuses, you escalate your disagreements to their audit manager.
   C. You accept the audit report and respond to all the recommendations with target dates for closure except to the recommendations that you disagree with. You just inform the auditor that you disagree with them.
   D. You accept the audit report and respond to all of the recommendations with target dates for closure. You also respond, in writing, with the rationale as to why you are rejecting the recommendations that you disagree with. You need to document as to why you feel that they do not make sense or are not feasible in your opinion.

6. The audit report should include:

   A. The scope of the audit
   B. The names of the auditors

C. The audit start date
D. All of the above

7. The executive summary is usually just a statement of opinion on audit results without any substance.

A. true
B. false

8. Every audit report must be signed by the audit client executive.

A. true
B. false

9. You are the audit client and you receive a draft of the audit report. You see only negative statements but nothing positive on what your organization is doing well. What action do you take?

A. You don't agree with the audit report and will recommend to your director not to sign.
B. You escalate your concern to the audit committee.
C. You escalate your concern to the audit manager.
D. You ask the lead auditor to include positive statements for which you have supporting evidence.

PART II

Controls Overview

Chapters 2–5 that comprise Part I of the textbook describe the audit process this is essential for all future audit clients to be familiar with. Part II begins the student's education on controls.

"The Only Thing Worse Than No Control is the Illusion of Control" - anonymous

It is important to realize that if we don't recognize that we have problems and exposures, we will not put corrective actions in place to correct these issues and rectify any control concerns that do exist. There are too many occurrences when managers and their staff assure executives that they are audit ready, that there are no significant problems, and then the world collapses and they are surprised, and stunned. They are presented with a failed audit report with many significant exposures, what a jolt.

Part I provided you with insight into the audit process—it is important that you are familiar with the process. The next step to be audit ready is to be aware of the controls that are expected and essential to obtain well-controlled processes and effectively executed procedures. This leads you to Part II that includes a discussion of types of audits and controls such as preventive, deterrent, and detective controls; physical controls; administrative controls; system and application controls; operational controls; access controls; and separation or segregation of duties.

Knowledge of the controls above will be important to you regardless of what process you own. When and if you are subjected to an audit, it would be beneficial if you were familiar with as many controls that could benefit your department and have a positive effect on the execution of their functions. This textbook will cover controls that have been or could be established in your department and controls within any service organization that you might be relying on. This knowledge benefits all business managers including IT managers, accounting managers, etc. There is a possibility that any manager who owns a process, financial or non-financial, can be audited, some more likely than others. Whatever the likelihood is of your being audited, it is essential that you are prepared.

CHAPTER 6

Types of Audits and Controls

To believe all men honest is folly. To believe none is something worse .—John Adams

Types of Audits

There are various types of audits that can be conducted. Examples of these audits are:

- Financial Statement Audits
- Information System Audits
- Information Technology Audits
- Operational Audits
- Forensic Audits
- Compliance Audits

The audits performed by internal audit organizations that this textbook focuses on are Financial Statement Audits and Information System Audits.

- Financial Statement Audits review formal records (e.g. balance sheets, income and expense statements, P&L reports) and supporting financial activities. The auditor gathers evidence about business transactions that have occurred and about the account

E. Danter, *Audit Defense*, Palgrave Studies in Accounting and Finance Practice, https://doi.org/10.1007/978-3-030-92466-9_6

balances where the transactions have been accumulated. Management makes assertions about the financial statements and the auditor compares the evidence to the assertions made, contained in the financial statements, looking for discrepancies. The auditor looks not just for errors and exposures, but for material misstatements in financial statements when conducting the audit. He or she should cite the misstatements and reasons for the errors, which can be due to missing or incomplete procedures or control weaknesses. Financial audits target SOX compliance.

Financial statement audits will focus on[1]:

- Occurrence: Whether all recorded transactions and events have occurred and pertain to the entity.
- Completeness: Whether all transactions and events that occurred during the period have been recorded.
- Authorization: Whether all transactions have been properly authorized.
- Accuracy: Addresses whether amounts and other data relating to recorded transactions and events have been recorded appropriately.
- Cutoff: Relates to whether transactions and events have been recorded in the correct accounting period.
- Classification: Concerned with whether transactions and events have been recorded in the proper accounts.

Financial statement auditors who will be examining financial statements will be utilizing analytical procedures to evaluate financial information through analysis of plausible relationships between financial and non-financial data.

You should be aware of the potential opinions that can be concluded as a result of financial audits. These are:

- An Unqualified Opinion: This is the result for an audit that is clean or free from material misstatements. As an audit client, this is the most desirable opinion.

[1] Adapted from ninth edition *Auditing & Assurance Services—A systematic Approach* by William Messier, Steven Glover, Douglass Prawitt.

- A Qualified Opinion: The auditor concludes that except for specific matters explained in the audit report, the financial statements give a true and fair view.
- An Adverse Opinion: The auditor concludes that the financial statements do not give a true and fair view.
- A Disclaimer of Opinion: The auditor concluded that the extent of their inability to obtain sufficient appropriate audit evidence is such that it is not possible to form an opinion on the financial statements.

Information Systems Auditing is the process of collecting and evaluating evidence to determine whether a system safeguards assets, maintains data integrity, allows organizational goals to be achieved effectively, and uses resources efficiently. Information System Audits will examine information system design, information systems controls, and execution of controls.

The results of an information systems audit will be different from a Financial Audit opinion. The results will generally be "an unsatisfactory opinion" or "a satisfactory opinion."

Some companies might even use the option of "a marginal opinion," which lies between a satisfactory and unsatisfactory audit.

You should be cognizant that there are two different information systems audits that you can be subjected to if you are or become a manger or a key staff person in an information technology organization. The first audit is an audit of a system that has not yet been installed but is still in a design and test phase. The second is a system that is already operational. The controls that we will discuss later will address both scenarios. For a system still being developed, auditors will key in on whether it is likely that the systems will be delivered on time, within budget, and will be meeting design requirements. With regard to systems that are operational, auditors will look to see if the applications within the system are running efficiently, effectively, and if they are meeting customer expectations.

An Information Technology Audit is different from an information systems audit. The technology audits can be thought of as a large umbrella with systems audits being a subset. There are no hard rules in defining these audits. Technology audits have many different descriptions and if you ask 10 different professionals what they consider information system components to be, you will probably get 10 different responses. In addition to reviewing information system design, information systems controls and execution, internal information technology auditors can broaden their audits and also specifically examine the following items, just to name a few additional areas:

- Data center facilities
- Networks
- System platforms
- Databases
- Applications
- Security
- Software
- Hardware

As an audit client, you will most likely be the recipient of either a financial statement audit or information systems audit. Realize that you can also be the recipient of a more specific audit that was previously referenced such as a forensic audit and compliance audit. There certainly are differences among the audits but the way you need to interface with your internal audit staff will be very similar no matter which of these audits you are faced with.

Auditors, whether financial statement or information system auditors, will be looking for controls over initiating, authorizing, recording, processing, and recording transactions.

Although many of the controls that will be audited are the same, there are distinctions—contrasts exist between financial statement and information systems audits. The controls that the auditors will review have differences and naturally since the processes, procedures, and controls do not always line up, the pro-active audit readiness measures that you will need to implement will also differ.

Control Importance

The importance of controls is significant no matter what processes you are responsible for in your company. One of the surprises that occur when you are being audited is that auditors will hold you accountable, not only for knowing if the controls are adequate within your department, but in knowing if other departments that you are dependent upon also have well-established effective controls. For example, if you are the manager of the Purchasing Department in your company and many of your functions are automated, you will most likely be dependent on your Receiving Department to have reliable processing and effective controls. If there are control exposures within the Receiving Department that affect you, auditors can hold *you* accountable. Accountability is one area where audit clients are vulnerable. A lack of knowledge on the part of a process owner on the controls within a service organization supporting them can be harmful and result in unsatisfactory audits. You need to be and should be comfortable that there are established controls in any department that you are dependent upon and that they are effectively being executed.

Every corporate executive, or future corporate executive, should realize that controls have always been important, and have not become important from the emergence of Sarbanes Oxley. SOX has raised the importance and accountability of controls but controls have always played an essential role when processes and procedures were in focus. However, throughout the last couple of decades, it seems that everyone's concern has been elevated, with controls becoming an integral part of the strategic plans in many organizations. You can even hear controls being discussed around the water cooler in the office. Controls should not be an afterthought, as they sometimes are, in the design and in the development of new applications or in planning application maintenance and IT operational support. The audits conducted today are much more comprehensive; then, they ever have been in the past.

Let us take a look at why controls are so important.

- One of the most detrimental results stemming from inadequate controls in a company is the loss of revenue resulting from inadequacies in correcting errors and processing omissions. Without adequate controls, the losses can be significant, more than most people can imagine.
- Adequate control design and effective execution are mandated by federal legislature given teeth by SOX with significant penalties imposed for noncompliance. Executive management now has an increased legal liability. The mandate by the federal government is not new, but Sarbanes Oxley legislature has given it a mouthful of teeth.
- Computer crime, fraudulent activity, and cyber security have become major sources of concern and risk. How many of the corporate scandals of recent years might have been detected, if not prevented, if basic controls had been in place? How many of the Enron,

WorldCom, and other scandals would have occurred had there been adequate controls and accountability? Not an easy question to answer, but certainly one that should be asked.

- As business organizations convert their old systems to modern systems and databases, the failure of conversion, without adequate control, can be catastrophic to the company. Conversion must be successful and planning is critical up front to ensure that controls are in place, with checks and balances along every step of the conversion process.
- Controls are needed to protect breach of privacy and to protect a corporation's confidential or proprietary information (HIPAA compliance). With hackers more numerous, better educated, smarter, more dangerous, and more brazen than ever before, protection via security controls is not a luxury that only very profitable corporations can afford, they are a necessity. Hacking is a game to some, a challenge to others, but destructive and unaffordable to most enterprises. Even if confidential or proprietary information is not breached, disruption to the company's operation by hackers breaking into systems can be catastrophic. We will be talking about cyber security later on in this text.

You probably have been introduced to controls at a very early age. You probably remember the story of the three little pigs. The process was the building of houses for the pigs that would protect them from the big bad wolf. The procedure was that the three pigs were going to separately design and build their own house in line with their own specifications. The preventive controls were that they each chose a design that was suppose to be strong enough so that it could withstand attempts by the wolf to blow the houses down. The first pig built his house out of straw but when tested, it failed. The wolf blew it down. The second pig built his house out of sticks, but it too failed its test and the wolf blew it down. The third pig had a stronger control. He built his house from bricks and it passed the test. It was strong enough to stand up even after many attempts by the wolf to blow the house down.

Later in life, you were introduced to processes, procedures, and controls. If you look at your lives currently, they include political elections. The process is to elect our government officials. The procedure is to have our people vote by completing ballots and selecting those individuals chosen for office for various levels of officials all the way up to the presidency. The voting can either be done in person or by mail in ballots. The controls for both choices of voting differ. There are manual controls in place for the manual functions such as the distribution of ballots to all eligible voters, completion and verifying the legitimacy of the ballots entered ensuring that a voter submits one and only one ballot, etc. These controls should ensure that only registered voters submit ballots, that there are no duplicates, that the ballots can be read, that the results are all entered on time, that there are at least two individuals responsible for processing the ballots (deterrent controls), etc. There are also controls in place for the automated functions within the voting process. For example, if voting is done electronically how do we ensure that the systems have been sufficiently tested to ensure that duplicates are not entered? How do we verify that the ballots are valid? If ballots are rejected are there procedures for resubmission (corrective controls) and are the algorithms working correctly for tabulating the results? Then, there are the security controls that protect the ballot selections once entered. There needs to be assurance that the systems cannot be tampered with. And of course there needs to be security on the databases where the results are stored before final tabulation. The databases need to be protected from hackers and outside malware, viruses, worms, etc. (preventive controls). There are also audit trails to examine the data before and after entry to detect if there were errors or fraud (detective controls).

Whether we are looking at our election systems, accounting systems, information systems, or any corporate process, we need to be concerned with the adequacy of controls and understand their importance, and they need to be sufficiently tested.

Control Benefits

Now let us take a look at the benefits of having well-established and convincing controls in place.

- Controls can position you to comply with federal legislature. This is especially true with regard to SOX and should help keep you from being subjected to penalties and/or heavy fines.
- Controls can help you to pass audits. There is no guarantee that you will pass an audit with adequate controls, but you certainly will improve your odds.

- They provide early warning of processing problems. The earlier the detection of processing errors, the lower the cost of correction. The cost of fixing errors rises exponentially with the passing of time. You will want to identify problems as soon as possible, and with the right detective controls in place, you should be able to.
- Well-designed controls can deter fraudulent activity. The installation of adequate controls is a potential deterrent.
- Controls should reduce maintenance costs. Effective controls can prevent application and system failures, resulting in a reduction of costs associated with the maintenance required to ensure that applications are up and running.
- They reduce costs associated with administrative corrective action. If application errors increase because of control weaknesses, you will likely be spending more money on the administrative actions required for corrective action than you could have imagined.
- Well-established controls provide assistance in evaluating performance and efficiency.
- Controls should provide measurements to evaluate end user satisfaction. Throughput, timeliness, and accuracy measurements can be of significant help to you and your customers.
- Effective controls should provide recoverability in case of disaster. Hurricanes, tornadoes, floods, power outages, terrorism, and other disasters can bring your operations to a halt without recovery controls.
- Established and well-placed controls reduce operational costs. The better controlled your applications and systems, the less expensive it will be to keep them operational.
- Controls will improve completeness, timeliness, and quality of processing. Having adequate controls in place can play a major role in achieving these objectives.
- They will help provide accountability. Controls should help audit clients establish competent accountability.
- Controls should provide auditability. If controls are implemented effectively within the process, you will have audit trails generated that will demonstrate auditability.

Control Axioms

These are a few control axioms that are useful to know. They are:

- The primary accountability for overall control resides with top management. SOX assigns accountability at the highest level of management and that is where it should be. Top executives can no longer plead ignorance and take the position that they were not aware of the actions of their management teams. Their management teams might be responsible for having adequate controls being executed within their departments but the accountability is at the top.
- Application controls must be reviewed before and after installation. Controls need to be independently reviewed before implementation and during design and development. Controls should not be an afterthought with the intent of designing and installing them later. This will be discussed in more detail later. However, even with well-designed controls, you can have ineffective execution. Reviewing controls after a new application or system is operational for a reasonable period of time is extremely beneficial.
- Management must set objectives and assign accountability for effective implementation of adequate controls. The only way that an infrastructure within a corporation can effectively achieve a sound audit control posture is if there is full support and endorsement from the CEO, CFO, CIO, and other executives. Your management teams cannot be effective in enforcing controls if the CEO is not behind them 100%. Top management needs to set objectives and put an infrastructure in place for the effective implementation of controls.
- Controls must be audible. If you cannot demonstrate the design and execution of your controls with adequate documentation, you will be in jeopardy of failing an audit. Auditors are extremely skeptical and need to be shown proof. You should have audit trails to provide evidence. Auditors need to verify.
- Controls should be jointly developed by users/owners and IT personnel. For many process owners, the dependency on IT is much greater today than it ever was. More than ever, it is an essential partnership. Controls need to be developed by everyone who is in the game and who has a role. It is a team effort. Controls

should not be established without taking all users into consideration. For example, if you are an application development manager designing controls for application recovery, you should design these controls with operational personnel who will probably be relying on well-documented run books with instructions for keeping applications and systems running in case of failure. You should also consult process owners and end users who understand business needs regarding the availability of critical applications and can help in establishing necessary recovery requirements and acceptable application downtime parameters. When designing controls, consulting with other organizations you interface with is a positive step and should be strongly considered.

- Application controls are not to be compromised in order to meet schedules. Corners should not be cut—you will pay for it in the long run. For example, if a new billing application being developed is under a tight schedule, controls should not be compromised and the focus should not be totally placed on meeting installation deadlines. You can meet the scheduled date of installation but spend an inordinate amount of time putting out fires and keeping the application running after it is installed. Because of control absences or weaknesses, the application can frequently abort and you might need to resolve problems at all hours. Do not let controls be an afterthought—you will pay the price in the long run.
- It will be exponentially more expensive to retrofit controls into projects after they have been designed and are operational. If you compromise controls to meet an implementation schedule, it will be much more expensive to retrofit the controls into the system after it went live then if you had designed the controls up front. It is analogous to building a new house. It's a lot cheaper to put a solar heating system into a house when it is being built than after construction is completed. To use an old adage. "Pay me now or pay me later."

Control Principles

There are principles of controls that should enlighten you as to actions that you should take to benefit your company's business success as well as position you to improve audit readiness. They are described here but referred to in greater lengths within subsequent chapters of this book. This is just an overview at this time to drive these points home.

- Separate responsibilities

The most effective, basic control that every auditor searches for is segregation of controls, also referred to as separation of duties. Both terms refer to the establishment of separate roles and responsibilities. If adequate separation of duties exists, you will most likely need to have collusion between multiple parties to circumvent controls that result in fraudulent activities. If you own a process within a company, whether you are an accounting manager, information technology manager, inventory manager, etc., you should be aware of the need to ensure adequate separation of duties. Separation of duties is discussed in more detail in a subsequent chapter for both financial statement audits and information technology audits.

- Use manual controls where automation is not possible

Manual controls are more prone to human error. There is no doubt that automated controls are more effective. However, manual controls are an integral part of any controls review and should not be overlooked. They should be used where it is not possible to use automated controls and, needless to say, are better than not having any controls. If automated controls are not possible or feasible due to technology issues, you need to ensure that there are adequate checks and balances on the manual control activities. They can also augment automated controls that are in place, increasing overall effectiveness. In some cases, you will be combining automated and manual controls. For example, you might have a system-generated report that identifies everyone who has access to your accounts payable system, but you might need a manual review to validate their business needs and to initiate action to remove unwarranted access.

- Conduct annual reviews to see that the controls are still valid and that they are executing effectively

As business processes, environments, and personnel change, documented control procedures will most likely have to change as well. Not only should control procedures and control points be reviewed at least annually, but they should be reviewed more frequently if and when you become aware of changes. You will need to validate not only if they are still of value and if the documentation requires updating, but control activities should be executed at least annually to ensure that they are still effective. Controls are only worthwhile if they are being executed effectually.

- Mitigate business risks wherever possible by establishing controls

Business risks need to be frequently re-evaluated to determine their severity. If there is greater business risk due to control weaknesses being identified, then a new control procedure might have to be established, or an existing control procedure enhanced, to mitigate the risk. The same will hold true if the business environment changes—the risks could be affected due to these developments.

- Document controls and control points

Once processes and procedures are documented, it is essential to identify and document where controls need to be established (control points) and then to document the control procedures corresponding to each control point. It is an exercise in futility to try to establish controls without reviewing documented processes and procedures to determine where exposures might exist without adequate controls.

- Keep controls simple

If you design overly complex, difficult to execute control procedures, they may lose their effectiveness. This can occur with a new system that was designed and programmed by IT personnel. The controls can be so difficult to understand and execute that there is dependency on one expert who understands them. When that individual is not available, there is a lack of understanding and confusion as to how they work—the controls are not practical. Keep controls effective but as simple as possible.

- Localize and reduce exposures

Establish as many control points as needed, as close to each other as possible to ensure maximum control with the fewest exposures. Be careful not to over control but be sure that all exposures are addressed.

- Consider cost effectiveness

Establishing controls can be very costly. Manual controls might need additional resources to be hired and automated controls might require a significant amount of programming efforts and a possible delay with implementation that can be costly as well. However, you can't ignore the need to have IT controls designed and implemented because failure to do so will probably cost you more later on. Recovering from control problems and retroactively establishing controls after applications and systems are operational could result in considerable costs, more than you anticipated. It is of paramount importance that one realizes that the cost of adding controls is often more than justified by the savings achieved.

Managers can say that their companies cannot afford the expense of adding all of the controls that are recommended by auditors. This is where a risk assessment, referred to below, comes into play. Control requirements (e.g. SOX) that are mandated by the federal government probably will not afford you the luxury of not complying with them. Again, there will be exceptions after risks are analyzed and documented.

You will be faced with difficult decisions, weighing the costs of adding controls versus the benefits of a more established control environment. You will need to do what is right for your organization and balance controls with business needs. Neither the establishment of controls, nor the execution of control procedures, is an exact science, and they are riddled with challenges that will put you to the test. You will need to ensure that you are audit ready and in compliance with control regulations. It will be necessary to design controls or be accountable if delegating that responsibility and to validate that the controls are cost justified. If the cost of adding control is more expensive than the business loss associated with the exposure than reevaluate and redesign. There are many ways to implement effective control activities, use good judgment and explore all possibilities.

- Don't over control

As indicated above, you want to establish as many control points as needed to effectively address and reduce operational exposures. But don't over control. If one control will suffice instead of two, then use one. This is a judgment call, but an important exercise, as over controlling could be detrimental to your processes executing timely and accurately. Over controlling could bring your business to its knees. Too many controls can extend the time needed for your processes to execute. You will then have a very well-controlled environment but business functions could take a lot longer to execute than you would like and/or will be able to afford.

- Conduct risk assessments

You need to know that risks apply both to auditors and to audit clients.

Auditors have a risk that when conducting their audits, that they could be missing identifying exposures that exist. There might even be situations of fraud or exposures to fraudulent activities that fall through the cracks. Auditors could be negligent in identifying existing control issues when reviewing business processes and procedures. Failure to call out these weaknesses can be very damaging.

Exposures identified by auditors will result in recommendations cited in audit reports that in the auditor's opinion require corrective actions. It is important to understand that these are the auditor's recommendations and do not have to be accepted by management who is being audited. There are times when the recommendations will not make sense. All recommendations will require a response. They can be accepted or rejected. If rejected, there needs to be justification. This is when audit clients should conduct a risk assessment. A risk should be evaluated and utilized to assist you in discerning whether or not corrective action is warranted, in your opinion. You will need to notify the audit staff of your conclusion and have your risk assessment documented. The process for conducting and documenting a risk assessment will be discussed in more detail in a later chapter.

If you are a process owner and become an audit client, auditors will be examining how efficacious your controls are and if they are effectually and timely being executed.

It is important that every process owner understands what the different control choices are so that they can make an educated decision on the controls they should establish.

Controls can be put in place to prevent, deter, or detect not only fraudulent activity but also unintentional erroneous processing. Most issues arising in a company do not result from fraud but from inadequate controls in everyday processing to catch processing errors. Most errors are a result of a lack of education or compliance by honest business people who are well intentioned and trustworthy. Preventive controls, as we will see below, are the first line of defense and probably the most beneficial. However, the other types of controls discussed are very important and can be established and executed in conjunction with preventive controls. The best scenario at times is to have multiple types of controls established, reinforcing each other.

We will look at defining some of these controls on a high level before getting into more detail later on.

Preventive Controls

created by Brett Sayles

Companies should maintain internal controls that provide reasonable assurance that fraudulent or erroneous processing can be prevented. Preventive controls mitigate or stop an event from occurring. These are designed at the point of entry. Preventive controls are usually passive. They are close to 100% effective. When breached, they lose their effectiveness and need be backed up by additional controls, usually detective controls. Examples of preventive controls are:

- Passwords that stop unauthorized access to systems or applications.
- Badge readers that are required to gain access to buildings.

- Edits and rejections of erroneous data before it is entered into applications (e.g. duplicate transmissions of data).
- Assurance that sensitive records requiring approvals before being processed are actually approved (e.g. payroll payments of excessive amounts).
- Door locks that prevent unwarranted entry to homes or to rooms containing sensitive equipment or documents (e.g. locks on doors of computer rooms or where company strategies are stored).

Deterrent Controls

created by Ellie Burgin

Deterrent controls discourage or restrain one from acting or proceeding through fear or doubt. They can also curtail or hinder an event. Examples of deterrent controls are:

- The knowledge that systems are password protected can discourage someone from trying to hack into a particular system.
- Security guards sitting at entrances to buildings or a security guard within a bank can also be a deterrent control.
- A sign on a window of a car warning of an alarm system.
- A sign on a winding road that says "slow down, steep hill ahead."
- The existence of an independent audit committee.

Detective Controls

created by Nataliya Vaitkevick

Detective controls reveal or discover unwanted events and offer evidence of trespass. Detective controls find errors for later correction. They are generally the least costly. They often necessitate rework or investigation after the error or incident has been identified. They are usually very effective and can be an auxiliary control to a preventive control. If a preventive control or deterrent control does not stop an unwanted event from occurring, the detective control should be an indication that the first line of defense did not work but that the incident was detected. Examples of detective controls are:

- Overdrafts on banking accounts.
- After hours security checks.
- Unsubstantiated accounting entries.
- Absence of documented authorizations when reported.
- Various types of alarms (e.g. smoke alarms, fire alarms).
- Data base reconciliations.
- Identifying out of balance records/accounts.

Reporting Controls

Reporting controls document an inexcusable event, an undesirable situation, or a trespass. Upon detection of an unwarranted incident, it is essential that some sort of report can be generated. Examples of reporting controls are:

- Reports being generated for out-of-balance records or irreconcilable accounts.
- A process to prevent violations or suspicious activity to executive management. An example would be a list of unauthorized access attempts to the payroll file.
- Preparing audit reports where exposures are identified.

Corrective Controls

created by Daria Sannikova

Corrective controls remedy or set right an unwanted event. These controls detect errors and attempt to correct them immediately. Examples are:

- The automated or manual correction of rejected computer processing.
- The submission of omitted records.
- The enforcement of disciplinary action against personnel engaged in fraudulent activity.
- Firemen putting out a fire.

Recovery Controls

Recovery controls regain or make good the effect of an unwanted event. This type of control is used mainly in situations of hardware errors but can be used in the case of software failures. They are automatic. Examples of recovery controls are:

- Software automatically recovering and restarting communication circuits when there is a communication failure.
- Automatic restart of application programs in the event of failure.
- Disc rereads.

Summary

It is important that every corporate manager understands what different control types exist so that they can make an educated decision on the controls they should establish. It does not matter what process in the company you are managing, you will need to establish effective controls. Controls will be examined when auditors conduct financial statement audits, information systems audits, information technology audits, operational audits, compliance audits, forensic audits, etc. It does not matter what process is being audited.

Controls are put in place to prevent, deter, or detect not only fraudulent activity but also unintentional erroneous processing, which is most likely. Most control deficiencies are not a result of intentional errors but are a result of a lack of education or compliance by honest people. If preventive controls or deterrent controls cannot be put in place, then detective controls should be installed. The best scenario is to have as many types of controls established as possible, where they reinforce and support each other.

Corporations perform functions that they need to accomplish. If these functions are executed repetitively, we consider them to be processes. Processes describe *what* functions should be achieved (e.g. payroll system where employees are to be paid for their work). And processes have procedures that describe *how* the process is to be executed (e.g. cutting bi-weekly checks for all employees, except senior executives who get paid monthly). The procedures have controls that are designed and established to ensure that all procedures are effectively executed.

This chapter introduces us to Financial Statement Audits and Information Systems Audits, There are other types of audits but these audits and their processes, procedures, and controls are highlighted in this text. Financial Statement Audits opinions will result in a conclusion of the report being: Unqualified, Qualified, Adverse, or a Disclaimer. Information Systems Audits will have a different result of being Satisfactory or Unsatisfactory.

The following are the types of controls that the audit client needs to be familiar with: preventive controls that mitigate or stop an unwanted event from occurring; detective controls that reveal or discover unwanted events; deterrent controls that discourage one from acting through fear or doubt; reporting controls that document an unwanted event after it occurs; correcting controls that remedy an unwanted event; and recovery controls that regain or make good an unmated event.

Guidance

1. Document all of your processes from input origin to output destination.
2. Using your process documentation, indicate what controls should be established and where they need to be installed.
3. Spend the additional time when a system is designed to focus on controls. Controls should not be an afterthought when designing and promoting a new system. It will be a lot more costly if you try to retrofit them in later.
4. Understand the different types of controls that you can have imbedded in your processes.
5. Do not hesitate to put more than one control in a procedure for the same function. For example, it is beneficial at times to have both preventive and detective controls in place at the same control point.
6. Understand the risk involved with not having a control inserted at a specific junction where exposures are known to exist.
7. Weigh the cost of establishing any control versus the risk of not having it.
8. Conduct annual reviews of documented processes and controls to determine if the controls are still valid.

Chapter 6 Exercises

1. You have recently been promoted to be the manager of the inventory department. The previous manager was never audited but you received a notification yesterday that the internal audit department is planning to audit your department in three weeks. Your director asks you if you will be audit ready and if you think that you will pass the audit. What do you tell him and why?

2. As the accounts payable manager, you are dependent on your IT department for a significant amount of automated processing. You receive an announcement letter from internal audit that you are scheduled to be audited next month. You know that you have adequate manual controls established in your department and that they are effectively being utilized. Your IT manager says that she is audit ready. Do you take her word and don't worry because you trust her and hold her accountable? Is this the right decision? Please explain.
3. You are an IT manager who has been commissioned to design, program and install a new billing system by June 1. Your team is behind schedule and the situation is worsening every day. You hire more employees (doubling your staff) to meet the schedule. You decide to get the new system installed by June 1 and meeting your schedule. You have not had the time to include controls in your design but have decided to add the controls in later. Explain why this is not the right decision.
4. You are an accounts receivables manager. What are five reasons as to why you should ensure that controls are established and effectively working within your department?

Chapter 6 Questions

Please choose the best answer:

1. You are the purchasing manager. If the IT department is providing a service for you and has automated many purchasing functions, are they accountable for the controls in their department?

   A. true
   B. false

2. Are the edits within an application that have been designed and working:

   A. Detective controls
   B. Reporting controls
   C. Preventive controls
   D. Deterrent controls

3. You have a process where you reconcile your payroll database monthly. What type of control is this?

   A. A preventive control
   B. A detective control
   C. A deterrent control
   D. A correcting control

4. You are an order entry manager and have asked your IT department to design a new order entry system since there are many shortcomings with the existing system. Who should be designing the controls?

   A. The IT department
   B. Your department
   C. The audit committee
   D. Both your department and the IT department

5. You have recently been audited and there is a promise to deliver the audit report to you by the end of the week. What type of opinion are you hoping for:

   A. A qualified opinion
   B. An unqualified opinion
   C. A disclaimer
   D. An adverse opinion

6. When financial statement audits focus on completeness they are determining:

   A. If all recorded transactions and events have occurred and pertain to the entity
   B. If all transactions have been properly approved
   C. If all transactions and events that occurred during the period have been recorded
   D. If amounts and other data relating to recorded transactions and events have been recorded appropriately

7. If an auditor, when conducting a financial statement audit, concludes that except for specific matters explained in the audit report, the financial statements give a true and fair view, it is called an unqualified opinion.

A. true
B. false

8. You should review application controls:

A. Before installation
B. After installation
C. At least on an annual basis
D. Before and after installation

9. You are the manager and process owner of the inventory process. The inventory system needs to be replaced. You will require the services of the IT department to develop a new automated system. The controls for the new system should be designed by:

A. You, the process owner
B. The IT department
C. The internal audit staff
D. Yourself (process owner), users, and IT

10. Adequate control design and effective execution are mandated by the following federal legislature:

A. Sarbanes Oxley
B. Dodd Frank Act
C. COBOL
D. All of the above

Reference

Messier William, Glover Steven, Prawitt Douglass (2014) *Auditing & Assurance Services—A systematic Approach*, 9th edn. McGraw-Hill.

CHAPTER 7

Administration Controls

We should not rely solely on automated controls for our processes. Sometimes it is also necessary to depend on manual controls. When we speak of manual controls, administrative control is an important element. We are referring to controls that the employees exercise who are responsible to ensure the accuracy and efficiency for their processes.

Administrative controls typically change the behavior of people. The controls can be preventive, detective, or deterrent. Administrative controls are procedural or policy designs that lessen the threat of a processing exposure or weakness (unintentional or fraud) that can be detrimental to the company's business.

When examining administrative controls, we will concentrate on service level agreements, password controls, and user id administration.

Service Level Agreements

A service level agreement (SLA) is an agreement between two or more parties, where one is the customer or client and the other is a service provider. This can be a legally binding formal or an informal "contract" (e.g., internal department relationships). The agreement may involve separate organizations, or different departments within one organization. Agreements between the service provider and other external third parties should not be called SLAs. Because the level of service has been set by

E. Danter, *Audit Defense*, Palgrave Studies in Accounting and Finance Practice, https://doi.org/10.1007/978-3-030-92466-9_7

the (principal) customer, there can be no "agreement" between third parties; these agreements are simply "contracts." In some companies these contracts, with external organizations can be referred to as documents of understanding (DOUs) or Memorandum of Understandings (MOUs). These are usually legal contracts. However, the principle above is not always followed. Many companies, however, use SLAs when engaging with either internal or external organizations. There does not seem to be an iron clad rule on how to refer to service agreements but its intent is what is important, more so then the nomenclature.

A service level agreement is preceded by service level objectives. The objectives are intentions that the customer, or the audit client/process owner, solicits from the service provider. Negotiations usually go back and forth between the parties involved until agreement is reached—it is when agreement is achieved that a service level agreement needs to be documented. If some aspect of a service has not been agreed to with the customer, it is not an "SLA".

When auditors arrive, initiate the audit, and start questioning the process owner they could find issues and concerns that they have with the process. They will most likely ascertain after reviewing the process documentation and conducting various interviews if there are any service exposures that have led to or can lead to erroneous and/or delayed processing.

A well-defined and typical SLA will contain the following components:

- *Type of service to be provided*:
  It specifies the type of service and any additional details of type of service to be provided. For example, in case of an IP network connectivity, type of service will describe functions such as operation and maintenance of networking equipment, connection bandwidth to be provided, etc.
- *The service's desired performance level, especially its reliability and responsiveness*:
  A reliable service will be one that suffers minimum disruptions in a specific amount of time and is available at almost all times. A service with good responsiveness will perform the desired action promptly after the customer requests it.
- *Monitoring process and service level reporting*:
  This component describes how performance levels are supervised and monitored. This process involves the gathering of different type

of statistics, the frequently of when statistics will be collected and how the statistics will be accessed by customers.

- *The steps for reporting issues with the service*:
  This component will specify contact details as to who and when to report the problem to. The contract will also include a time range in which the problem will be reviewed.
- *Response and issue resolution time frame*:
  Response time frame is the time period by which the service provider will start the investigation of the issue. Issue resolution time frame is the time period by which the current service issue will be resolved and fixed.
- *Repercussions for service provider not meeting its commitment*:
  If the provider is not able to meet the requirements as stated in SLA, then the service provider will have to face consequences for the same. These consequences may include customer's right to terminate the contract or ask for a refund for losses incurred by the customer due to failure of service.

SLAs commonly include many components, from a definition of services to the termination of agreement. To ensure that SLAs are consistently met, these agreements are often designed with specific lines of demarcation, and the parties involved are required to meet regularly to create an open forum for communication. Rewards and penalties applying to the provider are often specified. Most SLAs also leave room for periodic (annual) compliance reviews to make changes.

If you are an audit client who will be audited and you are dependent upon IT for your service or if you are an IT manager who is being audited and dependent upon another organization for support (e.g. Human Resources) you will probably need a documented service level agreement.

Service level agreements are established to satisfy service level objectives. There are usually objectives that a process owner has with a service organization that are needed to ensure a smooth and effective operational environment. Auditors can ask the process owner what the objectives are. Once these objectives are known and documented, the process owners will attempt to reach agreement with the service organization and document these agreements in a service level agreement. Auditors will look for evidence of these agreements and check to make sure not only if the agreements are documented but also if they are signed off by the process owner and the service organization management. They can also validate if there is a procedure for at least an annual validation and if there is evidence that the annual validation was actually conducted (e.g. documented meeting minutes),

Let us explore what a service level agreement should address in two different scenarios. The first being where you, as the audit client, are an accounting process manager and the second, where you, as the audit client, are an IT manager who is subjected to an IT audit.

Case Study on Service Level Agreements

Suppose that you are the manager of the accounts receivable department. The accounts receivable application that had been operational for 12 years was recently replaced with a new application that was programmed, tested, and installed last month. Unfortunately, the application aborts frequently, on the average once every two weeks, and there are numerous editing and balancing errors that have resulted. There are exposures where processing is constantly delayed or transactions that are missing, causing erroneous, and delayed revenue recordings.

If auditors arrive, initiate an audit, and start questioning you and your staff, they will probably find these issues and cite the various concerns that they have with the A/R process and existing control weaknesses. You tell them that the A/R application that had been operational for many years was recently replaced with a new application last month. They will most likely arrive at the conclusion that this could account for the issues and exposures cited above.

The auditors can ask you if there is an agreement between you and the IT department. If there is an agreement, they could ask to see it and examine it to see if it was signed off and if it is current. If there is no agreement, they will probably ask you why it was not established and hopefully you will have a plausible explanation.

Some examples of what could be in an agreement reached with the IT department reinforcing your objectives that you had that were requested before the new application went live are:

- Applications should be operational for a designated percentage of scheduled time (e. g. ninety-eight-percent of the time).
- Critical errors need to be resolved within a specified number of hours (e.g. four hours). This is usually the responsibility of the

programming department, in the case of a software malfunction or inadequate testing, or it could be the operational staff that needs to resolve the problem in case of a hardware or network problem.

- Number of outages during a period of time and total hours where the application is down should be agreed upon (e.g. less than three total hours outages in a month for less than one hour of down time). If the applications or systems are inoperable for an extended period of time without resolution, there could be negative repercussions affecting the company's business. The process owner as well as the end-users are highly dependent on the continuous and uninterrupted application processing.
- Number of errors generated as a result of code changes is a minimum agreed to number based on the number of promotions (e.g. five percent of all promotions result in corrections). This is the responsibility of the programming department to further improve the quality of their testing.

As we can see from the above, the requirements in the agreement are the responsibility of either the service organization or the process owner. The owner of the SLA, in this case, the A/R process owner, needs to ensure that these requirements are clearly stated, documented, and agreed to by both parties. It would be the same if you hired a contractor to repair your roof. You should have a documented agreement that holds the contractor responsible for the quality of the work but guess who your family will hold ***accountable*** if the work is not done right and if there is no documented agreement as to the quality of the work as well as the cost. Your family will hold you accountable and not the contractor. It is you who hired the contractor and not the other way around.

Audit could not only ask to see and verify the existence and currency of the SLA agreement but they will also probably ask you and the IT department manager for any documentation that provides evidence that the items in the agreement have been monitored. Of course, they will probably want to validate that monitoring took place. You should have documentation for any review that took place, what the results were and if and when any penalties were imposed on the IT department for failing to adhere to the requirements that are reflected in the SLA.

As the A/R manager you might also have service level agreements with other organizations in the company. For example, if you have eight people on your staff, some might have been recently hired and some might be there longer than you have been. You might even have to let one or two employees go because of poor performance. You might want a SLA with Human Resources so they can let you know that they removed any employee from the payroll database after you alerted them that you had to fire someone. Another example would be if you hired a new employee, you might want confirmation that they have been added to the payroll database. This is just another example of when a SLA would be appropriate.

Now let's look at the second scenario. If you are an IT development manager or programming manager being audited and you are the audit client. The audit staff might ask you if you have an SLA with the operational department.

Some of the elements in an SLA that the auditors could be looking for are:

- If the application is to be running 24/7, then there should be adequately trained operational personnel.
- If there is a disaster at the site where the application is operational and the site is damaged or destroyed then a business recovery plan should be documented and a site designated where the application and system can be operational again. The SLA might also have a stipulation as to when the application needs to resume operation again after a disaster occurs.
- Are there audit logs maintained for the application that indicate if and when there are any hardware of software errors?
- Are there run books that are used by the operational personnel to run the application effectively?

It is important to note that if auditors find issues with lack of an agreement with a service organization, they will hold the process owner accountable for not having a signed SLA and not the service provider. In this scenario, the process owner would be the development or programming manager—be prepared.

Following is an example of a SLA that you can use as a guide.[1]

[1] Example of SLA Agreement components adapted from "Service Level Agreement (SLA) Examples and Template Blog"—December 24, 2019; Muhammad Rehan Raza (Stockholm technology consultant).

I will start with a Table of Contents that is followed by: a SLA Introduction; Definitions and Abbreviations; Purpose; Contractual parameters; Examples of Client Responsibilities; Examples of Service Provider Responsibilities; Service Level Priorities; KPIs and Metrics; Version Details and Document Change History; and Document Approvals (Table 7.1).

Table 7.1 Service Level Agreement Table of Contents

1. Agreement Overview
    1.1. SLA Introduction
    1.2. Definitions, Abbreviations
    1.3. Purpose
    1.4. Contractual Parameters
2. Service Agreement
    2.1. Responsibilities of client
    2.2. Responsibilities of service provider
    2.3. Service Level Priorities
    2.4. KPIs and Metrics
3. Service Agreement History
    3.1. Version Details
    3.2. Document Change History
    3.3. Approvals

Table of Contents

SLA Introduction

Include a brief description of the agreement, concerning parties, service scope, and contract duration. "This is a Service Level Agreement (SLA) between (customer name) and (service provider name), The document identifies the services required and expected level of service from MM/DD/YYYY to MM/DD/YYYY".

Definitions and Abbreviations

Service Level Agreement (SLA)—the agreement of service between the client and provider of service.

Key Performance Indicators (KPIs)—indicators that help support the SLA. For example, availability, reliability, timeliness of issue resolution.

Purpose

This section defines the goals of this agreement such as:

- Agreed service targets.
- Criteria for target fulfillment.
- Roles and responsibilities.
- Duration of scope and renewal of the SLA.
- Supporting processes, limitations, exclusions.

Contractual Parameters

You should define the policies and scope of this contract related to applications, renewal, modification, exclusion, limitations, and termination of this agreement. For example:

- Contract renewal must be requested by the (client name) at least 45 days prior to expiration date of this contract.
- Modifications, amendments, extension, and early termination of this SLA must be agreed to by both parties.
- (Client name) requires a minimum of 60 days notice for early termination of this SLA.

Examples of Client Responsibilities

- (Client name) should provide all necessary information and assistance related to service performance that allows the (service provider name) to meet the performance standards as outlined in this document.
- (Client name) shall inform (service provider name) regarding changing business requirements that may necessitate a review, modification, or amendment of the SLA.

Examples of Service Provider Responsibilities

- (Service provider name) will act as primary support provider of the services identified except when third party vendors are employees who shall assume appropriate service support responsibilities accordingly.

- (Service provide name) will inform (customer name) regarding scheduled and unscheduled service outages due to maintenance, troubleshooting, disruptions, or as otherwise necessary.

Service Level Priorities

These are examples of service level descriptions, priority, and response targets (Table 7.2).

Table 7.2 Severity level priorities

Severity level	*Description*	*Target response*
1.	Outage (e.g. server down)	Immediate
2.	Critical (e.g. high risk of server down)	Within 30 minutes
3.	Urgent (e.g. end-user impact initiated)	Within 2 hours
4.	Important (e.g. potential for performance impact if not addressed	Within 3 hours
5.	Modification (e.g. code problem, issue addressed but potential future impact)	Within 48 hours

KPIs and Metrics

An example of what you can have (Table 7.3).

Table 7.3 KPIs and metrics

Metric	*Commitment*	*Measurement (%)*
Availability	99% throughout month	98
Reliability	95% throughout month	96
Code errors	2% of all changes throughout month	3

Version Details and Document Change History

This is example of what the SLA could use to track version control and change history (Tables 7.4 and 7.5).

Table 7.4 Document details and change history

Version	*Date*	*Description*	*Authorization*
Version 1	April 15, 2018	Change in client responsibilities	Client manager
Version 2	August 13, 2019	Severity response time changes	Client Manager
Version 3	March 1, 2021	Availability metric changes	Service provider manager

Table 7.5 Document approvals

Name	*Role*	*Signature*	*Date*
Ali Mayan	Accounting director		04/26/2018
Ali Mayan	Accounting director		12/10/2020
Seth Vale	IT director		12/10/2020

Document Approvals

Last review and approval MM/DD/YYYY
Next Scheduled review MM/DD/YYYY

Password Controls and User ID Administration

Typically in an authentication process, user ID is used in conjunction with a password. The end-user must provide both credentials correctly to gain access to the system or application. Moreover, system administrators utilize user IDs to assign rights, track user activity, and manage overall operations on a particular system, network, or application.

Let us assume that you are the newly designated owner of the inventory process. You need to be aware that there are passwords and user ids that allow for individuals to access the inventory files and databases and to the system that the inventory application is running on. The SLA that you should have with the IT department should indicate that it is your responsibility to ***approve*** access to the inventory files and databases utilizing user ids and passwords and that the IT department's administrators have the responsibility of ***granting*** access after reviewing your approval of the request.

Request for Access

The request for access to your application needs to be completed by individuals in your department or any other department who need access. A simplified form to gain access could look something like this (Fig. 7.1).

When an individual needs access, they need to complete a request for access, similar to the example above. Their manager needs to first approve their access. You, as process owner, will then need to approve the access as well, sign and date the request. You should then forward the approval to the IT administrator who will grant access.

Auditors can verify the following with you:

- That there was a request form completed for each individual who has access to the inventory system, they can sample a number of employees who have access and ask you for their request forms.
- That the form was signed by their manager and by you, the process owner.
- That the form was properly dated
- That the business reason for approving access is still valid with the individual still performing the same functions as when they first requested access—there should be evidence of a least an annual revalidation of the business need.
- That the individual is still in the department/company.

Requestor's Name: ______________________ Date: xx/xx/xxxx
Department: ______________________
Manager's Name: ______________________
Reason for Access: ______________________
____
____
____
Manager's Approval: ______________________ Date: xx/xx/xxxx
Process Owner's Approval ______________________ Date: xx/xx/xxxx

---

Fig. 7.1 Access request

The IT department, as mentioned above, has responsibilities that they need to comply with as stated in the SLA. You should validate that they are performing their responsibilities. You are the process owner and the auditors will hold you accountable to see if you are monitoring IT compliance with the SLA. Some items that the auditors might expect to see in the SLA that you should check for are:

- Has IT established unique IDs for system access?
- Are there guidelines stipulating that user IDs not be shared?
- Is there a formal procedure to establish user IDs and passwords to gain system access?
- Does the procedure require management approval on a submitted request and is IT responsible to check the signature?
- Is there a process to revoke user IDs if they are inactive for a certain time frame (e.g. six months)?
- Are there rules established for passwords regarding physical characteristics that will tighten control (e.g. length, acceptable characters)?
- Are there rules that require passwords to be changed frequently?
- Are there system controls that will check that passwords are changed to comply with established security guidelines?
- Are there different rules for password change requirements based on job function?
- Are user IDs and passwords revoked automatically when there is a suspected compromise or when an individual no longer has a business need for access? Is there a requirement that the process owner notifies IT to revoke access?
- Are there automated checks to see that passwords are not trivial?
- Are levels of access established and assigned to user IDs based on business need or are all requestors granted the same level of access?

Password Guidelines

Weak and insecure passwords are a security concern and a gateway to breaches that can affect more than just the targeted users. It is important to create keys that strike the right balance between being easy to remember and hard for others (intruders or impostors) to guess, crack, or hack.

A good password is one that the user finds easy to remember but is difficult for potential intruders to guess. Several studies have found that about two-thirds of passwords fall into one of these three categories:

- Names of family members or pets.
- Important numbers in user's life (e.g. social security number, birthday).
- Keyword patterns (i.e. ASDF).

Better choices are:

- Passwords of two or more words that have several letters omitted (NWYOR).
- Passwords that are spelled backward.
- Passwords that include characters such as numbers and punctuation marks.

Summary

If you are going to be audited, you probably will most likely not be able to answer all questions that the auditors have. Most processes are dependent, to some degree, on the Information Technology Department for automated processing. You could also be reliant on other departments in your company to support you. Other departments might be the Human Resources Department for payroll functions or control of master employment databases, the Purchasing Department for equipment you might need, and other accounting processes that either feed you data for processing or departments that you are sending data to for downstream processing. For all departments that you are dependent upon, you should have service level agreements (SLAs) in place that detail the responsibilities for each party. These SLAs need to be readily available to present to the auditors if and when asked. The auditors, in addition to looking at the responsibilities of both parties and validating that the designated parties are fulfilling their responsibilities, will look for signed signatures from management indicating agreement. They will look at the date the SLAs were signed to see if they are current and if there is a procedure for review and revalidation. If there are functions that you are dependent upon that have been outsourced to another company (e.g. payroll), then you should have a signed contract available to show the auditors. This contract is frequently referred to as a "Document of Understanding (DOU)" and is different from an SLA that is internal between departments within the company.

With regard to passwords and user ids, you will be responsible for approving the business need for those employees and users who need access to your application's files and databases. There should be a procedure that requires individuals within your company who need access to fill out a form indicating the business need required to have access. The procedure should be compulsory that you and their manager, if the manager is not you, sign the request form that approves access, and then forward the form to the IT department to grant access. The IT department should check for the requester's manager's signature as well as your signature, as process owner, and grant access based on the approvals. When an employee is no longer in need of access, it is incumbent on the process owner, to notify IT to remove their access. The audit staff can not only check to see if there is a request on file for those employees who have access but they can verify that they still need access and even verify with H/R that those employees are still working in the same department or even still employed in the company. The auditors can refer back to the SLA between the process owner and IT to see who has responsibility for approving and who has responsibility for granting and removing access.

You need to ensure that concerns with passwords are limited. Password rules need to be established regarding triviality, frequency of use, password length, the number of characters contained in the password, the use of alpha and numeric characters, requirements for changing passwords, deactivation, etc. If you have a critical application, it is even more essential that password rules and controls are established and adhered to. The process owner decides who has a business need to have access via passwords and user ids but the responsibilities for granting and removing access by IT should be spelled out in the SLA between the process owner and IT. Remember, as process owner, you are the audit client and the internal audit staff will hold you *accountable* to ensure that all responsibilities are identified and that there is evidence that effective execution is being monitored, as stated in the SLA.

Guidance

1. Make a list of all departments within your company that provide a service to your department.
2. Validate that you have a service level agreement with any service organization and that it identifies the roles and responsibilities of both your organizations.
3. Validate that management signatures are evident on all SLAs.
4. Ensure that the SLAs are reviewed at least annually.
5. Make sure that there is a documented process for anyone to obtain a user ID and password wishing to gain access to your files or data.
6. Validate that your procedure requires your approval to submit the request to a systems programmer who will grant access after the form is received.
7. Verify that the individual who requests access has a valid business need that is stated on the request form.
8. Revalidate the business need, at least annually (more frequently if the access is to critical data).
9. Take positive steps as soon as you receive an audit announcement. Review all access and remove access for those who left the company or department or who no longer have a valid business need. This action alone, by minimizing an access exposure that could lead to fraudulent activity, can possibly save your job.
10. Inform your employees to change their passwords frequently to avoid trivial passwords and to ensure their secrecy. Passwords should not be exposed and easily accessible to unauthorized individuals. I have seen passwords stuck on the bottom of laptops, written on calendars, posted underneath blotters, etc.

Chapter 7 Exercises

You are the purchasing manager and the purchasing application used within your company has been operational for 13 years. There are numerous concerns that have surfaced over the last year and they have reached a crescendo. There are too many errors in the selection of vendors, the application has been out of balance five of the last 6 months, and the application aborts at least once every two weeks. Senior management has decided that a new application is needed. You speak to the IT manager about developing a new system. You draw up a SLA between your organizations.

1. State four IT responsibilities that you would include in the SLA.
2. Mention three responsibilities that you think you should include in the SLA for your organization.

Chapter 7 Questions

1. You hired 3 new employees recently and last month you had to fire one of the employees for poor performance and another one of your staff left for maternity leave. Which department in your company do you think you should have an SRA with to best address responsibilities for the above scenario between your departments?

    A. Accounts payable department
    B. Human Resource department
    C. IT department
    D. Accounts receivable department

2. You have outsourced your payroll to an outside firm. This firm generates bi-weekly payments for your staff but you need to ensure accuracy and timeliness of their processing. What action do you take?

    A. Generate a SLA for agreement to be reached on the responsibilities of both parties.
    B. Insist that an SR holds them accountable for late payments.
    C. Generate a document of understanding that defines the responsibilities of both parties.
    D. All of the above are applicable.

3. The accountability for a service level agreement or document of understanding being generated belongs with:

    A. The service organization
    B. The process owner
    C. The audit committee
    D. The legal department

4. You need to have one of your staff initiate purchase orders, with your approval when he or she requires access to the customer database. The individual will need passwords to get access to the database. There are password requirements that IT has established and you instruct the employee to establish a password. The password that was established is indicated below. Which one of the four passwords is the best?

   A. 8765432
   B. Christmas
   C. Children
   D. ginPeels

5. If there is a former member of your staff who still has access to the purchase database with a list of all your vendors after they left the company, and the auditors have an issue with this, who would the auditors hold accountable?

   A. The IT department for not removing access
   B. The executives in your company as per Sarbanes Oxley
   C. The process owner even though they do not remove access
   D. The H/R department

6. Service level agreements are established:

   A. To correct previously erroneously processing
   B. To pass audits
   C. To satisfy service level objectives
   D. To satisfy federal regulations

7. All service level agreements should state that all critical errors be resolved within 24 hours.

   A. true
   B. false

8. You might find KPIs within a service level agreement. These are:

   A. Key process indicators
   B. Key performance issues
   C. Key process issues
   D. Key performance indicators

9. Which of the following statements is true?

A. The process owner approves and grants application access passwords.
B. The IT department approves application access passwords.
C. The process owner approves application access passwords and IT grants access.
D. The IT department approves application access and grants application passwords.

10. All requesters, if they have a business need to gain application access, are granted the same level of access.

A. true
B. false

Reference

DRaza Muhammad Rehan (December 24, 2019) Service Level Agreement (SLA) Examples and Template Blog. https://www.bmc.com/blogs/sla-template-examples/.

CHAPTER 8

Physical Controls

As process owners and current or possibly future audit clients, you need to be aware of the physical security as well as technological controls that are in place to protect your data and resources. This is an area that is frequently overlooked or one that is given less attention than non-physical controls—don't ignore the possible exposures that could exist in this arena.

Physical security describes security measures that are designed to deny unauthorized access to facilities, equipment, and resources and to protect personnel and their property from damage or harm. These incidents could result from espionage, theft, terrorist attacks, vandalism or revenge, etc. Physical security involves the use of multiple layers of interdependent systems that can include TV surveillance, security guards, protective barriers, locks, access control, perimeter intrusion detection, deterrent systems, fire protection, and other systems designed to protect employees and property.

Access controls include access to physical sites as well as access to data, services, and networks. We will initially look at building access.

E. Danter, *Audit Defense*, Palgrave Studies in Accounting and Finance Practice, https://doi.org/10.1007/978-3-030-92466-9_8

Building Access

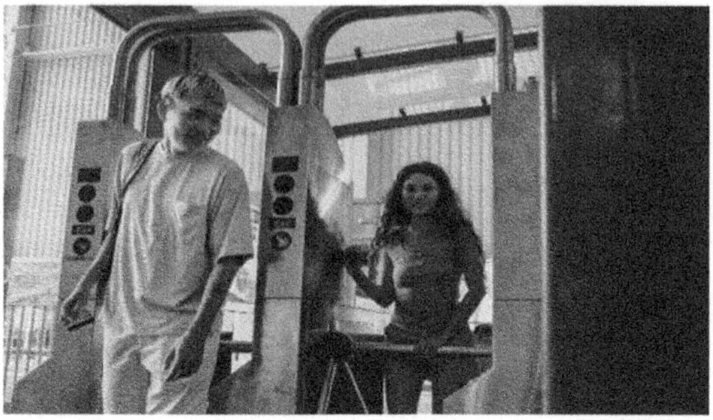

created by Samson Katt

Years ago physical access was controlled by being requested to sign in at a desk in the main lobby or with the issuance of employee badges. All employees were given badges that identified them as employees, and they were required to show their badge to a security guard to gain building access—they were to display and present their badge whenever requested. When a visitor entered the building, he or she was requested to sign in at the desk and in most cases was given a visitor badge and was even escorted while in the building. The only way that they could gain access to the building was via the main entrance, which was guarded, and all other entrances were locked.

Two problems surfaced in the early 1980s at many corporations. First, exit doors that could only be opened from the inside could be left ajar and accessible to unauthorized visitors. Second, in many complexes with multiple buildings, there were entrance and exit doors within the complex between interior buildings without security guards behind desks. Tailgating into buildings within these complexes was easily achieved.

The remedy that evolved, which became very popular, was the installation of badge readers that had to be used to gain entrance through every door into every building. There was no need to have a guard at every entrance. The only exception was the entrance door in the main building where visitors could gain entrance and request to sign in, or if employees forgot or lost their badges, they could gain access through the main entrance. In some buildings today, you cannot even leave a building without a badge to unlock a door. You need to be prepared for questions that an auditor could ask with regard to building access. Examples are:

1. Does every door, with the exception to the main building, require badge access?
2. Are all visitors requested to sign in?
3. Are visitors requested to indicate whom they wish to visit?
4. Is a log maintained indicating what time visitors enter and leave?
5. Are visitors required to be accompanied by an escort while they are visiting the premises?
6. Are visitors given temporary visitor badges?
7. Are these badges clearly designated as visitor badges?
8. Are employees displaying their badges? (auditors could walk around to determine what the procedure is at the site and if it being followed)
9. Is there a policy requiring every employee to badge in and out and not tailgate?

An additional problem arose that necessitated remedy. It was still possible for disgruntled employees or other dangerous individuals to drive and crash their vehicle through front doors of buildings and gain access, bypassing badge readers and security guards. This was addressed by the installation of pillars or other barriers, placed close enough to each other, so that a vehicle could not drive directly into the building. A personal incident that I had that was a wakeup call to the dangers of inadequate building access is described below:

Personal Experience 8.1

I was a fairly new auditor. I was sent by my manager to conduct an audit at one of our principal sites at a building in another state where our billing systems were developed and installed. I arrived at the local airport and drove to the site. I announced the audit via an announcement letter a few weeks earlier and had arranged to meet the audit interface whose responsibility was to schedule meetings with the manager and his staff.

I had never previously met this individual. I just spoke to him over the phone. I anticipated our meeting and was anxious to start my audit. I parked my rental car and walked into the building. I was shaken up by what I noticed as I entered. I saw blood stains, that still remained, over the interior walls. I remembered that a few months back there was a horrific shooting incident at the site, but knowing this did not prepare me for the tragic scene that was in front of me. A disgruntled previous employee had a grievance over workman's compensation. He had driven his car through the front glass door of the building, got out of the car, armed himself with a automatic gun and began shooting anyone in sight. In addition to the automatic rifle, he had a shotgun and 2 handguns. There were 600 employees in the building at the time. Three employees were killed by the gunman as he spayed dozen of rounds throughout the building, and seven others were wounded. The audit interface that I met filled me in on some of the gruesome details. It was first-hand knowledge since he was there when the shooting occurred and bolted himself in his office, hiding behind his desk. He personally knew many of the victims. He was one of the lucky ones the day of the shooting—he survived. He was understandingly very traumatically affected himself. He was the interface on a few other audits that I participated in over the next three years and somehow he was able to focus on his daily responsibilities. I have not spoken to him in years but would not be surprised if it still haunts him to this day. The police arrested the shooter. My company realized a need to take immediate action to secure the safety of the hundreds of people who were working at that facility. They had steel columns built and installed in front of the building. They were placed close enough so that a vehicle could not be driven through the building entrance. Building access was and still is a prime concern. This was an experience for many of us that will always be remembered.

Restricted Space Access

created by Pew Nguyen

If you are subjected to an audit you may not be too concerned with building access since, in most cases, this will not be your direct responsibility. Your company should have a security department who will be accountable for securing access to the building. However, if you are an IT manager you can be directly responsible for access to restricted areas it they are under your purview. Within your sphere of responsibility, you might have control over access to computer rooms, tape libraries ,or printer rooms. And if you are a financial manager you might be responsible for securing access to rooms or restricted areas where confidential and sensitive financial data is stored.

Computing installations and supporting facilities must be protected and have restricted physical access when continued operation is considered essential and vital. This is also especially true whenever critical data and information are on the premise. Let's examine computer room access first and then tape library control—you need to realize that in many companies, the tape library is situated within the walls of the computer room so we have a restricted area located within a restricted area.

With regard to computer room control, the audit client should ensure that at a minimum, the following control questions, if asked, could be satisfactorily answered:

- Individuals that have access to the computer room are individuals whose primary job functions require routine access to the computer rooms. Is there a computer access list that identifies who should have access to the computer room?
- Is routine access limited and granted on the basis of verifiable and documented management-approved business reasons?
- Is access to the computer room protected with its own badge reader or other security measures (e.g. combination lock)?
- Are unique badges supplied to those individuals who require routine access? These badges could be a special color, have a special tag, or indicate that these individuals require computer room access. These unique badges would give them access to both the building and the computer room.
- Is there a visitor's log that was established and is it maintained requiring visitors to sign in and out of the computer room?
- Is the visitor' log checked daily by a third person and initialed after being reviewed?
- Is there a procedure requiring visitors to be escorted at all times?
- Is there a procedure requiring that when a computer door is left open that someone be present to prevent unauthorized access?
- Are all uncontrolled exit doors alarmed and clearly labeled?
- Are contractors who are admitted to the computer room supervised and monitored?
- Are contractors required to sign in?
- Is there a requirement that contractors be escorted while working on the premises?
- Are master keys adequately controlled?

Tape libraries although frequently located within restricted computer rooms require additional access controls, a further level of control. That extra control is needed because not every individual who works within a computer room needs access to the tape library. For example, computer operators might need access, but not necessarily contractors who are working on an electrical problem in the computer room.

Tapes used in business processes are assets and need to be adequately protected, and tapes that contain classified information need to be protected even at a higher level. Access must be limited to fewer individuals than who even have access to the computer room. Each person who has access to the tape library must have tape library responsibilities or a business need. Auditors will attempt to ensure that controls exist for tape library access and that tape assets are adequately controlled. Tape inventory controls are essential.

It is important to realize that all portable storage media must be inventoried and adequately controlled. Each tape must be uniquely identified and accounted for. There needs to be an individual responsible for taking inventory and to ensure adequate separation of duties—the inventory should be taken by more than one individual and reconciled and signed off by management. Physical tape inventory is an arduous job, but it must be done periodically, at least annually, or when there is a large increase or decrease in tapes or movement to another site.

There are three functions that must be performed before a tape inventory control system can be considered complete and auditable.

1. Maintain an inventory.
    - Take the final inventory record count from the previous inventory.
    - Add to it all tapes added since.
    - Subtract all tapes from this number that have been removed since the last inventory. This should result in the number of current tapes in your inventory.
2. Reconcile the inventory that you have to what is actually in the racks.
    - Start with your current inventory status, which is your physical inventory that is reflected in your day-to-day record keeping and is on your books.
    - Physically compare this current inventory status to what is in your racks, taking into account any tapes that are currently in use.
3. Reconcile any differences between the two procedures.
    - Both of these steps should yield the same results. If they do not, reconcile any differences and document the reconciliation.
    - The result is the current inventory that becomes the opening balance or input to the next inventory.

Some of the questions that an auditor can ask that you should be prepared to answer, or have someone else available to answer are:

- Is the tape library a separate room within the computer room?
- Is there an authorized list of those who have access to the tape library?
- Did management approve this list?
- Is this list current? Auditors can take sample names from this list and ask you to verify that these individuals still have a valid business need to have access to the tape library. They can also follow the same verification for access to the computer room. There are situations where there are individuals who still have access and who have retired or have been transferred into other departments and no longer have a business need for access. You need to verify access before the auditors possibly find a problem with access. You can perform the verification, once you receive the audit announcement letter and if the computer room and tape library are in scope.
- Is there a person who controls visitor access to the tape library indicating who entered and when they entered and left?
- When was the last tape inventory taken?
- Was the inventory reconciled to the previous inventory?
- If it was not reconciled, were all discrepancies explained?
- Who performed the inventory?
- Was there more than one person involved in the inventory process?
- Were inventory results reviewed and signed off by management or a supervisor?

In many companies printers are located in separate rooms that are accessible by all employees. The printers could be accessible to all employees working on the floor and there might be many employees from many different departments having access to the shared printers.

The material being printed and picked up can be general business information or classified/confidential data. This room should be a restricted area if the latter is true.

Be prepared to answer questions that an auditor might have regarding printer rooms. For example, he or she might ask:

- Is the printer room(s) locked?
- If it is locked, then who has access?
- Is there a key lock or combination lock used?
- Who has custody of the key or combination?
- If a combination lock is used, how often is the combination changed?
- If it is not locked, is there a procedure for classified documents to be secured?
- Is there a requirement that employees must pick up classified documents within a specified time period (e.g. within one hour)?

In addition to computer rooms, tape libraries, and printer rooms, other restricted areas might exist where financial departments are located and possibly exposed. These areas should have restricted access to individuals with a business need due to the confidentiality of journals, budgets, strategic plans, and other sensitive financial information. These areas also need to have adequate access control.

There are other restricted areas, aside from the financial department that also need to be controlled. This is necessary if they contain confidential or sensitive information or assets. If you are responsible for these areas within your company, you will also need to be audit ready. Examples of these other areas are areas that house your legal department, laboratories, payroll department, medical department, or various other departments where restrictions to data should be enforced. Controls in these areas are basically the same. Only authorized personnel or escorted visitors with a business need should have access. All sensitive information needs to be secured.

Proprietary, Confidential, and Personal Information

Physical controls also need to be in place for proprietary, confidential, or personal information even though this data may not be contained within restricted areas. The data needs to be adequately protected.

With the importance of data privacy and security, it is critical that sufficient controls are in place to adequately classify, store, destroy, transmit, and otherwise protect data and information that are located within your work areas. This is not only true in your company, specifically if your department is a candidate to be audited, but also critical if you are outsourcing any of your processing to a service organization. The service organization then has a responsibility to protect the client's data—however, you will have the accountability from an audit perspective. For example, if you are the manager of the payroll department, being audited and payroll processing has been outsourced to a service company, you will be held accountable if the company's employees are not being paid accurately or timely. The same is true if you are outsourcing your processing and any confidential, personal, or sensitive data is sent to an outside company. Again, a DOU that addresses responsibility for protection would be a plus in these situations.

During audits, auditors will rarely ask question regarding the classification of data (e.g. unclassified, confidential, or highly confidential classification decisions). They usually leave it up to the process owner to determine the proper classification. However, they can and probably will inquire about the protection of data. The higher the classification of data, the more extensive the controls are that are needed to be established and effectively executed. Controls need to be put in place to secure not only company's confidential data but personal and sensitive data as well. This is especially true with medical information. You need to ensure that your employee's personal, sensitive, and medical data is adequately protected within your department or within your HR department. The Health Insurance Portability and Accountability Act (HIPAA) was put in place to protect and restrict access to individuals' private medical information. There is a legal obligation to protect this information, and a serious exposure can exist if personal health date is not protected from unauthorized access. We will further be discussing HIPAA in a later chapter.

Suggestions of personal, sensitive, or confidential data of your employees that you need to protect are:

- Individual's social security information.
- Driver's license numbers.
- Bank account numbers.
- Credit card numbers.
- An individual's religious or philosophical beliefs.
- Data concerning physical and mental health including state of health, illness, and disabilities.

You still need to ensure that there are policies, procedures, and controls that protect confidential and sensitive information even if they are not located within restricted areas. Some protection guidelines might involve requiring your employees not to leave confidential or sensitive information exposed but to secure it in locked cabinets or locked desks. Placing confidential documents that are no longer needed in locked bins for document disposals may not be sufficient. You need to realize that there may be contractors who have keys because their job is to empty these bins at night so your documents are not really secured. A better alternative and more robust policy might be to require that these documents be shredded.

Some inquiries that an auditor may have with regard to protection of confidential, sensitive, or personal data are:

- Are documents properly classified?
- Are there guidelines for the accessing and processing of confidential, proprietary, and personal information?
- Do guidelines exist for electronically transmitting confidential data?
- Are there encryption guidelines that state when it is necessary to encrypt?
- Are there security precautions for mailing such information?
- What controls are in place when these documents are printed?
- Are there distribution guidelines for computer-generated proprietary and confidential documents?
- Are there guidelines for the destruction of classified information?

A personal experience that I had indicates that everyone no matter their position in the company should be protecting confidential, sensitive, or personal information.

Personal Experience 8.2

I was the lead auditor conducting an audit at one of our remote locations, a facility where numerous top executives had their offices. After every audit, we had a procedure of conducting "clean desk reviews" to ensure the security of confidential, sensitive, or personal information. These documents, according to our company's policy were to be secured. We waited until after the normal workday ended to inspect the work areas, cubicles, or offices of our employees. We checked to determine: if the employee' password was exposed; if desks or credenzas were unlocked containing these sensitive documents; if keys to desks, cabinets, or credenzas were easily obtained; if there was sensitive documentation left on desks in plain site; or if confidential documents were thrown into trash baskets and were not shredded. We documented violations and reported concerns to management the following day. We left notes on the employees desks that indicated what, if any, violations we found or if there were none. It was a Friday night, just after 5, and we conducted a review. We walked up and down the aisles checking each office and I found myself at the end of the corridor in front of a vice president's office. I knew that the building security manager was still in the building. I called him. It was our practice to have building management accompany us as we conducted our clean desk reviews, we did not want to be accused of writing up violations without a witness. I asked the security manager what the security policy was in the building regarding securing confidential documents and if locked offices were sufficient to secure all documents—the vice president's office was locked. He told me that locked offices, by themselves were not secured, since most of the cleaning personnel in the building had keys, as did he, so that they could clean offices. I asked him if he could open the vice president's office—he obliged. The vice president usually worked late but this was a Friday evening and he left early, before five for an extended weekend. We entered his office and found strategic confidential documents just lying on top of his desk. I told the security manager that I deemed this to be in violation with the building security guidelines that were distributed to all employees. I asked him if he was in agreement. He said yes and I asked him to take one or two of the confidential documents as evidence to be returned to the VP on Monday. He agreed. I concluded my review and left. Monday came and all hell broke loose. The VP was furious. He wanted to know who gave him a violation and where were the two missing confidential documents that were taken. The security manager advised him that even as vice president, he should be following the security guidelines. The VP accepted the fact that there was an exposure and quieted down, He needed to set a good example.

Summary

We cannot rely on automated controls to adequately protect our data and resources. We also need to focus on physical controls. Auditors will hold you accountable if they are auditing your process to see if you are aware of physical controls that should be in place, established either by you or by another organization within your company.

The first area of concern that auditors might have is in assessing whether there is sufficient access control to the building where your resources and data are housed. This might not be your direct responsibility but you can be negatively affected if control is nonexistent or weak. It is your responsibility to know if there is adequate control even though direct responsibility might lie with building security. Auditors might want to know if there are badge readers and/or sign-ins required for everyone entering the premise. They may want to know what is the policy for tailgating.

You also need to ensure that effective controls are in place and effectively being executed for restricted areas such as computer rooms, tape libraries, and printer rooms. You should also have procedures and controls to protect proprietary and confidential information that might be stored in your work area. It is not just company sensitive, confidential, or highly classified documents that need to be adequately secured but personal information for your employees as well. This will include health information that is under the purview of federal HIPAA requirements.

Guidance

1. Verify that if your work area is located in a restricted area, that there are adequate controls for access.
2. Inform your staff that if they are printing confidential documents, that they remove the documents from a printer as quickly as is feasible. If the documents are printed at a location other than their own work area (e.g. printer room that is accessed by many employees), instruct your staff to retrieve them as soon as possible. Check to see if there are company policies for retrieval, and if so, that they are being followed.
3. Make sure that your employees are aware of securing confidential, sensitive, or personnel documents when they leave their work areas.

4. Have members of your staff conduct after hour reviews to check on whether your department members are securing confidential, sensitive, or personnel documents. They should be secured in locked desks, cabinets, credenzas, etc. A locked office is not necessarily secure.
5. Instruct your staff to properly shred confidential, highly classified, and personnel documents that need to be discarded.

Chapter 8 Exercises

1. The building that you are working in has badge readers on every door and security cameras on every entry. Do you think that the building is secure enough? If not, why not and what would you do to enhance security?
2. The physical tape library is located within the computer room. The computer room has a badge reader and sign in desk in addition to badge readers on building access. Do you think that the tape library needs additional security? What is the reason for your answer?
3. You are a financial manager and your department calculates budgets for the upcoming year and prints the budget for executive review. What security measures would you ask your staff to follow?
4. There is a policy in your company that confidential documents that are no longer needed by employees are to be placed into a locked receptacle that is emptied every night. Do you believe that this is sufficient security? If not, why not and what would you propose?

Chapter 8 Questions

1. You are about to enter your building and are running late for a meeting that you are scheduled to attend one morning. You get to the side door that has a badge reader and you put your badge in your hand to gain access. As you insert your badge and the door opens, you hear a voice behind you scream "please hold the door". You recognize the individual being someone you worked with last year. What do you do?

   A. Hold the door open
   B. Close the door, lock them out, and require them to use their own badge

C. Stop, turn around, apologize, and ask them to use their own badge
D. Call security

2. According to HIPAA guidelines, you need to have extra security for which set of the following documents:

   A. Strategic plans
   B. Personnel health information
   C. Payroll information
   D. All of the above

3. As the Accounts Payable manager for your company, you do not have to worry about physical security as security guidelines and enforcement lie with the security department.

   A. true
   B. false

4. You are the payroll manager and you have a list of every company employee with their names, social security numbers, and other sensitive payroll information. You need to leave for the weekend 2 h before the workday ends. What should you do?

   A. Lock all of the documents in your desk or cabinet.
   B. Lock your office on your way out.
   C. Give the confidential documents to your colleague who works next to you and ask him to lock the documents in their work area before he leaves.
   D. Inform your manager that you are leaving early and that you did not have time to clean your desk.

5. There is no problem with every computer operator who has access to the computer room in also having access to the tape library that is secured within the computer room.

   A. true
   B. false

6. Three departments on your floor use the same printer room. Which of these controls make the most sense?

   A. The printer room should always be locked with badge access necessary for entry.

B. Everyone should be required to sign in and out of the printer room.
C. There should be a time limit as to when confidential documents should be picked up from the printer room.
D. There should be an individual assigned full time to be stationed in the printer room to monitor document pickup.

Reference

Davis Chris, Schiller Mike (2011) IT Auditing—Using Controls to Protect Information Assets, 2nd edn. McGraw-Hill.

CHAPTER 9

System and Application Access Controls

System Access Controls

When referring to systems, we are talking about any system from mainframe to personal workstation to laptops where any application is installed and operational, used for the purpose of conducting business related functions. For example, there can be many applications (i.e. a payroll application, an accounts receivable application, an inventory application) that reside on a mainframe system. Then there are application developers or programmers who code the applications, end users who need to gain access to the applications as well as IT personnel who are responsible for maintaining the systems and establishing system controls that grant and remove access.

System controls are preventive controls that address logical access such as password controls and levels of access, protection of systems from hackers, viruses, and unauthorized individuals. System access controls are the first line of defense against unauthorized access. As a process owner, you will depend upon IT professionals to provide you with system controls that you will rely on. These responsibilities that IT personnel are empowered with should be detailed within SLAs that you have established with the IT department.

E. Danter, *Audit Defense*, Palgrave Studies in Accounting and Finance Practice, https://doi.org/10.1007/978-3-030-92466-9_9

As a process manager within your company, you will be expected by auditors to be accountable to ensure that system access is effectively being administered by IT if one of your applications is being audited. You should have procedures that request the level of access needed for each of your employees to gain entry to the system where your applications and data are housed. And you need to instruct your staff on establishing acceptable passwords based on IT rules. It is IT, however, who has the staff, expertise, and responsibility to actually grant passwords and levels of access to the systems. IT will also have responsibility to grant and remove access, monitor access, establish rules for password length, password acceptable characters, frequency of change, removal for inactivity, etc.

There is day-to-day required system access for individuals who need to do their jobs. This might include end users or application developers who need system access to further access the application data that resides on the systems. Application access controls will be discussed separately later on. There are also individuals who are required to have special access, a very high level. These individuals who require privileged access are referred to as individuals having *keys to the kingdom*. Within the IT department, there are individuals who themselves are required to have system access and some need to have this elevated level of access. Their access is essential for them to do their jobs. Auditors will review their access very closely to see if they have been authorized, if there is an excessive number of individuals with special access and if there are adequate controls in place to monitor their activity. The authorization of approving as well as granting access to these individuals with privileged access usually resides within the IT organization.

Figure 9.1 will hopefully depict the relationship between systems and applications and the personnel who need to have access.

The individuals with system access include but are not limited to:

- System administrators (privileged users) who establish the system controls and manage system access.
- System support personnel (privileged users) who maintain systems.
- Programmers who design and maintain applications running on the system.
- End users who need system access to access the application data.

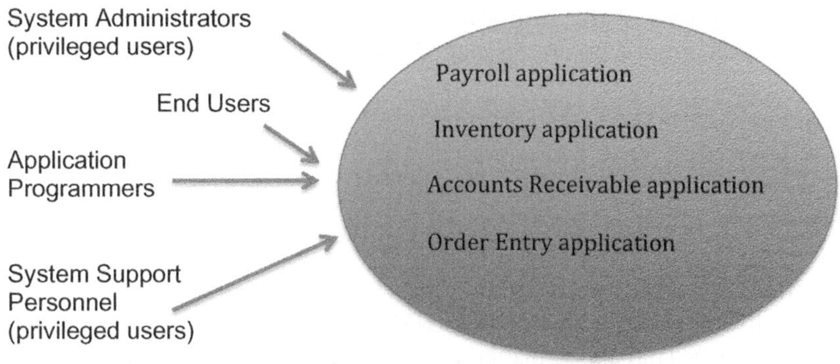

Fig. 9.1 Mainframe system

When we talk about system access, we need to have:

- Procedures addressing how users are authorized and are granted access.
- A procedure that periodically reviews the business need for continued access.
- Procedures to identify and authenticate users.
- Procedures documented that define and classify resources to be protected.

There need to be tighter controls surrounding the privileged users because of their level of power that exceeds those with normal system access.

Controls need to be in place that:

- Grant privileged access when required.
- Review continued business need for privileged access on a regular basis. Revalidation should not be done semi-annually or annually as it should be required for regular users, but more frequently, perhaps quarterly or monthly, since there is more risk involved.
- Remove access when no longer required.

Some indications of the authorities of systems administrators and system support personnel who are privileged users and their capabilities are[1]:

- Users with SYSADM authority.
- Users with SYSCTRL authority.
- Users with SYSMAINT authority.
- RACF administrators.

SYSADM authority is the highest level of administrative authority for an employee. Individuals with SYSADM authority can run utilities, issue database and database manager commands, and access the data in any table in any database, within the database. It provides the ability to control all database objects including databases, tables, views, indexes, packages, servers, database partition groups, data types, buffer pools, and event monitors. Only a person with SYSADM authority can perform the following functions:

- Migrate a database.
- Change the database manager configuration file, including specifying the groups having SYSCTRL or SYSMAINT authority.
- Grant database administrative (DBADM) authority.

SYSCTRL authority is the highest level of system control authority. This authority provides the ability to perform maintenance and utility operations against the database. These operations can affect system resources, but they do not allow direct access to data in the databases.

Only an individual with SYSCTRL authority or higher can do the following:

- Update a database.
- Force users off the system.
- Create or drop a database.
- Drop, create or alter a table space.
- Restore to a new database.

[1] Excerpts on privileged users from "IBM Administration Handbook", https://www1.columbia.edu/sec/acis/db2/db2d0/db2d036.htm.

SYSMAINT authority is the second level of system control authority. This authority provides the ability to perform maintenance and utility operations against the database. These operations can also affect system resources, but they do not allow direct access to data in the databases.

Only a user with SYSMAINT or higher system authority can do the following:

- Update database configuration files.
- Backup a database or table space.
- Restore to an existing database.
- Perform a roll forward recovery.
- Start or stop an instance.
- Restore a table space.
- Run a trace.
- Take database system monitor snapshots of a database manager.
- Query the state of a table space.
- Update log history files.
- Quiesce a table space.
- Reorganize a table.

Last is the RACF (Resource Access Control Facility) administrator. This is an IBM term. In a mainframe environment, it is the RACF administrator who controls access to datasets. These are production datasets that should not be accessible to developers unless process owners have authorized their access on an as needed basis. Anyone who needs access to a dataset in a mainframe environment should complete a request for authorization that is approved by the owner and granted by the RACF administrator. Auditors will review access lists to determine if access is still needed or if it should have been removed. One of the most common findings of auditors is that individuals who had once been granted access based on valid business needs have since switched departments, or even worse left the company, and no longer have a business need—yet their access was never revoked.

Application Access

It is important to realize that once systems are secured and system access controlled that we need to peel back the onion, look at the next level of access, and ensure that applications, residing on systems, are secured.

Underneath system access rules and restrictions there are application access rules and further restrictions. As a result, it is here that we address additional preventive controls, known as application access controls in addition to system access controls. Individuals might need to have system access but another level of control should exist to see if they need to have authorizations to access application code, application data, tables, and libraries. Application access controls will focus on process owner responsibilities, the authorization process, and separation of duties. Process owners, in many situations are also referred to as application owners. Let us realize that these process/application owners are responsible for the security of application data as well as the integrity, accuracy, and timeliness of application processing.

Since there can be various applications running on a system, it is incumbent on you, as a process/application owner, to establish application access limitations that allow only those individuals access to your application who have a valid business need. For example, let us assume that you are the manager and owner of the order entry system. If the order entry application and accounts receivable application reside on the same system then if a user of the order entry application has access to the order entry application there should be controls so that they should not automatically have access to the accounts receivable application. Only those with a business need, administrators with privileged access, that we discussed before, need to have access to all of the applications that are on a system. We would have a conflict of interest in this case if non-privileged personnel have access to all applications on a system. There would be an exposure to a possibility of fraud via unauthorized access.

This is an area where as process/application owners you will need to work closely with the IT organization. Process owners authorize access that is granted by the IT department. Process owners are dependent on the IT organization to implement controls that the process owners deem necessary. Auditors will ask the audit client, who is the process owner, how access to applications is secured. The auditors will ask who controls system access to mainframe or servers where applications reside as well as application access and we do not want to appear paralyzed and unable to respond. The best approach is to describe how security is controlled on a system level and then on an application level and to provide the auditors with any documentation that is available. It will be necessary and advantageous at times to invite IT management and key personnel to meetings with the auditors when access controls are discussed to be able to provide a smooth process flow and clearly define responsibilities. This is of vital importance to auditors, yet many hours and days can be wasted before the right personnel is present to help explain the total process. The auditors in many meetings with different personnel and after talking to many individuals can realize that not all of the essential personnel who are present at the meetings are able to satisfactorily answer their questions and they need to extend additional invitations for numerous subsequent meetings after being given additional names of key personnel.

Responsibilities of the application owner should include but are not limited to the following functions:

- Determining who needs to have access to the application and communicating requests for granting access to the IT organization. This access can be granted to end users, developers, and other management or individuals, based on business need.
- The application owner should approve valid access requests and there should be a documented audit trail of such approval. This approval can be in the form of a note, text, or email.
- The application owner also has the responsibility of notifying the IT organization of those individuals whose access needs to be removed with the lapse of their business need.
- The application owner should control the updates to any table that is read and used by applications in granting access.
- The application owners should, at least annually, be asked to validate the continued business need for application access for each individual and be asked to document such approval. It is common to find instances where individuals who needed to access application data for business purposes were still on the access list even after they had left the department and no longer had a business need for access or left the company. Application owners who never bother to revisit and revalidate the access list to their application after the initial determination can lose effectiveness of managing access control putting their data and information in jeopardy.

The process of authorizing and granting access to applications is an extremely important control. We are not talking about system access, usually controlled by the IT organization as indicated above, but rather to the applications running on a particular system where the application data resides and where there can even be sensitive or confidential data. Many applications have built in logic or tables that add another level of access beyond system access control. It is not necessary for everyone who has been given access to a system to have access to each and every application running on that system. Another example would be if the inventory application and payroll applications were running on the same system. It could be a breach in security for those individuals who have a business need to access the inventory application to also, by default, automatically have access to the payroll application for which they have no business need.

The access process usually starts with a request for access to the application and this access can be a view of data or a request to have authority to update the data. The request is initiated by the end user and should be signed by the end user's manager as well as the application owner.

The auditor could ask, "Who controls access to the application?" and "How is access controlled?" What is important to the auditor is how well the process is controlled and if there is adequate separation of duties. Some of the questions that an auditor might ask that you should be prepared to answer are:

- Is there a formal documented process or request form used for requesting application access?
- Does this process include approval by the requester's manager?
- Is application owner approval required?
- Does the request form indicate view or update capability?
- Does the request form indicate the business need?
- Are request forms retained as an audit trail?
- Is there adequate separation of duties with regard to requesting, approving, and granting access?
- Is there a formal process for removing access?
- Is there, at a minimum, an annual revalidation validating the need for those who have access?

Auditors during an audit of a selected process, will probably choose a sample of the most sensitive financial or confidential data and ask for a list of those individuals who have access. From this sample, they will most likely ask for access requests and approvals for selected individuals. The auditors will review the date that employees were granted access and validate that there is still a valid business need as well as when access was last validated. Unfortunately, there are too many instances when access exposures occur where individuals without a current valid business need still have access. This results from constant changing environments, movement of personnel to other departments, and personnel leaving the business. Access lists are not reviewed and in many cases administrators are not timely notified of the need to remove access. The revalidation is a detective control to identify individuals who no longer have a business need for access. Unfortunately, there is a gap and lapse in time from when an access report is generated (e.g. semiannually process) and when the report is generated again. So at any time that an auditor arrives at a site and conducts an access audit, there could be personnel who should have been removed but have not been removed because their access still needs to be determined. If revalidation of access occurs annually, or semi-annually there can be an individual who left the department one month after the last revalidation and the auditor might arrive three weeks or perhaps two months after the last revalidation but before the next revalidation and removal. This is a timing issue. The most advisable action is to conduct a revalidation as soon as an audit is announced and to remove all personnel without a business need as soon as possible. The same will hold for system access.

System Security

When examining system and application access controls, we focused on the responsibilities of both process owners and IT organizations and highlighted their partnership, necessary to successfully avert an unsatisfactory audit. There is another responsibility that needs to be addressed by an IT organization.

That function is to protect systems from hackers and to foil any attempt to gain unauthorized access. The protection of today's systems has become more of a daunting task with the need for effective cyber security, the sophistication of hackers, and their use of malware and even ransomware, where hackers penetrate our systems and hold processing hostage until a ransom is paid. We will be discussing cyber security in a later chapter when we discuss current and future challenges.

As a prospective audit client, as mentioned earlier, you need to ensure adequate protection of your applications and validate that the systems that they are running are secured from unwanted penetration. The data and information that is processed, utilizing the systems, networks, and servers and residing within your application files/databases, needs to be guarded. As a process owner, you will need to be dependent on the controls that IT has established and is utilizing. This dependency, along with responsibilities, should be addressed within a service level agreement with the IT organization. If you are an IT manager and it is you who is directly being audited then this will be a significant challenge and of paramount importance. As an IT manager, who is supporting a process owner, or a potential audit client yourself, you will also need to be audit ready when it comes to security.

All audit clients need to understand the threats that exist before they can verify that effective controls have been implemented.[2]

Let us look more closely at the security threats.

Malware is software that is intentionally designed to cause damage to a computer, server, client, or a computer network. By contrast, software that causes unintentional harm due to some deficiency is typically described as a software bug. This can result from the occurrence of a coding error. When we talk about malware we need to be familiar with viruses, worms, and Trojan horses.

Computer viruses are self-replicating programs written to alter the way a computer operates, without the permission or knowledge of the user. Management should understand the problems that viruses present as well as understanding what steps can be taken to protect systems from harmful code.

A worm is a piece of software that uses computer networks and security flaws to create copies of itself. A copy of the worm will scan the network for any other machine that has a specific security flaw. It replicates itself to the new machine using the security flaw and then begins scanning and replicating. Worms are programs that replicate themselves from system to system without the use of a host file. This in contrast to viruses, which

[2] Malware references in "CISA—All in One" (2012), Peter Gregory.

require the spreading of an infected host file. Although worms generally exist inside of other files, often Word or Excel documents, there is a difference between how worms and viruses use the host file. Usually the worm will release a document that already has the worm macro inside the document. The entire document will travel from computer to computer, so the entire document should be considered the worm.

A Trojan horse is an imposter that claims to be something desirable but in fact, is malicious. Rather than insert code into existing files, a Trojan horse appears to do one thing (e.g. install a screen saver, or show a picture inside an e-mail) when in fact it does something entirely different, and potentially destructive, such as erase files. Trojan horses can also open back doors so that computer hackers can gain access to passwords and other personal information stored on a computer. Although often referred to as such, Trojan horses are not viruses in the strict sense because they cannot replicate automatically. Examples of how a Trojan horse spreads is that it can be invited into a computer by the user opening an e-mail attachment or downloading and running a file from the Internet.

Let us take a closer look at viruses. Some viruses are programmed to damage the computer by damaging programs, deleting files, or reformatting the hard disk. Others are not designed to do any damage, but to simply replicate themselves and make their presence known by presenting texts, video, or audio messages. Even these benign viruses can create problems for the computer user. They typically take up computer memory used by legitimate programs. As a result, they often cause erratic behavior and can result in system crashes. In addition, many viruses are bug-ridden, and these bugs may lead to system crashes and data loss.

Virus detection is an important element of computer system security. Two resources available for virus detection are vigilant users and watchful programs. Users should be cognizant of unusual or unexpected symptoms and utility programs should be installed to provide assistance.

Some signs that users should be watchful for and alerted to are:

- Unexpected changes in the lengths of files.
- Programs running longer than expected.
- Programs taking longer to start than usual.
- Unexplained decreases in amount of available memory.
- Files vanishing.
- Workstations mysteriously rebooting without reason.

- Unusual displays or messages.
- Any other unexpected program behavior.

Programs should be installed that scan for specific characteristics or behavior of known viruses. These programs should signal the presence of many known viruses. As new viruses are identified, these anti-virus programs are updated and the latest versions of these anti-virus programs should be installed as needed.

Virus detection is one thing, but it is also very important to recover from virus infections. Recovery needs to address the replacement of every infected object in the system with an uninfected version and restore any other object that a virus may have damaged. Uninfected files should be restored from backups. It is important during restoring procedures to avoid reintroducing the virus into the system. Questions that an auditor can ask you that you should be prepared to answer are:

- Are users educated with regard to security threats and computer viruses?
- Are users informed of how to identify a virus, whom to call, and what to do if they discover that they have been infected?
- Are backups kept of all critical data?
- Are backups maintained for all programs?
- Have recovery procedures been tested using backups?
- Where possible, have critical systems been isolated from sources of infection?
- Are programs that are added to a software library checked by authorized and knowledgeable personnel for possible infection?
- Are anti-virus software programs used to ensure that programs added to software libraries are virus free?
- Are programs that are vital to the business (e.g. accounts payable programs) tested on isolated systems before being moved into software libraries to see if they show any signs of infecting other programs?
- Are the latest anti-virus software versions being used?
- Has a response team been established to quickly react to virus threats?
- Is there a procedure to remove viruses from infected systems once detected?

- Is there a procedure to isolate infected systems until they can be cleaned to avoid infecting other systems?
- Is there a procedure to record the characteristics of the virus and the steps to take to prevent its spreading, once it is identified, in case the same virus is detected again?
- Are anti-virus tools available for easy access by any computer network user?
- Are there security practices for network connections to outside organizations?
- Is electronic mail communication limited to non-executable files?

In today's corporate environment, many networks are now connected to the Internet, which has enabled organizations to conduct new ways of doing business. This is a current challenge facing business processing throughout our workforces today. These functions range from advertising products and services, to exchanging information and processing transactions over unsecured or inadequately secured network components.

We hear of more incidents every day of hackers entering our systems, and unfortunately we do not know when they will be intruding into our networks and gaining access to our websites, systems, applications, and data. With the internet being used more and more for financial transactions, including electronic payments being made using social security numbers, and more detailed individual security information becoming available, we are more vulnerable to hackers than ever before.

We are no longer just talking about mischievous and malicious viruses penetrating our systems by pranksters and technological pundits who are trying to outsmart the systems, but about being vulnerable to theft and even cyber terrorism. The amount of damage, destruction, and financial impact can be accomplished by professional hackers entering into our systems is beyond scary. We must be audit ready.

All that we can do is be prepared and take adequate measures to protect our systems from invasion and minimize their vulnerability. We have become more and more aware of the dangers of hackers who intrude our systems and access confidential and proprietary information. We need to protect our networks from unauthorized personnel.

IT departments have become more sophisticated in developing and installing firewalls, which are preventive controls against unauthorized access, and in the installation of anti-virus software that is both a detective and corrective control.

What is a firewall? It is the first level of defense. Its intent is just like a door lock or security guard at the entrance to a corporation's building. Its purpose is to keep unwanted people out of your network. The firewall functions as a filter or as a choke on the type of information that can be exchanged. The risk that we are faced with today is not limited just to accessing a company's network. You need to realize that there is a large portion of a company's employees who work from home today. As cable modems, satellite hookups, and other high-speed access to the home become more popular, the risk of being attacked grows proportionally. I am not suggesting that auditors will necessarily be reviewing networks in your home, but a way to increase the level of security for processing your company's data is by using a firewall that will protect network connectivity to your company from various locations.

As mentioned above, firewalls are preventive controls. Firewalls are software applications or hardware systems (routers) that enforce security and prevent inappropriate access to and between internal networks. Firewalls consist of rules that review each packet of data as it passes through the firewall. The rules can range from what is the source of data to what is the destination to the time of day the packet arrives. In simplistic terms, if the packet passes all the rules then it is allowed to pass, otherwise it is turned away. All incoming requests for different network services such as file transfer protocol (FTP), and hypertext transfer protocol (HTTP) regardless of which host on the internal network will be the final destination must go through the firewall.

Firewalls are very technical and complex and few auditors will have the knowledge to perform an in-depth audit in this area. The auditors who will perform these audits must know how firewalls work if they are engaged in these reviews. If the auditors do not possess the technical knowledge and skill, they will probably solicit help from subject matter experts (SMEs) to participate on the audit team. Realize that auditors will, when needed, enlist the help of SMEs to assist them in conducting audits where additional expertise is needed. And you, as an audit client, can also request the help of personnel outside of your department, when necessary (e.g. IT department). You should request their assistance and their participation when their knowledge and expertise can be beneficial in your being audit ready and in responding to audit questions and requests. Responding to an auditor's requests is frequently a team effort. Do not hesitate in bringing in additional support.

An auditor, or a SME on the auditor's team, to ensure that the organization's firewall is protecting the company, could ask the following questions that you should be prepared to respond to, with assistance if needed, and avoid being caught by surprise:

- Does the company's Internet policy ensure adequate protection?
- Does an internet policy permit any service unless it is explicitly denied?
- Does the Internet service deny service unless it is specifically limited?
- Is the firewall flexible in accommodating new services?
- Does the firewall contain advanced authentication measures, and/or allow for the installation of advanced authentication measures?
- Does the firewall have filtering techniques to permit or deny services from specified host systems as needed?
- Does the firewall log traffic and suspicious activity?
- Are there procedures for reading and analyzing log results?
- Is there a procedure to update the firewall with software fixes?
- Does the firewall language filter as many attributes as possible, including source and destination and inbound and outbound interfaces?
- Does the firewall use proxy services for services such as HTTP and FTP so that advanced authentication measures can be employed and centralized at the firewall?

A firewall is necessary and can prevent intrusion but it is no guarantee against intrusion. Keeping that in mind, it is important to realize that if a computer contains information that is highly classified, extremely sensitive, or confidential, it should not be connected to a network, especially not connected to the Internet.

Auditors will probably spend time validating not only that there is effective anti-virus software that will recognize known viruses and correct their damage but also that there are adequate firewalls to protect systems, applications, and applications from unauthorized access.

Summary

If you are or will become a manager within your company, responsible for data you are processing, as a custodian, you will be concerned with the security and safeguarding of the information entrusted to you. In order to be audit ready, you will be either directly or indirectly responsible to ensure adequate access controls surround the systems and applications where your data resides.

Some of these controls will be your direct responsibility, and for other controls, you will need to depend upon successful implementation and execution of controls by your IT organization.

You will be accountable for the security of access to the applications supporting your processes but these applications will reside on systems (e.g. servers, mainframes) and the responsibility for access to these systems will most likely lie with your IT department. It is a partnership—both you and the IT department need to support each other and function as a team. This is essential for your company to have effective auditability and access controls in place for adequate protection.

There can be many applications running on one system. You will not be responsible for system access, unless you are an IT manager, but only responsible for authorizing access to your application and its supporting data. The IT department will be responsible for granting access to all applications running on the system. To clarify, if you are a Purchasing Manager and the Purchasing Application and an Order Entry Application are housed on the same system then you will only be responsible for authorizing access to the Purchasing Application and the Order Entry Manager will be responsible for authorizing access to the Order Entry Application. However responsibility for authorizing system access will reside with IT—IT will be in partnership with you as well as with the Order Entry Manager.

Within the IT department, there will be individuals who will be responsible for controlling system access. These individuals will have privileged access so that, when requested by you or any other process owner, they can grant access to the system, remove access when requested, monitor access, establish password rules, control frequency of change, remove access for lack of activity, update databases, maintain systems, update table space, reorganize tables, etc.

These individuals, system support personnel or system administrators, will be prime candidates for auditor review. Their privileges are very powerful and auditors will most likely question and review controls and monitoring of their activity, authority, and business need.

The auditors will look to you, as process owners, to control access to the applications supporting your processes. This will include authorizing access to applications, databases, and tables, requesting IT to grant access and then having procedures in place to request that IT revoke access, when it is necessary.

Auditors may also ask many questions on the security of systems, applications, and networks. They may be concerned with preventive and detective controls to prevent, deter or reveal any individual who attempts unauthorized access via hacking. They might want to validate the existence of anti-virus software, malware controls, firewalls, trojan horse controls, and ransomware prevention. Cyber security is a major challenge today and all of the security areas discussed above will probably draw a lot of attention and focus from auditors.

Bottom line, if you are an audit client, don't panic—be prepared to answer access inquiries and solicit help from your IT department to provide support in answering the auditor's questions. There can be technical questions where the input and explanations of the IT department might be critical and vital in achieving a satisfactory audit.

Guidance

1. Have a list of who can access the system(s) where your data and applications reside.
2. Make sure that there is a documented process to authorize, grant, and remove access for individuals to the systems where your data and applications reside.
3. Know what controls are coded within your applications to gain access to tables.
4. Ensure that you have a process for reviewing who has access to your application(s) at least on an annual basis and retain any reviews.
5. Request and be certain that access is removed, if necessary, just before the auditors arrive. Do not wait for the next review according to your schedule.
6. Verify, via documentation, that separation of duties exists as to who can authorize access and grant access to your data, applications, and tables.

7. Ensure that there is a procedure to educate your employees on security measures (e.g. the awareness of hackers, viruses) and have evidence of any education that they have received.
8. Obtain documentation to demonstrate that critical data is backed up and that recovery procedures have been successfully tested.
9. Review your SLA with the IT department, if necessary, to make sure that systems and networks are secure, preventing unauthorized access to your data and applications and that it is current.
10. Work closely with your IT department to review and validate essential security controls that IT has installed to provide protection from malware, viruses, worms, and the installation of effective firewalls.

Chapter 9 Exercise

You are the billing manager for a large corporation and are notified that your processes and procedures, including security, will be audited next month. You were promoted to your managerial position six months ago. The Billing Application, currently in operation, was developed and installed 3 months ago, due to frequent delayed and erroneous billings with the previous application. In addition, there were 3 identified instances of fraudulent activity and successful hacking into databases where the hackers gained access to a list of customers, potential sales data, and other classified data. You feel that you are audit ready to address the controls that you now have in place to ensure accurate and timely billing but you do not feel comfortable in addressing security controls. What three steps do you take to improve your comfort level?

Chapter 9 Questions

Please select the best answers to the questions below.

1. You are the Accounts Payable manager in your company and need to prepare for an upcoming audit in your department next month. You were told, when the announcement letter described the scope of the audit, that one of the functions that will be reviewed by the auditors will be security over your data and processing security. What should you do to prepare for this phase of the audit?

A. Explain to the audit lead that the security of your system, application, and data is the responsibility of the IT organization and they should be audited, not you.
B. Ask your director to contact the audit manager and let the auditors know that you do not agree with the scope.
C. Review any service level agreement that you have with your IT department and ask the IT manager to participate in the audit to explain their responsibilities regarding security.
D. Do nothing since your last revalidation of access was performed 8 months ago and your process requires annual revalidations.

2. Auditors will not question system administrators as to why they accessed the mainframe during the audit time period since as a result of their job description, they need to have permanent access, to maintain the integrity of the system.

A. true
B. false

3. You are the payroll manager and there are payroll databases and tables supporting your application and payroll processing. Since this is a critical application, what functions should you be allowed to perform if the payroll tables are wrong and the payments are going out incorrectly?

A. Authorize and grant access to your developer to fix the table
B. Authorize access for your developer to make the change and ask IT to grant their access
C. Have IT authorize your developer to have access and you grant the access
D. None of the above since all of your developers will have automatic access

4. If the Order Entry Application and Accounts Receivable Application run on the same system then whoever has access to one application should automatically have access to the other application.

A. true
B. false

5. Which of the following is true if you are the purchasing process owner and own the Purchase Application?

A. You determine who needs to have access to your application and communicate requests for granting access to IT
B. You should approve access and there should be a documented audit trail of such approval
C. You have the responsibility of notifying the IT department of those individuals whose access needs to be removed with the absence of a business need
D. All of the above

6. If you need to have a specific user be granted access to your application, you should:

A. Verbally approve access and then call IT and request the access
B. Grant the user access and get their manager's approval
C. Complete a form authorizing access and then grant access
D. Complete a form authorizing access and then route it to IT to grant access

7. Whose responsibility is it to ensure that there is anti-virus software on the system where your application is housed?

A. Your responsibility as application owner
B. The IT organization
C. The legal department
D. The audit committee in your company

8. A firewall a:

A. Detective control
B. Deterrent Control
C. Preventive Control
D. Reporting Control

9. Which of the following is true?

A. Privileged users should always have system access with minimum controls in order to do their jobs.
B. Privileged user access should be revalidated annually, the same as regular users. There is no need to revalidate their access more frequently.
C. The need for privileged users to have system access should probably be revalidated more frequently than regular user access because of the greater risk.

D. As an application owner, you will be responsible to revalidate the business need for privileged users to have system access.

References

CISA—All in one (2012) Peter Gregory, pp. 504–510.

IBM Administrative Handbook. https://www1.columbia.edu/sec/acis/db2/db2d0/db2d036.htm.

CHAPTER 10

Operational Controls

IT management (programming or operational personnel) can be the recipient of an audit or the audit client can be a non-IT process owner who owns an application or process being audited. In either situation, there needs to be a partnership and strong relationship between the two entities. This is especially true when auditors are auditing operational controls. If the audit client is IT management, then IT will be accountable for the adequacy of controls and if the non-IT process owner is being audited, then he or she will be accountable for the adequacy of controls. However, if one organization is being audited, there should be a dependency on the second organization for support. The primary audit client will be accountable and the secondary manager will be responsible for effective controls. They need to work closely together and reinforce each other during an audit. This, in many instances should be a team effort. There will probably be questions that can best be answered by the department that has the most expertise. A strong service level agreement clearly defining responsibilities, as we discussed in a previous chapter, is advisable. Both departments should be readily available to provide help in answering audit questions during an audit, if called upon for assistance.

E. Danter, *Audit Defense*, Palgrave Studies in Accounting and Finance Practice, https://doi.org/10.1007/978-3-030-92466-9_10

When auditors are reviewing operational controls, they will most likely be examining the processes of: change management, library control, code migration, issues management and business recovery/continuity. There can be other processes that can be reviewed as well but for this textbook we will focus on these processes and controls.

Change Management

Change management is a crucial process within any audit. What is important is that the audit client can demonstrate that all work is approved by authorized individuals; that there is documentation throughout all phases of the change management process; that there are documented business decisions and rationale as to why various testing is or is not conducted; or if any of the accepted process steps are not being adhered to. Auditors will focus on assuring executives that there is no issue with separation of duties that has or can result in unauthorized change and possibly fraudulent activity.

One of the most rigorous components of many audits is a review of change management controls. Frequently this is where many exposures are identified and unfortunately this review results in an unsatisfactory or failed audit.

Application changes start with a request for a work effort to most likely change or introduce coding. These requests can be initiated either by a programmer, process owner, end user, or anyone who recognizes the business need for a change. The request can be called a change request (CR), a system request (SR), a program change request (PCR) or any other terminology decided on by a company. The term SR will be used throughout the remainder of this textbook.

The SR is a request for enhancement or maintenance work and should be generated and authorized prior to almost all work efforts. Emergency changes are an exception. For an emergency change, a SR may not always be required prior to the change being made, because of time constraints. However, even though there may not be an SR before the coding change, the request for a work effort should still be documented (e.g. an operations ticket if the application aborted) with the necessity for a coding change, if required, being explained.

Auditors will want to validate the existence of an SR for work efforts they sample or choose to review. If there was no SR, they need to examine the documentation as to why the change was made (e.g. emergency change). If the work effort is not an emergency, the SR should have a documented process with a form that is required to be completed for authorization of the work to be done. If it was an emergency (e.g. a critical application that aborted and needs an emergency fix in the middle of the night) then there will be little or no time to acquire authorization with an approved signature before the change is made. In this case, the SR should still be generated as soon as possible and signed the next day. What usually occurs is that there are temporary libraries where emergency code changes are placed and then moved from the temporary library to the production library the next day, after authorization is obtained from the process owner. During the interim, the application will be executing the changed program from the temporary library.

Another instance where there might not be an individually approved SR is something referred to as a "blanket" SR. The company might use this term or another term that provides the same function. The concept of a blanket SR refers to work to be done without explicit owner approval for each and every change. An example of a blanket SR might be for code changes that are for repetitive requests. Suppose that every month a new Accounts Receivable report needs to be generated with the only change in appearance being the name of the month. A blanket SR can be generated at the beginning of the year with a one-time owner approval. The blanket SR would ask for a new report to be generated every month. A blanket approval would eliminate the need to generate a SR every month.

The process owner, who can also be the application owner, should authorize the change and then it should be forwarded to the programming staff where the authorization is verified before coding begins. Auditors will focus on two controls: evidence of the SR and its approval by an authorized individual. A process owner can delegate another individual to authorize the SR when they are absent. However, this delegation needs to be documented, not just verbal. The SR is then routed to the programming department where the authorization is validated before coding begins. SRs need to be retained for the period of time that is indicated in the company's change management process.

Once SRSs have been approved, they should enter a queue. The process owner or application owner then needs to control the prioritization and sequencing of the SRs to be worked on. This will depend on the needs of the business. The auditor will attempt to verify that the application owner is prioritizing the work, not the programmer. The auditor can look for evidence of regular communication with the owner where the SR queue is discussed and determinations made as to which SR should be worked on next. This can be an email, text, or minutes from a meeting. In addition to decisions being made as to which SR is next in the hopper, there should also be communication between the programming department and the owner to track the progress of the work being conducted.

What you might be up against when the change management process is audited is that the audit can follow a similar scenario to the one that follows.

An auditor requests a sample of ten SRs covering a specified period of time within the audit scope. When the auditor looks at the SRs they will probably ask for evidence of who authorized the work that had to be done. The auditor will then examine the SRs that can fall into the following groups:

- one project SR
- four corrective maintenance SRs
- three large enhancement SRs
- one emergency SR
- one minor enhancement SR.

If one of the corrective maintenance SRs does not have an owner's signature, the auditor could ask, "*why not?*". You might tell the auditor that there was verbal approval but the auditor probably will still want to see some form of documented evidence. If the other SRs have signatures, the auditor could ask for a list of names of individuals who are authorized and then compare the names to the signatures on the SRs. If the auditor notes that the programming change for one of the SRs started on November 1 when the SR was signed November 15 then he or she will want an explanation. Do not be surprised if auditors conducting thorough reviews are asking one question after another. They keep digging—it seems like there is no end.

Library Control

If you are a billing manager and you have the IT department develop a new billing application for you, based on your requirements, there are controls that you should be aware of and comfortable with before a billing audit is scheduled to begin.

Programmers will write application code for the billing application and place the code in a development library. When ready to be promoted, the code will be moved to a production library. The development library should be separated from the production library. We will discuss the migration of code from the development library to the production library later. What is important is that you understand that the developer should not have access to the production library unless he or she receives special authorization. This ensures adequate separation of duties and minimizes the exposures to fraud. If a developer needs access to the production library, there should be documented authorization by management.

If a change is needed to be made to support a SR, a programmer should be required to request access to the development library to retrieve the code, make the change, and move it back into the development library for testing. Auditors will look at source program code to see if there are comments as to what the last change was, who made the change, and when it was made. This is an audit trail. Auditors consider this to be a manual control, and that a developer who is about to make a change by looking at the comment in the source code will know if the change had already been made, by whom, and when. Adding a comment to the code is an added control but not always used or required.

Auditors will look for version control to provide an automated control that the proper version of the program was accessed, worked upon, updated, and ready to be moved to production. Version control will help ensure that only one individual can be working on a change to the same program at the same time. It would be very confusing if two or more programmers were working on the same program at the same time, and difficult to ensure that the correct version was promoted. Version control will also help in controlling and ensuring that there is a comfort level that the correct components are in place. This can include data tables, job control language, and other program modules that are needed in support of the promotion of the program currently being changed. All elements needed for satisfactory promotion must be current, available, and effectively packaged prior to moving the correct program version from the development library to the production library. The programmer will not move the code from the development library to the production library. The movement of code will be assigned to another individual, as we will see when we discuss code migration, below.

Code Migration

Auditors will spend a significant amount of time on code migration or promotion of code to production libraries. They will be looking for adequate separation of duties or preventive controls to ensure that there are controls in place to control separation of tasks in this area. This will be true if they are looking at a mainframe, UNIX, SAP, Oracle, or Web application environment.

In many companies, a separate group or department, non-programmers, will be responsible for the migration of code from development to production libraries. This is done to provide adequate separation of duties. An individual in this group, responsible for code migration, is usually referred to as a *librarian*. The golden rule that should be adhered to, if possible, is that programmers should not be permitted to promote code to production libraries. If this tenet is broken and developers' access to production is to be accepted, you will need auditors to agree to a secondary control process that you have established.

This secondary control might be needed in small shops where they do not have the luxury of being able to afford hiring a librarian or a separate group that will promote code to production. An example of a secondary control could be a second programmer, who did not write the code, being responsible for moving code to production. A secondary control could be as follows:

1. An independent programmer who did not code the change could ask for a generated list of all code promotions in the last month.
2. The independent programmer could verify that there is a corresponding documented change request for each program version.
3. The reviewer could then compare the program version level in production to the version level in the development library and ensure that they were the same.
4. The next step would be to inspect documentation where the owner approved the migration of code to production (this is usually done after all testing is satisfactorily completed).
5. Once validated, the independent reviewer would need to sign off on the results of their review.

You will need to be able to demonstrate the execution and effectiveness of this manual control. Keep in mind that the starting point must be the production library and not the development library since the purpose of this control is to validate authorization of all code promoted. There is no interest in seeing what is sitting in the development library if it was not promoted. There are many times that code could be sitting in the development library still being tested and not ready for promotion. There would be no exposure in this situation if the code was not installed in a production library. To establish a strong secondary control and minimize your exposure, this review should be done more frequently than monthly.

We need to look closer at the controls that need to be recognized and effectively executed for change management, library control, and code migration because of the high degree of attention in this arena being paid by auditors. Imagine the following scenario that you could be faced with when change management is being audited:

The auditors request a list of all mainframe promotions in the last six months for the process being audited and a list of all distributed promotions in the last four months. They select forty changes in total from the two platforms and require the following:

- The SR supporting each change.
- A screenshot from production showing the version and date of the program promoted for each change.
- Documentation of who is authorized to approve the changes.
- Evidence of the individual who performed the promotion.
- The authorized approval for each promotion.

After reviewing the forty changes, auditors have the following questions:

- The individual who promoted eleven of the SRs was a developer and they want to know why.
- Five of the programs associated with the SRs have different dates in the development library than the production library. For three of the programs they found that program change dates in the development library had later dates than in the production library and they want to know the reason.
- Why did two of the programs have later program versions in the production library than in the development library?
- There was no evidence of authorized approval for fourteen of the SRs before promotion and the auditors ask you for a reason.

- Three of the changes had no SRs associated with the promotions and you need to explain.

You attempt to answer their questions with the following explanations:

- The developer, who migrated code to production, was supporting UNIX applications. There is a limited staff and she had access to production libraries.
- The three programs with later program dates in the development library had not yet been approved to be moved to production—they were waiting for approval.
- The two programs with later version numbers in the production library were an indication that the changes had not yet been tested. They were emergency changes that occurred in the middle of the night. There was not enough time to test the changes in the development library since the test data could not be created fast enough, so they were tested in the production library.
- Five of the fourteen SRs had no approved signatures and that was an oversight.
- Nine of the fourteen SRs that were approved by individuals prior to promotion could not be found on the authorized list. Individuals who transferred to other jobs or left the company had approved the SRs. They were authorized at the time of approval.
- The three SRs were emergencies and did not have SRs for the changes.

Follow-up questions by the auditors were:

- Since it was a common practice for UNIX developers to promote code, what secondary controls (either preventive or detective) are in place to address the exposure of the developers promoting their own code?
- Do you have a documented decision that bypassed regular testing for the two programs that required changes in the middle of the night, and were emergencies?
- Do you have evidence of notifications that the nine approvers had changed jobs or left the company?

- Is there proof that the three changes that were emergencies without SRs were emergencies and post approved?

And the audit process continues and your answers are:

- Programmers who promote code in the UNIX environment are not supposed to be the same individual who did the coding. However, there is no secondary control for an independent control to review the changes made prior to migrating the changes to production to verify that they were authorized.
- For the two SRs that were emergencies in the middle of the night, there was verbal concurrence but no written concurrence that it was okay to test in production.
- There is notification on only three of the nine that the approvers had changed.
- There is documented evidence that two of the three SRs with post approvals were emergencies and had approvals after the changes were promoted to production.

As you can see, the auditors were not easily satisfied and they kept asking question after question. As a result of their review of change management code migration and library control, findings could very likely appear in the final audit report with a request that corrective action plans be developed.

Be ready to answer the following questions that an auditor can ask on the controls that we just covered:

- Is there a formal documented process to control changes made to production?
- Are all change requests authorized by the process or application owners or their designees?
- Is there a readily available list of authorized change request approvers?
- If there is a list of approvers, is it current?
- If authorization is delegated, is there documentation supporting the delegation?
- Are there separate development libraries established for testing rather than using production libraries?

- Is version control used to ensure that the correct program version is always promoted to production?
- Is there a requirement that programs should be documented with a description of the changes made?
- Are programs documented with an indication of who made the change and when?
- Do all production changes, including emergencies, adhere to a change control process?
- Is there overall adequate separation of duties with regard to change management with limitations placed on programmers' library access.
- Are programmers restricted from promoting code from development libraries to production libraries?
- Are there secondary controls in place if programmers need to migrate code from development libraries to production libraries?
- Do librarians or a separate group of individuals, not programmers, migrate code from development libraries to production libraries?
- Are the librarians restricted from writing code and placing it in the production libraries?
- Are temporary libraries used when emergency code changes are made and are overrides pointing to these libraries restricted to a specified time period?
- Are all non-emergency changes reviewed and approved by application owners prior to moving code to production?
- Are all emergencies changes authorized as soon as possible after migration to production? Is there a process that requires post approval if pre-approval can't be obtained for emergency code changes?

As we can see there are numerous inquiries that can, and do surface when auditors are looking at change management. This is an area that frequently has issues. You need to be prepared to minimize exposures and realistically aspire to have a satisfactory audit result.

Issues Management

Auditors will ask to see an issues management process that addresses software or hardware issues during all phases of testing or operational problems. Issues need to be recorded as a result of self-assessments, peer reviews, production problems, audits, or any controls review in addition to any coding problems. Not only do all issues need to be recorded and a corrective action plan documented but also an individual needs to be assigned who is responsible for the corrective action, with an indication of target date and actual completion date. Open issues need to be evaluated, and if past the target dates, then the reason why corrective action plans are late. The issues management process should require that escalation to executive management be required, when issues are excessively late.

Be prepared. An auditor might ask you if you are the audit client, the following questions regarding an issues management process:

- Is there a documented issues management process?
- Does the process require all issues to be recorded and tracked?
- When are issues recorded?
- Are issues flagged if open for an extended period of time?
- Are there target dates for remediation?
- Are issues recorded as being closed after being resolved?
- If results need to be validated after testing, who performs the validation?
- Is there an assigned individual responsible for establishing and implementing corrective action for each issue?
- Is there a target date indicated for closure?
- Is there an actual closure date recorded?
- Are open issues analyzed and corrective actions that are late reported to higher management?

Business Recovery and Continuity

What do you do if a disaster occurs? This question was never more daunting than after September 11, 2001 and currently with the growth of cyber security attacks across all of our infrastructures and companies. Not only terrorist attacks, but floods, hurricanes, power failures, fire, and earthquakes all make us realize that we need to address the reality of disaster and the challenge of business continuity.

According to the *Internal Journal of Government Auditing*, the overall objective of producing and maintain a business continuity plan is to "maintain the integrity of the organization's data together with an operational service and processing facilities and, if necessary, provide a temporary or restricted service until normal services can be resumed. Your businesses must be restored and operational after disasters strike. This entails people, systems, hardware, networks, telephone lines, and data".

Business continuity or disaster plans need to ensure that critical business functions of the company are able to continue or restart in the event of unexpected circumstances with minimum disruption of service. Disaster plans must be developed that will address how to bring systems back up, how to restore data, what sites will be used, and where people will work. Not only do controls need to exist and a disaster plan documented, but it must also be kept current and tested to ensure that it is designed well.

Business continuity plans are developed by application owners or process owners, operational management and their key staff, as well as key personnel and management from all critical departments. It is a company wide effort. Business continuity plans take time to develop and when completed should be signed off and agreed to by all affected parties.

It is not only essential that a company has adequate business continuity plans but critical that they have been tested. As a process owner, it will be incumbent on you to ensure that this is certainly true for your process. You need not only establish and review plans but you should review test results. Business continuity plans need to be tested on a regular basis to ensure readiness and successful execution. And they need to be updated when needed. At a minimum, they should be tested annually. However, business continuity plans should be tested more frequently if and when key locations and personnel change. Unfortunately, in many companies, business continuity is not a priority until disaster strikes—it is too late then.

Some questions that an auditor might ask regarding business continuity that you should be prepared to answer are:

- Can your systems be restored from backup media in case of a disaster?
- Can backup media be retrieved promptly from off-site storage?
- Is there a current copy of the disaster recovery plan maintained at a secured off-site location?
- Does the disaster recovery plan identify a critical recovery time when business processing must be resumed before suffering significant or unrecoverable losses?

- Have you verified that if emergency operations are used that there are appropriate supplies, computers, and telecommunications connectivity?
- Are emergency communications addressed in the plan and contacts listed with phone numbers?

Summary

In this chapter, we covered operational controls that you could be asked about during an audit. These functions included library control, code migration, change management, issues management, and business continuity.

The important aspect of library control is to ensure that development libraries, where programmers do their testing, are separate from production libraries. Programmers should, as a rule, be restricted from accessing production libraries. Production code and production data should be segregated from development code and development data and access to the production library should be adequately controlled. If there are access exceptions and programmers or other usually unauthorized personnel need to have access to the production libraries, then there should be secondary controls established where authorizations are documented, retained and access granted but only on a temporary basis. Access should be revoked once it is no longer needed. Version control should also be utilized to safeguard that the correct version of the program and its components are promoted to production.

Code migration, the migration of code from the development library to the production library, should be assigned to a librarian to provide for adequate separation of duties—the possibility of fraudulent activity should be minimized. If a programmer or any other individual needs to move code to production, then there needs to be documentation authorizing production access and the movement of that code. ***Again, as a general rule, programmers should not be permitted to migrate their own code to production.*** In small shops, due to limited resources, adherence to this separation of duties with the hiring of a librarian or another individual to migrate code might be a problem. In this situation, you should establish a secondary control where perhaps another programmer can migrate the code of the first programmer. In this situation, there should be an audit trail and reports generated of the code change that can be reviewed by a third party or manager, ensuring that there was independence in the migration of the code.

One area where the auditors will spend a significant amount of their time reviewing and opining on is change management control. Process owners should authorize all changes where either service requests, change requests, or program change requests are utilized. Auditors will examine the authorizations on the requests to see if there are valid signatures requesting the changes. They will most likely look to see if there are process owner approvals of the testing and sign-offs once testing is completed and before changes are promoted to production. The only exception should be emergency changes where there is little or no time to generate change requests and acquire signatures before promotion. If this occurs, then the auditors will expect to see post approvals, as soon as possible, after promotion to production. Auditors usually sample a large number of change requests, since this is where many problems can surface and possible fraudulent activity or the potential of fraud can exist.

Auditors will expect to see documented procedures for library control, code migration, and change management. The lack of documented procedures can result in audit issues. Try to avoid this from occurring.

All issues originating from audits or reviews as well as coding should be recorded and tracked from identification to closure. Target dates for resolution need to be indicated as well as individuals assigned to address the issues/exposures.

Business recovery and continuity plans require documented plans in case of disasters (e.g. fires, hurricanes, floods). There should be evidence of testing disaster recovery plans, at least annually, with results recorded and documented evidence maintained. Updates should be made to the plan when and if they were necessary.

Guidelines

1. Make sure that you have a documented procedure for change management.
2. Ensure that the change management process addresses who has to initiate a change and who has to approve a change.
3. Validate that the change management process addresses regular changes as well as emergencies.
4. Have a list of who can authorize all changes (e.g. managers or delegates).

5. Verify that the list of authorizers is current.
6. Make sure that you maintain all change requests for a period of time indicated in the process documentation and that the requests are readily available to any auditor.
7. Ensure that the change management process addresses prioritization.
8. Establish separate libraries for development/programming and testing versus production.
9. Make sure that there is separation of duties controls on who can access both libraries and that it is being employed.
10. Document your process for version control.
11. Ensure that adequate separation of duties controls exist and that the controls are documented for code migration. Assign a librarian or independent party to migrate code.
12. Establish a documented procedure where all identified issues from audits and all reviews as well as from coding errors are recorded and tracked and make sure that all issues are being effectively managed, till closure, by utilizing the documented procedure.
13. Make sure that you have a documented business recovery or disaster plan.
14. Validate that the plan covers personnel, equipment, software, and all necessary components.
15. Verify that the plan requires at least annual testing.
16. Ensure availability of evidence of all testing that was done and test results.

Chapter 10 Exercises

1. You are the accounts payable manager in a small company with a limited staff. You are dependent on the IT department, which is also limited in size, to develop, code programs, make any necessary changes, test them and promote them to production.

    - Describe what controls you establish before changes are made.
    - Describe the controls and audit trails you would ask IT to have before code is migrated to production.

2. You are an IT manager but your IT site is located in a high-risk area where floods have frequently occurred. What steps do you take

regarding a disaster recovery plan to ensure business continuity in case of a catastrophic event occurring?

Chapter 10 Questions

Please choose the best answer for the questions below:

1. Any change to program code can only be migrated to production if properly authorized before promotion

   A. true
   B. false

2. An SR (system request) is approved, covers the entire year and does not require subsequent approvals. The SR could be utilized, for example, when only the name of the month needs to be changed for a monthly report. The SR is called a (an):

   A. covering request
   B. inclusive request
   C. on time request
   D. blanket request

3. If a program aborts in the middle of the night and there is no time to follow the procedure to get approval for the change before promotion then:

   A. A SR must be generated regardless
   B. The SR needs to be authorized by the owner ASAP
   C. The change made should be independently reviewed the next day
   D. All of the above

4. The control used to ensure that the most current change to a program is updated to the production library if two programmers are changing the same program is known as:

   A. code migration control
   B. version control
   C. library control
   D. separation of duties

5. The individuals who move code from test or development libraries to production libraries are known as:

   A. system programmers
   B. operators
   C. developers
   D. librarians

6. A business continuity plan or disaster plan includes:

   A. communication equipment
   B. software
   C. networks
   D. all of the above

7. All coding changes need to be authorized by:

   A. the programmer making the change
   B. the programming manager
   C. the process owner
   D. the programmer and the programming manager

8. It is sufficient to test business continuity plans annually.

   A. true
   B. false

9. When should issues be recorded in an issues control log?

   A. issues identified during an audit
   B. issues identified during self-assessments
   C. issues that occur during testing
   D. any of the above instances

Reference

Davis Chris, Schiller Mike (2011) IT Auditing—Using Controls to Protect Information Assets, 2nd edn. McGraw-Hill.

CHAPTER 11

Separation of Duties

If you are a current or future process owner, you should realize that auditors will vigorously focus on whether or not you have established and are effectively administering adequate separation of duties (SoD) controls. SoD, also referred to as segregation of duties, is a basic underlying preventive control. It is a key internal control area of focus. Establishing and executing SoD can be costly, however, it will provide increased protection from fraud and errors. You need to balance the benefit of SoD with the increased cost/effort required of establishing this central control.

In essence, SoD implements an appropriate level of checks and balances upon the activities of individuals.

The primary objective of separation of duties is the prevention of fraud and errors. This objective is achieved by disseminating the tasks and associated privileges for a specific business process among multiple users.

Separation of Duties to many is a prime concept in internal control frameworks, in financial reporting and in regulatory compliance, specifically the Sarbanes Oxley Act. It is a component of an efficacious control environment.[1]

[1] Adapted from Protiviti KnowledgeLeader on Thu, Mar 19, 2020 @ 04:45 P.M.

E. Danter, *Audit Defense*, Palgrave Studies in Accounting and Finance Practice, https://doi.org/10.1007/978-3-030-92466-9_11

SoD is one of the most successful leading controls that can be implemented for the protection (via segregation of job functions) and detective (via manual checks and balances) of unwanted events. If adequate SoD is established, it will require collusion, in most situations, for fraudulent activities to take place. Almost every audit will target separation of duties and as the audit client, you will need to not only state that SoD has been effectively established, but you will need to validate and demonstrate credible execution of SoD. To many an auditor, it is the foremost control that needs to be corroborated.

One of the most commonly used excuses for not installing adequate separation of duties is that it is a resource detriment. There are many companies that believe that they cannot afford the expense of hiring additional personnel to provide for SoD. However, separation of duties can sometimes, although not always, be accomplished without additional resource. All possibilities should be explored to see which functions can be split, so that the same individual is not performing two or more critical functions, resulting in a separation of duties conflict.

When you are undergoing any audit, SoD is looked upon as one of the most effective preventive controls that can be implemented. However, it is not a guarantee that fraudulent or erroneous processing will not take place, but it is recognized during an audit as one of the most essential controls and is closely examined and scrutinized by auditors. Be careful, inadequate SoD can be a red flag, possibly a show-stopper, resulting in a failed audit.

The overall effectiveness of management's internal controls depends on SoDs to a large extent. For fruitful internal controls, there needs to be an adequate division of responsibilities.

The basic idea underlying SoDs is that no employee or group of employees should be in a position both to perpetrate and conceal errors for fraud in the normal course of their duties. The specifics of which duties should be segregated from others will vary by company, however, the general idea is that the responsibilities for initiating, authorizing, inputting, processing, and checking data should be segregated so that one person does not have the ability to create a fraudulent transaction, authorize it, and hide the evidence. In other words, you're attempting to prevent one person from being able to subvert a critical process. In general, the principal incompatible duties to be segregated are:

- The custody of assets
- The access to assets
- The authorization or approval of transactions affecting those assets
- The recording or reporting of related transactions
- Verification of the asset
- Performance of independent checks

Traditional systems of internal control rely on assigning certain responsibilities to different individuals or segregating incompatible functions. The general premise of SoDs is to prevent one person from having both access to assets and responsibility for maintaining the accountability of those assets. It's important to keep in mind, as mentioned above, that SoD, which is most beneficial, does not prevent collusion.

Why Is SoD Important?

SoDs help minimize the risk and possibility that an organization does not achieve its goals, provide reliable financial data, and/or comply with laws and defined policies. Administrative or other recording errors may not be detected timely since an independent/objective review of transactions may not be occurring or inappropriate, or unauthorized (fraudulent) transactions are permitted to occur since one individual controls a major portion of the revenue, expenditure, payroll, or other functions.

Sarbanes Oxley and other regulatory issues are forcing companies to increase their awareness and accountability of their employee's actions within the company. Recent privacy laws and prosecution of security violations are bringing new awareness to monitoring and controlling security and access to data within organizations.

What Is the Risk?

Inadequate segregations of duties could make fraud prevention, detection, and investigation difficult, which could possibly lead to misstated financial statements, regulatory punishments, damage to the company's reputation, and reduced investor trust.

There is also the risk of misappropriation of assets, which involves third parties or employees in an organization who abuse their position to steal from the company through fraudulent activity.

If internal controls cannot be relied upon, this can increase testing by audit, translating into additional costs to the organization. More serious findings could lead to an evaluation by the auditor that the company has a significant deficiency or material weakness.

Lastly, if SoDs are not present, it raises the question of whether the information and evidence obtained is reliable, free from errors or may suggest that a material misstatement exists. As a result, the auditor may increase sample sizes, lower substantive testing threshold, or increase audit procedures overall.

SoDs should commensurate with the size and complexity and overall risk of a company's operations and financial reporting environment. It is important to always first consider the risks to the organization. Businesses are continuing to increase reliance on IT, further making SoDs important in efforts to reduce fraud and increase operational effectiveness. Compensating/mitigating controls may exist to mitigate the risks resulting from a lack of appropriate segregation of duties. These controls include audit trails, reconciliation, supervisory reviews, and transaction logs.

Traditional systems of internal control rely on assigning certain responsibilities to different individuals or segregating incompatible functions. The general premise of SoD is to prevent one person from having both access to assets and responsibility for maintaining the accountability of those assets. As stated before, and emphasized here, is that SoD although one of the most effective preventive controls, does not prevent collusion. SoD controls can be circumvented when collusion exists. However, it can significantly improve your odds of reducing the possibility of fraud and erroneous transactions, but it is not a guarantee.

Every process owner within a company needs to be cognizant of the importance of SoD. This is especially true for finance, accounting, and IT personnel. When auditors are examining various processes within a corporation they can find SoD control issues in both accounting and IT departments within the corporation. Since there is a strong dependency on IT processing by management, in most large or significant sized companies, it is essential that process owners understand and can validate the successful execution of SoD controls in the IT arena. There is a dependency on a constructive and committed synergy between process management and the IT organization to work closely together in order to be audit ready; responsibilities should be clearly defined in a Service Level Agreement.

We are going to first examine SoD implementation in the IT community and then focus on SoD for accounting organizations. These are not the only areas where auditors will be reviewing SoD but these departments are primary points of focus.

Separation of Duties in IT

As stated before, SoD is the segregation of responsibilities and duties to various functions within an organization and applies to IT as well as accounting functions.

Many corporations in the US find that an unexpectedly high proportion of their SOX internal control issues stem from IT. If you are a manager and own a process in any other department in a company other than IT, you might be a candidate to be an audited. And if you use IT as a service organization, you should be aware of SoD compliance within the IT organization. SoD is an area that you should include in an SLA with IT. If you are an IT manager and are being audited yourself, you certainly need to be able to explain to an auditor what functions are performed by IT personnel, ensuring adequacy of SoD controls.

SoD plays an important role among operational personnel, application programmers, system programmers, data base administrators, and support personnel. Illustrations of SoD controls are:

- Prohibiting application programmers from having access to production data/libraries unless authorized by owners
- Preventing operational personnel from writing code to be promoted

- Preventing an operator, application, or systems programmer from authorizing and/or granting access to production data
- Assuring that a developer/programmer does not have privileged access to production data to support a production environment, as does a systems programmer
- Determining that there are adequate controls to prohibit a systems programmer from writing application code

There is a unique SoD question that pertains to tables if the tables are used to grant access to databases and files. Access to these tables whether external to applications or internally coded within applications needs to be adequately controlled. If applications contain access tables, it is imperative that separation of duties be established. There should be controls to ensure that the people granting access are not the same as those requesting access. Usually an end user submits a request form, after they obtain authorization, to the individual who updates the access tables. There should be checks and balances intrinsic in the processes that require that the individual who receives the request is not the person who updates the access tables, and that the request contains authorized approval. Some questions that the auditor could ask are:

- Is the requester who wants access to databases or files the same person who updates the access tables?
- Is there an individual who checks for approvals and is the person different than the person who updates the application or application tables?
- Can programmers grant themselves access to the tables without a third party review?
- Can an individual delete a person's access without the application owner's or process owner's approval?

Smaller firms have more of a challenge than larger companies in ensuring adequate separation of duties. In a large company, there is a greater number of personnel among whom to distribute and disseminate functions. In a smaller organization, one person is usually performing functions that one, two, or many individuals are assigned to accomplish in a larger company—they wear multiple hats. They do not have the luxury of being able to establish the ideal separation of duties environment. Executives within these companies need to be aware of the risks involved and need to establish whatever separation of duties that they can afford. Check and balance procedures should be installed where separation of duties is limited and where possible, to mitigate risk. If one person needs to be responsible for multiple activities that are in conflict and a risk to the business, their actions should be reviewed by another individual, even a manager, if necessary.

Case Study (SoD in a Small Company)
You are the president of a small company. You have less than 50 people working for you with 20 people in your IT organization managed by Monica. Within Monica's organization there are 5 operational people and 15 programmers supporting the operation, development, and maintenance efforts for 24 applications. An outside accounting organization is conducting a SOX audit at your company and Monica has informed them that due to limited resources and budget constraints against hiring additional IT resources, there is a separation of duties exposure that she is aware of. There are two operational personnel who have database administration (DBA) responsibility, assign passwords, issue, and revoke user ids and monitor application performance as well. These two individuals back each other up. Apparently Monica documented a business risk assessment and obtained your approval.

Monica's programmers either write code and in some instances they promote code. You realize that the programmers should not be promoting code but your resource is limited with budget constraints. There is no one else who can promote their code. You need them to perform these tasks to keep the applications running and your customer has no problem with this separation of duties concern. You explain the SoD situation to the auditors. Do you think that they will accept it? They probably will not. They will most likely want to know why you can't have checks and balances such as one programmer writing code and another promoting that code. They will probably want to know why you can't have secondary controls exercised by an independent party that would detect if unauthorized code has been promoted, such as a manager or another programmer who checks the code being promoted.

Case Study (SoD in a Large Corporation)

You are the CIO at a fairly large corporation. Your outside accounting auditing firm previously notified you that they will be starting the fieldwork of their audit today. They have arrived at the headquarters of your IT organization, located about a half mile down the road from where the corporate offices are. Three months ago your IT organization underwent an audit from your internal audit staff that resulted in minor findings—you feel pretty comfortable that you are audit ready. The outside auditors (Ethan, Ali, Kristian and Mindy) have arrived at the headquarters of your IT organization.

The auditors start their interview process after you have had a kickoff meeting. Ethan and Ali want to talk to the application support senior manager and his staff. Ethan asks him if any of his programmers have access to the production library. He tells them that the mainframe programmers have read access to the production library where code is stored but not update capability, unless access to update is specifically granted by the owner of the data. Ali wants to know when programmers would need to update production libraries where production applications and programs reside. He wants to know the process for granting access to update the production libraries. Your senior manager tells Ali that, right now, none of the mainframe programmers update production program libraries. There is a librarian in place within the operations organization, who promotes code and none of the programmers promote code. Your senior manager feels that with two different organizations in place, duties are effectively segregated. He does not realize that he is going to be subjected to further inquiries.

Ethan then asks not if any of the programmers promote code but "can they promote code? Are there preventive controls in place to prevent them from accessing the production libraries?" The senior manager tells Ethan that there are preventive access controls in place. RACF is used to grant access and none of the programmers have RACF capabilities. The access is granted by a database administrator (DBA), who is not a programmer. The DBA works in the operations organization. Ethan, as most auditors will, wants to verify this. He asks to be shown a list of mainframe programmers and an indication of what functions they perform and what they have access to. He is told that he will have the list by the next day.

The senior manager reacts quickly and asks his programming managers for a list of each department's personnel and their access. He receives the lists and hands them over to Ethan and Ali. They are now joined by Kristian and Mindy, the other two auditors. They have been assigned to help with examining adequacy of separation of duties. Kristian asks how the auditors know if the lists actually represent the access that the programmers have since they were manually prepared. She asks for "system generated" lists. The senior manager goes back and asks his managers for "system generated" lists. Rather than one list being generated for each department, the RACF administrator generates a single access list for all mainframe programmers. After receiving the access list, the manager presents the list to Kristian and Mindy the next day.

Kristian and Mindy review the list the next day and ask the senior manager to identify production data sets. Mindy then asks why some of the programmers have update access to certain production libraries. Your senior manager is surprised to see this as he was told by his management staff that none of the mainframe programmers had update access to production libraries. He is embarrassed now and asks his managers for an explanation. After some research, it is discovered that two programmers have update access to production libraries because at one time they were database administrators. They changed their career paths but their accesses were never revoked.

Mindy makes some notes and then asks, "How often is access reviewed to validate that people who no longer have a business need to access production libraries have their access revoked?" Your management team answers that it is supposed to be done annually. Mindy then asks for a verification of the last revalidation. Your management team is able to produce it. It was done 11 months ago. Kristian then asks, "When did the two programmers change their careers and transfer from being DBAs to being programmers?" She is told that they transferred seven months ago. Then Kristian asks your management team, "Do you have a process in place to revoke access when employees transfer?" Your senior management replies that his management is supposed to notify the RACF administrator to revoke access if there is no longer a business need. Kristian and Mindy then verify with your senior manager that there was an exposure for seven months when the two programmers might have migrated their own code to production and he has to agree.

Kristian and Mindy leave production program libraries alone and ask about access to production data. It was stated earlier that mainframe programmers could have access but if they needed access to production data, the access would have to be approved by the owner of the data. There are times when programmers need to read and change production data in case of production emergencies and erroneous data. Mindy asks for the procedure and your management team shows it to her. She then asks if there is any monitoring done when anyone modifies production data. Your manager tells her that the owner of the production data has someone on her staff authorize a temporary ID to be granted to the programmer to access production data. The owner then reviews the change that was made, initials it and then ensures that the temporary access is removed. Your senior manager tells the auditors that programmers should never be able to update production data unless authorized and their access is limited and controlled by the owner.

Now Ethan and Ali ask you about the distributed environment. Your managers tell them that they have small staffs and that programmers promote their own code. RACF does not play a role for the UNIX and Windows environments that they support and they do not have the resources to separate responsibilities and ensure separation of duties. The auditors then ask a few questions focusing on checks and balances and on detective controls since there are no system controls in place to prevent unauthorized access. Your senior manager tells the auditors that one programmer is assigned to making coding changes to a specific application and another programmer promotes the code. For another application they switch roles. Ethan then asks your senior manager if the programmer who wrote the code could promote the code and how would that be detected. Your management team is asked if there is any manual monitoring to ensure that all changes that were promoted to production were in fact authorized. Your senior manager does not have an answer and sees Ali writing notes in his book. And it goes on and on; the questions keep coming. Most of your management team would opt for root canal rather than be subjected to this audit.

Following is an illustration of an IT Separation of Duties Matrix. This should give you an overview of where potential exposures exist and an idea of where segregating duties can be advantageous.

IT Separation of Duties Matrix

	Req access to prod data	Appr access to prod data	Provide access to prod data	Update prod data	Appr request to change code	Appr access to code	Change app code	Appr UAT code	Prom Code to UAT	Create dev UAT data	Execute UAT	Appr prod code prom	Promote code and tables to prod	Update ext tables that provide prod access
Request access to production Data		N	N	N	Y	Y	Y	Y	Y	Y	Y	N	N	Y
Approve access to production data (owner)	N		N	N	Y	N	N	N	N	N	Y	N	Y	Y
Provide access to production data (DBA)	N	N		N	N	N	N	N	N	N	N	N	Y	Y
Update production data (DBA)	N	N	N		N	N	Y	N	Y	Y	Y	N	N	Y
Approve request to change code (owner)	Y	Y	N	N		N	N	N	N	Y	Y	Y	N	N
Approve access to code (program mgr)	Y	N	N	N	N		N	Y	N	N	N	N	N	N
Change application code (prog)	Y	N	N	Y	N	N		N	Y	Y	Y	N	N	Y
Approve UAT code prom (owner)	Y	Y	N	N	Y	N	N		N	Y	Y	Y	N	N
Promote code to UAT (prog)	Y	N	N	Y	N	N	Y	N		Y	Y	N	N	Y
Create and develop UAT data (owner)	Y	Y	N	Y	N	N	Y	N	Y		Y	N	N	N
Execute UAT (owner)	Y	N	N	N	Y	N	N	Y	N	Y		Y	N	N
Approve prod code promotion (owner)	Y	Y	N	N	Y	N	N	Y	N	Y	Y		N	Y
Promote code/tables to production (operations)	N	N	N	N	N	N	N	N	N	N	N	N		N
Update ext tables that provide prod access (owner)	Y	N	N	N	N	N	N	Y	N	Y	Y	N	N	

Exhibit 11.1 IT SoD Matrix

Creating and implementing a SoD matrix is not an exact science and there will be different responsibilities assigned depending on your company's size, available resources, and organizational roles. For example, the creation, development and execution of User Acceptance Testing (UAT) can be performed by programmers or owner organizations (Exhibit 11.1).

Some notes on the matrix:

Request access to production data—This is the individual who requests read or update access to production data; he or she can be a programmer, database administrator, or end user. This individual should not approve access or provide access to production data.

Approve access to production data—This individual is the owner of the data, or it could be their delegate, who reviews the business reason for data access and approves access. This should not be the person who requests or provides access to production data nor should it be someone who can update production data.

Provide access to production data—This individual is usually someone in operations, a database administrator, who grants access to individuals who have been approved for access. This individual must not be an approver.

Update production data—A database administrator is usually approved to update production data as a result of a business need or in their daily job performance. A database administrator has pre-approval by an owner but there needs to be an audit trail of their activity. As a rule, programmers should not be able to update production data. This is known as the ***golden rule***. However, depending upon your organization's structure and resource limitation there might be a need for a programmer to update production data and correct it or discard the data in case of an emergency where erroneous data causes an application program to abort. If a programmer has to update production data, then his or her activity needs to be monitored by an independent reviewer to validate that the programmer was authorized, approved by the owner, and that the change(s) were valid. This secondary control, which is a detective control, requires that the independent reviewer sign-off after their review with the documentation maintained as an audit trail.

Approve request to change code—Application code that needs to be updated must be approved by a process owner, or their delegate. The request is usually submitted via a CR (change request, SR (system request), or PCR (program change request). The owner may or may not be the same individual who is the data owner. These roles need to be defined by each organization.

Approve access to code—If an application programmer needs to access program source code to make a change, then the programmer's manager needs to approve their access to the source code library. The programmer then extracts the source code, makes his or her change and moves it to the development library where it is tested. The individual who grants access should not be the same individual who approves access. You do not want an individual approving and then granting their own access. The programmer's manager should not be allowed to change application code unless access to the source code library is granted by another manager.

Change application code—Only a programmer should be allowed to change application code. The only exception would be an application programming manager, as indicated above.

Approve code promotion to UAT—Migrating code to a library where user acceptance testing (UAT) is performed should be approved by the process owner or their delegate.

Promote code to UAT—An application programmer promotes code to the development library where UAT is performed.

Create/develop UAT data—In some organizations, the programmers create UAT data and in some organizations (more common) the process owners create the UAT data. Realize that the two organizations can work together in creating UAT data.

Execute UAT—The execution of UAT can be done by the individual who created the test data or by someone else. However, this individual should not be the person who changed the code. Separation of duties should be evident in this case.

Approve code promotion to production—This can only be done by the process owner or their delegate. A programmer or programmer's manager can never provide approval. Approval should be obtained prior to moving the code to production. If there is an emergency and the owner's documented approval cannot be obtained prior to promotion, then in this situation there needs to be post approval after the code is moved to production.

Promote code to production—Migration of code to the production library should be done by a librarian, usually someone in operations, but certainly by an individual who is not the programmer who was responsible for this coding. In some smaller organizations, it might not be possible to have a librarian or another individual in operations perform the promotion. In this case, another programmer might have to promote the code with secondary controls in place and effectively executed. If the second programmer needs to promote the code, then the owner should authorize their access, which should be temporary access. A temporary ID should be assigned and removed after the code migration when it is no longer needed. An independent reviewer should ensure that the access was authorized for the actual code change being promoted. No other code should be changed other than the change authorized.

Update tables that provide access to production databases or production data need to be controlled. If tables are internal to applications, then the controls over table updates and the separation of duties controls are the same as code changes. Separation of duties or secondary controls needs to be in place for promotion. If tables that grant access are external tables, then the person who updates the tables is usually an administrator or end user and this individual should not have the capability to grant access and update production.

Having an IT separation of duties matrix is highly advisable and can be very advantageous during an audit. It can demonstrate to the auditor that you are cognizant of the need to separate responsibilities and that you have done so, wherever possible. What is also important as well as the documentation is to have evidence that there is a review of the matrix on a regular basis and that it is updated, if necessary, as personnel or responsibilities change and the matrix may be outdated.

Accounting Separation of Duties[2]

If you are or become a manager of an accounting or financial process within your company, you certainly need to be ready to address separation of duties. We focused on IT SoD but just as important, if not more so, will be establishing, documenting, and explaining your department's separation of duties. If you become an audit client there is almost a certitude that SoD will be a candidate for review within the audit scope. We will take a look at separation of duties in some major accounting processes.

Revenue

The first accounting process that we will look at closely with regard to SoD is the Revenue Process. The revenue process focuses on sale of goods and or services to customers. First, before we look at SoDs within the revenue process, we need to review and ensure that we understand the revenue functions. They are:

[2] Accounting SoD material and SoD matrices adapted from the ninth edition "Auditing & Assurance Services—A Systematic Approach" by William Messier, Steven Glover, Douglass Prawitt: Chapter 10 through Chapter 16.

Order Entry—Order entry is the action needed to record a customer's order into the company's order handling system. Once the information has been entered, it is typically classified internally as a sales order. The information in the sales order is then used to schedule all of the activities needed to fulfill the customer's order which may include materials procurement, production warehousing, shipping, and invoicing. In most companies, there is usually a separate order entry department.

Credit Authorizations—The credit authorization department checks to see if customers are able to pay for goods or service. There are usually credit limits established for customers and the credit authorization department determines that credit limits are not exceeded. If credit limits are exceeded, the credit authorization department might be able to accept authorization for payments up to a designated amount. However, if the amount that the customer is purchasing exceeds that established amount, the credit authorization manager might need to obtain additional management or executive authorization. This level of authorization can increase as the amount of the order rises above a designated threshold. The credit authorization function also has responsibility for monitoring customer payments. An aged trial of balance of accounts receivable should be prepared and reviewed by the credit department personnel. They should request payment from delinquent customers. In addition, usually the credit department is also responsible for preparing bad-debt write-offs. Bad debt write-offs might additionally require the authorization of executive management (e.g. treasurer) under certain parameters and applying to specific conditions.

Shipping—An exposure where controls are needed is to prevent goods from being shipped nor services provided without proper authorization. The shipping department manager and staff are responsible to ensure correct and authorized shipments are made with regard to product and quantity.

Billing—The main responsibility of the billing department is to ensure that all goods that are shipped and that all services provided are billed at authorized process and terms. The billing department personnel are also responsible for handling goods returned for credit. They should not accept goods returned for credit unless they satisfy acceptable criteria.

Cash Receipts—The collection function must ensure that all cash collections are properly identified and promptly deposited. Cash receipts are recorded in the company's cash receipt journal where cash is debited.

Accounts Receivable—Personnel in the accounts receivable department are responsible for ensuring that billings, adjustments, and cash collections are properly recorded in customers' account receivable records.

General Ledger—Accounting data is posted from journals and subledgers (e.g. accounts payable, accounts receivable, cash management, fixed assets) into the general ledger. A ledger account is created for each account in the chart of accounts for an organization and is classified into account categories such as income, expense, assets, liabilities and equity. The main objective of the general ledger function, in terms of the revenue process, is to ensure that all revenues, collections and receivables are properly accumulated, classified, and summarized in the appropriate accounts.

Segregation of duties is one of the most important controls across revenue functions. This is particularly important in the revenue process because of the potential for theft and fraud. Individuals involved in the order entry, credit, shipping, or billing functions should not have access to the accounts receivables records, the general ledger or any cash receipt activities. The revenue manager should establish a separation of duties matrix and the matrix should be reviewed regularly by higher management that shows that:

- The credit function should be segregated from the billing function. If an individual has the ability to grant credit to a customer and also has responsibility for billing that customer, it is possible for sales to be made to those customers who are not good credit risks, resulting in bad debts.
- Shipping should be segregated from the billing function. If an individual who is responsible for shipping goods is also in the billing department and responsible for billing, it is then possible for unauthorized shipments to be sent out. This can result in unrecorded sales transactions and worse, in a theft of goods. We need to prevent and avoid goods from being shipped without being billed.
- Accounts receivable functions should be segregated from general ledger functions. If an individual is responsible for accounts receivable records and also for the general ledger, it is possible for that individual to conceal unauthorized shipments. This can result in both unrecorded sales transactions and in a theft of goods.
- Cash receipts responsibilities should be segregated from general ledger responsibilities. If an individual has access to both cash

receipts and the accounts receivable records, it would be possible for cash to be diverted and the shortage of cash in the accounting records to be covered up. This can result in a theft of the company's cash.

There are different ways of formatting a separation of duties matrix. We will look at just two of them to give you a couple of ideas of the possible format you could choose.

Example I of Segregation of Duties Matrix for Revenue and Accounts Receivable

Department / Function	Order Entry	Credit	Shipping	Accounts Receivable	Cash Receipts	IT	Treasurer
Writing Customer Order	Y	N	N	N	N	N	N
Authorizing Customer Credit	N	Y	N	N	N	N	N
Shipping Goods to Customer	N	N	Y	N	N	N	N
Preparing Customer Invoice	N	N	N	Y	N	Y	N
Updating A/R Records	N	N	N	Y	N	Y	N
Receiving Customer Payment	N	N	N	N	Y	N	N
Updating A/R records for payment	N	N	N	Y	N	Y	N
Updating A/R aged trial balance	N	N	N	Y	N	Y	N
Authorizing write-offs	N	N	N	N	N	N	Y

Exhibit 11.2 First Revenue and A/R SoD Matrix

In the above example, the functions were listed down the rows and the departments performing the functions were listed across the columns (Exhibit 11.2).

Example II—Segregation of Duties Matrix for Revenue and Accounts Receivable

Name of individual / Function	Name 1	Name 2	Name 3	Name 4	Name 5	Name 6	Name 7
Writing Customer Orders	X						
Authorizing Customer Credit		X					
Shipping Goods to Customers			X				
Preparing Customer Invoice				X		X	
Updating A/R records				X		X	
Receiving Customer Payment					X		
Updating A/R Records for Payments				X		X	
Updating A/R Aged Trial Balance				X		X	
Authorizing Write-offs							X

Exhibit 11.3 Second Revenue and A/R SoD Matrix

In this example, the tasks or functions were listed down the rows and the names of the individuals performing the tasks were listed across the columns (Exhibit 11.3).

Purchasing and Accounts Payable

Let us look next at the purchasing process and its functions. After we review the functions, we can cite some separation of duties controls that should be established.

The principal business objectives of the purchasing process are acquiring goods and services at the lowest cost consistent with quality and service requirements and effectively using cash resources to pay for these goods and services. The major functions are:

Requisitioning—The requisitioning function is the initiation and approval of goods/services by authorized individuals consistent with management criteria. A requisition refers to the process of formally requesting a service or item, typically using a purchase requisition form. The requisition function is a standardized way of keeping track of and accounting for all requisitions made in the company. Each company should have a policy, requiring different levels of authorization for different requests for purchases—higher dollar value requests for purchases should require higher level of management approval.

Purchasing—The purchase department is headed by a purchasing manager and assisted by buyers. Purchasing is the formal function of buying goods and services. The function usually starts with a demand or requirements for inventory or service. A requisition details the requirements and a request for proposal (RFP) or request for quotation (RFQ) is then established. Suppliers or vendors send their quotations in response to the RFQ where the best offer from a vendor (typically based on price, availability, and quality) needs to be approved and is the basis for the purchase order.

Receiving—This function involves the receipt of authorized goods/services by a receiving department. The receiving department is the central receiving point for the delivering of merchandise and is responsible for verifying deliveries, inspecting for damaged goods and coordinating the delivering of merchandise to the ordering departments.

Invoice Processing—Invoice processing involves the handling of incoming invoices from arrival to payment. In this function, we have the processing of vendor invoices for goods and services received and processing of necessary adjustments for allowances, discounts and returns.

Disbursements—Disbursements involved the processing of payments to vendors. This involves the responsibility for preparing and signing vendor checks. Generally, dual signatures on checks over a certain amount are required. Disbursement is the actual delivery of funds from one party's bank account to another's.

Accounts Payable—The accounts payable department is responsible for accurately tracking what is owed to suppliers, vendors, ensuring payments are properly approved and processing payments. The accounts payable department records all vendor invoices, cash disbursements, and adjustments in individual vendor accounts.

General Ledger—Accounting data is posted from journals and subledgers (e.g. accounts payable, accounts receivable, cash management, fixed assets) into the general ledger. A ledger account is created for each account in the chart of accounts for an organization and is classified into account categories such as income, expense, assets, liabilities, and equity. The main objective of the general ledger function in terms of a revenue process is to ensure that all revenues, collections, and receivables are properly accumulated, classified, and summarized in the appropriate accounts.

Segregation of duties plays a very important role in Purchasing as it does with other entity processes. Duties should be assigned so that no one individual can control one or more phases of processing transactions in a way that permits errors or fraud to go undetected. A SoD matrix for Purchasing should indicate that the following functions should be segregated:

- The purchasing function should be segregated from the requisition and receiving functions preventing fictitious and or unauthorized purchases. If one individual is responsible for the requisition, purchasing, and receiving function, fictitious or unauthorized purchases can be made. This can result in the theft of goods and possibly payment for unauthorized purchases.
- The invoice-processing function should be segregated from A/P to help prevent overpayment for goods and services or theft of cash. If the same individual is responsible for the invoicing processing and the accounts payable functions, purchase transactions can be purchased at the wrong price or terms, or a cash disbursement can be processed for goods or services not received. This can result in overpayment for goods and services or the theft of cash.
- The disbursement function should be segregated from A/P to prevent unauthorized transactions from being recorded. If one individual is responsible for the disbursement function and has access to the accounts payable records, unauthorized checks supported by fictitious documents can be issued, and unauthorized transactions can be recorded. This can result in theft of the entity's cash.
- A/P should be segregated from the general ledger function so one individual can't conceal a defalcation. If the same individual is responsible for the accounts payable records and for the general ledger, that individual can conceal any defalcation that would normally be detected by recording subsidiary records with the general ledger control account.

Again, we will look at two different ways of establishing a separation of duties matrix (Exhibits 11.4 and 11.5).

Example I—Segregation of Duties Matrix for Purchasing and Accounts Payable

Department / Function	Purchasing	Receiving	Accounts Payable	Cashier	IT
Preparation and approval of purchase order	Y	N	N	N	N
Receipt, counting, and inspection of purchased materials	N	Y	N	N	N
Receipt of vendor invoices and matching them with supporting documents	N	N	Y	N	N
Checking of account distributions	N	N	Y	N	N
Updating of accounts payable records	N	N	Y	N	Y
Preparation of vendor checks	N	N	N	N	Y
Signing and mailing of vendor checks	N	N	N	Y	N
Preparation of voucher register	N	N	N	N	Y
Reconciliation of voucher register to general ledger	N	N	Y	N	N

Exhibit 11.4 First Purchasing and A/P SoD Matrix

Example II—Segregation of Duties Matrix for Purchasing and Accounts Payable

Name of person / Task	Name 1	Name 2	Name 3	Name 4	Compensating controls
Initiates Purchase Order	X				
Approves Requisition			X		
Prepare Purchase Order				X	
Manage inventory Records		X			
Approve Vendor Payments				X	

Exhibit 11.5 Second Purchasing and A/P SoD Matrix

Human Resources Separation of Duties

In a company, the Human Resources department is in charge of all employees and employee related activities. The HR department takes care of the organization's most valuable asset, its employees. The HR department makes sure that employees have everything that they need to perform their day-to-day tasks, and they are also responsible for creating a healthy working environment that attracts and retains qualified people. The human resources (HR) department includes the authorization of hiring, firing, wage rate and salary adjustments, salaries, and payroll deductions. HR maintains employees' personnel records and may be responsible for definition of job requirements, developing performance and evaluation criteria, and administering union contracts. Major functions within the Human Resources Process are:

Supervision—Supervisors or management are responsible for reviewing and approving employees' attendance and recorded hours. They are also responsible to monitor employee's productivity and managing payroll and employee relations. Their job also includes liaising with recruitment agencies, advertising job openings, and selecting workers with skills and interests aligned with the company's goals.

Timekeeping—Timekeeping duties involve preparing and inputting time and attendance data into the payroll system so employees can get paid for actual time worked, including overtime hours.

Payroll processing—Payroll refers to the process (manual or automated) by which employees receive their salary. Functions involve balancing and reconciling payroll data and depositing and recording taxes. This function is responsible for computing gross pay, deductions, and net pay. The recording and summarizing payments and verifying account distribution is also required. IT is used frequently to process payroll with some entities outsourcing their payroll. If IT is used there must be strong application controls stated in a service level agreement.

Disbursement—Disbursement means paying out money. The disbursement department is responsible for employee payments of services and benefits (e.g. stock options, retirement funds). The department is also responsible for the delivery of loans to a borrower, or the payment of dividends to shareholders. A disbursement is the actual delivery of funds from a bank account.

General Ledger—A general ledger is a means for keeping a record of a company's total financial accounts. Accounts typically recorded in the general ledger include assets, liabilities, equity, expenses, and income. The individuals with general ledger responsibilities accumulate, classify, and summarize payroll and benefit transactions in the general ledger.

Key separation of duties can prevent possible errors/frauds and is essential in HR. The following are examples of what functions should be addressed in a SoD matrix for HR:

- The supervision function should be separated from the personnel records and payroll processing functions. If an individual is responsible for supervision, personnel records, and payroll processing functions, fictitious employees can appear on the payroll records or unauthorized payments can be made. This is a major area where SoD is critical.
- The disbursement function should be segregated from the personnel records, supervision, and payroll processing functions. If there is one individual who is responsible for the disbursement function and also has authority to hire and fire employees, approve time

worked or prepare payroll checks, then payroll checks can be issued to unauthorized personnel.

- The payroll processing function needs to be segregated from the general ledger function. The reason for this is that if one individual is responsible for processing payroll transactions and is also responsible for the general ledger, that individual can conceal any defalcation that would normally be detected by an independent review of accounting errors made to the ledger.

Following is a simple illustration of a HR SoD matrix that you can use as a foundation for your matrix (Exhibit 11.6).

Payroll Separation of Duties Matrix

Tasks	Supervisor	Timekeeper	Payroll Processing	Disbursement	General Ledger
Review and approve employees attendance	Y	N	N	N	N
Prepares employee's time information for payroll processing	N	Y	N	N	N
Computing payroll payments	N	N	Y	N	N
Prepares and distributes payroll checks	N	N	N	Y	N
Accumulating, classifying, and summarizing payroll and benefit transactions in the general ledger	N	N	N	N	Y

Exhibit 11.6 Payroll SoD Matrix

Inventory

SoD is a critical control in the inventory process because of a potential for straightforward theft and fraud.

We need to first look at and understand the following major functions in the inventory process:

Inventory Management—Inventory Management refers to the process of ordering, storing, and using a company's inventory. This includes the management of raw materials, components, and finished goods, as well as warehousing and the processing of these items. What is involved with the inventory management function is the authorization of production activity and maintenance of inventory at appropriate levels. Purchase requisitions are issued to the purchasing department and represents the point at which the inventory management process integrates with the purchasing process.

Raw Materials Stores—Raw material stores play a key function in the custody of raw materials and issuance of raw material to manufacturing departments. When goods are received from vendors, they are transferred from the receiving department to the raw materials department.

Manufacturing—Manufacturing is the steps through which raw materials are transformed into a final product. There must be adequate control over the physical flow of goods and proper accumulation of the costs attached to the inventory.

Finished Goods Stores—When goods are completed by the manufacturing function they are transferred to finished goods stores. The goods have not yet been sold to the customers at this time. Finished goods stores are responsible for the custody of finished goods and issuance of goods to the shipping department.

Cost Accounting—Cost accounting is a set of procedures for recording and reporting measurements of the cost of manufacturing goods and performing services in the aggregate and in detail. It includes methods for recognizing, classifying, allocating, aggregating, and reporting such costs and preparing them with standard costs. Cost accumulation and variance reports are reviewed after processing into accounting records.

General Ledger—An inventory ledger is a document or computer record that tracks inventory transactions. The total of all transactions listed in this ledger should match the total for the corresponding account in the general ledger. This ledger maintains a beginning balance against which are netted all receipt and uses of inventory. The individual responsible for the general ledger is assigned the tasks of recording the accumulation, classification, and summarization of inventory and related costs in the general ledger.

These are separation of duties responsibilities that you should validate are adhered to if you are the manager who is responsible for inventory within your company:

- The inventory manufacturing function should be separated from the cost accounting function. If there is one individual who is responsible for inventory management and he or she also has access to the cost accounting records, production, and inventory costs can be manipulated. This can result in an overstatement or understatement of inventory and net income.
- The inventory stores function should be segregated from the cost accounting function. If an individual is responsible for controlling inventory and processing the cost accounting records, unauthorized shipments can be made or theft of goods can be covered up.
- The cost accounting function should be separated from general ledger functions. If one individual is responsible for both the inventory records and also for the general ledger, it would be possible for that person to conceal unauthorized shipments.
- One person should not be responsibility for supervising physical inventory and have responsibility for inventory stores functions. If the person is responsible for production management or inventory stores function and is also responsible for the physical inventory, it is possible that inventory shortages can be concealed by the adjustment of the inventory records to the physical inventory, This would result in an overstatement of inventory.

The following is a basis for an inventory management SoD matrix that you could use:

Inventory Managment Separation of Duties

Department / Function	Inventory Management	Raw Materials Stores	Manufacturing	Finished Goods Stores	Cost Accounting	G/L
Receives inventory	N	Y	N	N	N	N
Records receipt of inventory in inventory records	N	N	N	N	Y	N
Maintains custody of inventory (storage and control)	N	N	N	Y	N	N
Performs inventory count	Y (person A)	N	N	N	N	N
Reconciles inventory count to inventory records	N	N	N	N	N	Y
Reviews reconciliation of inventory count to inventory records	Y (person B)	N	N	N	N	N
Produces the product	N	N	Y	N	N	N

Exhibit 11.7 Inventory Management SoD Matrix

In this matrix format, we are defining the tasks or functions in the vertical column along the left axis and the departments responsible for these functions along the horizontal axis (Exhibit 11.7).

Financial Functions Separation of Duties

The last area when examining separation of duties within the accounting processes will be financial functions of capital assets; stockholders' equity;

and securities and investments. SoD needs to be established and successfully executed among the financing functions within the company.

A capital asset is property that is expected to generate value over a long period of time. Capital assets form the productive base of an organization. Examples are buildings, computer equipment, and machinery. Capital assets, for businesses, are assets with a useful life longer than a year that are not intended for sale in the regular course of the business operation.

Representations of capital assets SoD responsibilities are:

- Launching a capital asset acquisition should be segregated from final approval. If there is one individual who is responsible for initiating a capital asset transaction and he or she is also responsible for final approval, fictitious, or unauthorized purchases of assets can occur.
- The property, plant, and equipment records function should be segregated from the safeguarding or custodial function. If an individual is responsible for the property, plant, and equipment records and also has custodial responsibility for the related assets, equipment can be stolen and the theft can be concealed by adjustment of accounting records.
- The property, plant, and equipment records function should be separated from the general ledger function. If a person is responsible for the property, plant, and equipment records and is also responsible for general ledger functions, then that individual can conceal any defalcation that would normally be detected by reconciling subsidiary records with the general ledger control account.
- The function of an individual taking a periodic physical inventory of property, plant, and equipment should be independent of the custodial and record keeping functions. If an individual responsible for the periodic physical inventory of property, plant, and equipment is also responsible for the custodial and record keeping functions, theft of the entity's capital assets can be covered up.

For most companies, stockholders' equity includes common stock, preferred stock, paid-in capital and retained earnings. Major types of transactions that occur in stockholders' equity are issuance of stock; repurchase of stock; and payment of dividends. Many large entities, such as publicly traded companies, use an independent registrar, transfer agent, and dividend disbursement agent to process and record equity transactions—auditors will look for sufficient evidence by confirming documentation from these parties.

Stockholders' equity requires the following SoD:

- The employee responsible for issuing, transferring, and canceling stock certificates should not be engaged in nor have any responsibilities in any accounting activities.
- An individual who is responsible for maintaining detailed stockholders' records should not be involved in maintaining the general ledger control accounts.
- Appropriate separation of duties should be established among the functions of preparation, recording, signing, and the mailing of dividend checks.
- Functions of the individual responsible for maintaining detailed stockholders' records should be separated from the functions of also processing cash receipts or disbursements. One individual should not conduct both functions.

Entities frequently invest in securities of other entities. Such investments might include equity securities such as common and preferred stock, debt securities such as notes and bonds, and hybrid securities such as convertible bonds and stocks. Key separation of duties that should be established and executed with regard to investments are:

- The function of initiating securities should be independent from the final approval function. If the same individual is responsible for both the initiating as well as the approval of securities transactions, fictitious transactions can be employed, and there is a possibility that securities can be stolen.
- The responsibility for custody of the securities should be detached from that of accounting for the securities. If one individual has access both to securities and to the supporting accounting records, a theft of the securities is a possibility and can be easily concealed.
- Responsibility for maintaining the securities ledger should be partitioned from the responsibility of making entries in the general ledger. If an individual is responsible for both the securities ledger and general ledger, that individual can conceal a defalcation. This

embezzlement would normally be detected by reconciliation of the subsidiary records with general ledger control accounts.
- The individual who is responsible for the valuation-monitoring function should be segregated from the acquisition function. If an employee is responsible for acquiring and also monitoring the valuation of securities, securities values can be improperly recorded and escape being reported to management.

I had a personal incident when I was auditing, and I encountered a separation of duties exposure that is described below:

Personal Experience 11.1

Years ago, I participated in an accounts receivable audit at one of our remote sites. I was part of a team and about a month after the audit report was released, my manager came into my office and asked me if I had audited a particular employee in the A/R department. I said that I had and asked him why he was asking me. He told me that the woman was arrested—I asked him what happened. He told me that she threatened to commit suicide before she was arrested and I asked for more details. He told me that she was receiving checks made out to the company and also had the responsibility of depositing them. I will use fictitious names. Many of the checks that she received were made out to, for example, the ABC company rather than being spelled out and made out to the Allstate Baking Company. She had set up her own company. I don't remember the exact name of her company but for this scenario let us say that it was called Alicia's Breakfast Company. She was receiving the checks, endorsing them and then depositing them in a special account that she set up for her fictitious company. She had accumulated quite a windfall before her fraudulent activities were discovered.

My manager, knowing that I had not detected the fraud, asked me if I had at least identified the separation of duties exposure that could lead to a possibility of fraud. He told me that both of our jobs were on the line and fortunately, I had documented the SoD exposure. I breathed a sigh of relief, as did he, and he told me that we needed to check my audit work-papers. All auditors are supposed to keep audit work-papers for all audits that they were engaged in. The work-papers are an audit trail of the individuals that the auditors spoke to, when they spoke to them and what their findings were. If there were any exposures, they should have been reflected in my work-papers. He asked me to pull my work-papers to verify that I had included the separation of duties finding indicating an exposure to the possibility of fraudulent activity occurring. They were there, properly notated and cross-referenced to the audit report, as they were required to be. My audit trail was intact. And there was a recommendation stated in the final audit report that separation of duties needed to be established and effectively executed to prevent the likelihood of fraud with one individual being responsible for both receiving checks and depositing them. These functions, of course, should be separated, whenever possible between at least two individuals.

Summary

Separation or segregation of duties is one of the most effective preventive controls to prevent fraud and errors. This is a prime area that most auditors will focus on. As a process owner, who is or will be subjected to an audit, you will need to ensure that tasks within your department are adequately separated. The important thing to note is that the responsibilities for initiating, authorizing, inputting, processing, and checking data should be segregated so that one person does not have the ability to create a fraudulent transaction, authorize it, and hide the evidence. Inadequate segregation of duties could make fraud prevention, detection, and investigation difficult, which could possibly lead to misstated financial statements, regulatory punishments, and damage to the company's reputation and reduced investor trust. Large companies can probably afford SoD controls to minimize exposures but smaller companies, although understanding the risk, may not be able to afford the expense of hiring and training additional personnel to establish SoD. If this is true, then they will need to document the risk and establish secondary controls that could involve the establishment of audit trails and transaction logs that can be independently reviewed. Documented supervisory or management evidence of reviews would also help with auditor discussions and could prevent or mitigate audit concerns.

Every process owner within a company needs to be aware of the importance of SoD. This is especially true for IT, accounting, and finance management. SoD within IT requires that programmers should not have access to production data/libraries unless authorized by owners; the prevention of an operator, application or systems programmer from controlling or granting access to production data; or anyone writing code that can be promoted to production unless authorized and approved by an owner.

With regard to the Revenue Process, there should be SoD controls for the following functions: order entry, credit authorizations, shipping, billing, cash receipts, accounts receivable, and the general ledger. As far as the Purchasing Process, there should be SoD controls established for the following functions: requisitioning, purchasing, receiving, invoice processing, disbursements, accounts payable, and the general ledger.

There needs to be separation of duties within HR, especially the payroll function; within the inventory process including inventory management, raw material stores, finished goods stores, cost accounting, and the general ledger; and when you are involved with financial functions such as capital assets, stockholders' equity, securities, and investments.

It would be very helpful and beneficial to have a SoD matrix documented that explains roles and responsibilities within your organization where you could illustrate effective control.

Guidelines

1. Generate a SoD matrix defining the tasks and functions of all of your staff.
2. Review the SoD matrix to determine if there are any exposures.
3. If there are separation of duties exposures, separate functions to mitigate risk.
4. If the expense of hiring additional resources is cost prohibitive and functions can't be adequately segregated, then complete a risk assessment.
5. Obtain executive management approval on accepting the risk and/or establish secondary controls where there is independent review of activities.
6. If you are dependent on another organization for support (e.g. IT), then ensure that you have a service level agreement with them that addresses effective separation of duties.
7. Ask the service organization if they have a SoD matrix.
8. Review any SoD matrix that a service organization has in place that could affect the functions of your department.
9. If you see any exposures that a service organization has, document a request that asks the service organization to address the exposure.

10. Retain an audit trail of all documentation and correspondence that addresses any known exposure and planned actions to mitigate the risk.

Chapter 11 Exercises

1. You are an IT manager and your staff recently designed, programmed, and installed a new billing system. The new system has been operational for only one month, however there are numerous problems causing the primary application within the system to frequently abort. You get a call at four am one morning after the application terminated and the application needs to be fixed as soon as possible and back in operation. If not, there will be much consternation in the morning as there will be delayed or missing revenue once again. Your lead programmer needs to gain access to the production library, pull the code and fix the application. There is no time to wait for the process owner to approve and sign-off on a change request, initiate a change, and test it in the development library before promoting it to production. You realize that there is an SoD exposure—what action do you take?
2. You are the inventory manager in a small company and do not have needed resources to ensure adequate separation of duties. One of your employees receives merchandize for your company that she purchased, stores it and then takes a physical inventory every quarter. She reports the results to you when the physical inventory is completed. What separation of duties concerns are you aware of, what exposures are there to the company and what action do you take?
3. You are the accounts receivable manager. One of your staff has responsibility for shipping and also is responsible for the billing function. What separation of duties exposures do you see?

Chapter 11 Questions

Please select the best answer to the questions below:

1. Separation of duties prevents collusion.

   A. true
   B. false

2. Separation of duties in an IT organization should:

   A. prohibit operational personnel from writing code to be promoted
   B. prohibit a programmer from accessing production libraries
   C. prevent programmers from writing new code without owner's approval
   D. all of the above

3. Which is a SoD exposure?

   A. The person who approves a request to change code cannot be the same person who creates user acceptance test data
   B. A data base administrator who provides production access can't authorize production access
   C. The individual who creates user acceptance test (UAT) data can't write code
   D. All of the above

4. Which statement is true?

   A. IT cannot update accounts receivable records.
   B. The person who authorizes accounts receivable write-offs can be responsible for cash receipts.
   C. The person responsible for preparing customer invoices can't be responsible for shipping.
   D. The person who approves credits can also be responsible for preparing customer orders.

5. If an individual signs vendor checks they can be responsible for:

   A. cashier functions
   B. receiving functions
   C. purchasing functions
   D. accounts payable functions

6. If a programmer needs to make a coding change because a program aborts, they can access the source code library, extract the code they need, make the change, and test it in the development library. The only approval they need is when they want to promote the code to production.

   A. true
   B. false

7. The individual who approves access to production data can be:

   A. the programming manager
   B. the data base administrator
   C. the process owner
   D. any of the above

8. To prevent unauthorized checks from being recorded, the disbursement function should be separated from:

   A. the purchasing function
   B. the A/R function
   C. the receiving department
   D. the A/P function

9. If one person has the responsibility for supervising physical inventory and has responsibility for inventory stores function, it is possible that inventory shortages can be concealed. This would result in:

   A. an overstatement of inventory
   B. an understatement of inventory
   C. neither of the above

10. The individual who is responsible for maintaining detailed stockholders' records can also be involved in maintaining the general ledger control accounts provided that they don't issue stock certificates.

   A. true
   B. false

References

Messier William, Glover Steven, Prawitt Douglass (2014) Auditing & Assurance Services a Systematic Approach, 9th edn. (chapters 10–16).
Proviti "KnowledgeLeader" (March 19, 2020).

CHAPTER 12

Application Controls

Application controls surface and plays a key role in a vast number of internal audits that are planned and conducted. The design and effective execution of these controls cross over many company organizations and departments. Audits that are announced as business process audits, or IT audits will most likely effect both organizations. Business process owners can no longer respond to many audit questions that arise in today's environment without the help and assistance of IT management. IT plays a meaningful role in the collection, processing, storing, and distribution of data in the twenty-first century. And the reverse is true as well. IT management, when being audited, will depend on the business process owner—we need to remember that IT is primarily providing a service to the process owner. Effective audit readiness will frequently require close synergy between the business process owner and IT.

An application audit, to be truly effective, needs to be an integrated audit between IT and the business community. Auditors will attempt to validate that control activities are effectively designed, implemented, and auditable. The auditors, when conducting their audits, will be examining numerous controls: some of them will have been designed by the application development organization, some by the operations organization, and some by the business process owner who owns the applications within the processes being audited. In larger companies, there can be several application owners who own various applications that support a process—they

E. Danter, *Audit Defense*, Palgrave Studies in Accounting and Finance Practice, https://doi.org/10.1007/978-3-030-92466-9_12

report to a business process owner. For example, if you are the revenue process owner in a company you might have an order entry manager, a shipping manager, a billing manager and an accounts receivable manager, all application owners, all reporting directly to you, who are accountable for the efficiency and effectiveness of controls surrounding their applications. If you are a business process owner, in a smaller company, you might be wearing two hats—the business process owner might also be the application owner.

The responsibility for implementation of the majority of these controls will probably lie with the IT organization, even if they were requested by the business process or application owner. However, it is the business process owner, who is usually the audit client, who will have primary control accountability in the eyes of the auditors.

Each of the organizations plays a role during an application audit when application controls are reviewed. To be audit ready, the audit client should be aware of an application's control activities and needs to ensure that they are effectively designed, installed and auditable.

The objectives of control design are pretty clear. Their purpose is to ensure that the processing of all data is complete, accurate, and timely and that those assets are adequately protected. The objectives of auditability should also be fairly obvious. Auditability must address the documentation of controls and the traceability of results.

First let us look at an application, where hypothetically IA has verified that there are serious concerns where an application's processing is incomplete, erroneous, and untimely. In this situation, if the audit results are verified to be factual, the company's executives will presumably either want controls improved and concerns eliminated/mitigated in the existing application, or they may want a new application to be developed and installed, if enhancing the current application's controls will be too costly.

In either case, there will need to close cooperation between business process owners and IT. The executives can ask the process owners to work with their IT organization to either enhance existing application controls or to develop and promote a new application into production that will effectively address and improve upon the objectives of completeness, accuracy, and timeliness. Some of the challenges when improving controls in an existing application or addressing them in a new application will either be the same or they will differ, as we will see later in this chapter.

The chart below attempts to depict the relationships among the aforementioned organizations. In this chart, we are looking at a larger company where the application owners report to the business process owner. And the Application Development Department (developers and programmers) and the Computer Operations Department (operators and administrators) are supporting organizations that fulfill responsibilities of the Business Process Owner. The supporting organizations work directly with the Business Process Owners or work with the Application Owners. Note that the responsibilities of all the organizations should be defined in a service level agreement (Exhibit 12.1).

Application Controls

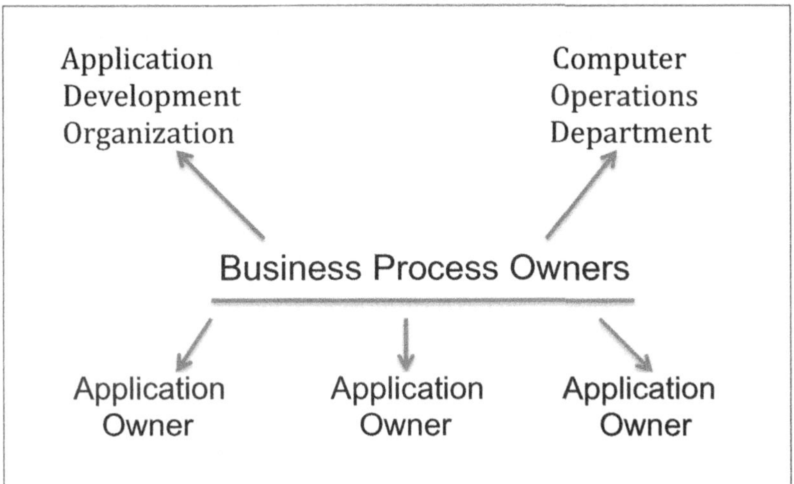

Exhibit 12.1 Realtionship between Owners and IT

In this chapter, as stated before, we will be reviewing application controls. The following application controls are not all-inclusive but should give you an idea of where the auditors can focus and what their expectations will be. The controls that we will examine cover the following functions: application documentation, project management, input/output, editing, error handling, application balancing, database reconciliation, application monitoring, and backup and restart procedures.

Before we look at the challenges let us understand application ownership. Business process owners are the customers for whom applications are developed and installed. They are, in many cases, users of the applications themselves but in most instances they control and manage end user activity and application processing via effective application controls. The application owners, sometimes referred to as business process owners (again, a process can consist of many applications and in smaller companies the business process owners are also the application owners) are involved with business strategies, establishing processes and objectives, and should play a significant role in requesting new application design or in the design of enhancements to existing applications.

The design, installation, and maintenance of these applications will directly support business processes. And for that reason, the applications must meet the ever-changing business environment. The application owner is usually involved with day-to-day operations or in interfacing directly with the IT development organization that is providing a service. In this chapter, the business process owner will be the audit client and will be accountable with IT being responsible.

Project Management

When an application is designed and developed or when major enhancements (sometimes called releases) are made, the objective for the process owner is to ensure that these efforts result in the new application or release being completed on time, within budget, and achieving quality processing in addition to satisfying requested requirements.

This, sometimes monumental task, is usually assigned to a project manager. This is an essential individual on any project and on whose shoulders expectations for success of delivery falls. The project manager has the responsibility of managing the project and ensuring that it is delivered on time (meeting scheduled delivery date), within an accepted quality level, within the budget.

Project management is a highly regarded role in today's business community and project management certification is an objective of many professionals. Project managers are sought after not only in application development organizations but throughout other organizations as well—anywhere projects need to be effectively managed to guarantee success. For example, opening a new data center, switching over to a new operating system, or transitioning to new hardware requires large work efforts with extensive, well-controlled projects that are established and managed by experienced project managers. One of the most taxing projects that I witnessed, an effort requiring a very able project manager was the successful conversion of hundreds of applications at the turn of the century. Most application programs were coded with just two yearly digits for the year. When we went from 1999 to 2000 we could not use "00" for the year or else most programs would perform calculations based on 1900 and not 2000. The programs had to modified to accommodate a four digit year. The entire country was apprehensive with regard to possible processing delays occurring during this transition from the twentieth to the twenty-first century. Everyone was extremely nervous and skeptical whether all programs could be changed and successfully tested with minimum disruption. This conversion was a herculean effort taking an extraordinary number of hours, coordination, and resource. There was a heavy dependence on an experienced project manager. I was directly involved with just one project manager faced with this task in my company but realized that throughout the entire country there were hundreds of project managers faced with the same challenge. The dependency of these project managers for so many companies was mind-boggling.

The efforts of a project manager include but are not limited to:

- Work management (project plan)
- Testing activities
- Metrics
- Quality management
- Task management
- Risk management
- Production change management
- Tracking work efforts
- Obtaining customer sign-offs
- Designing and ensuring implementation of effective controls

The last item above involves application controls. Too many times, controls are an afterthought and if this occurs, it can result in unexpected disasters. Controls need to be designed, coded, and tested as soon as possible during project development or else the consequences can be significant. See my personal experience below.

Personal experience 12.1

I was assigned to work on my first development project - it was a billing system. There were a half dozen programmers and a manager involved. We were given a set of requirements and asked to replace an existing billing system by a specific date meeting the requirements and budget allocated. This was a large billing system and required almost 2 years from the time specifications were written, programming completed (there were many programs involved), testing accomplished and installed. We met the target date when the system was to go live and stayed within budget. No additional resources or excessive expenses were incurred. However, we did not focus on controls. Our plan was to insert the controls, later on, as needed. This was unfortunate. We were considering establishing controls as an afterthought—this was a total calamity. We ran into problems shortly after the new application was installed and running. The programs were aborting on a regular basis due to coding bugs. We had not tested for all possibilities of erroneous data that entered into the system. Rather than rejecting the errors, the programs were aborting. Not only was our editing of data at fault, we never planned for recovery controls. To make matters worse, the programs were crashing and all processing came to a halt in the middle of the night. Because there was hundreds of thousands of dollars subjected to delayed or missed billings, time was of the essence. The programs needed to be fixed as soon as possible. The business process owner, the billing manager, was livid. Since I lived the closest to the operational site (remote coding fixes were not possible in those days), I was required to go to our building where our computers were housed and fix the coding, some of which I had coded myself and was familiar with and other coding that I had not written and was not familiar with. I still had to debug the programs and restore the processing. Sometimes, we just needed to bypass the records that were causing problems, reject them and store them in an error file for future correction. Naturally, we did not expect all this activity to be needed and restart procedures were lacking. The situation got so bad the first few weeks—the programs kept aborting, the system came down and I had to go in to fix the problem much too frequently. The phone rang too regularly. It got so bad that one night I dreamt that the phone rang. I went to answer it, thinking it was operations calling about anther problem, but there was no one on the other end of the line. This was a learning experience for us. In another few months, we were asked to develop a different type of billing system for different products. This time we knew that we had to establish, design and thoroughly test out all of the controls before the system went live. It was a painful lesson but one that I never forgot. I personally realized that maintaining systems that you install was a valuable experience. I was more assured of getting a good night's sleep with the next 2 systems that we were commissioned to design and install.

Input/Output/Interface Controls

Input, output, and interface controls are frequently reviewed by auditors during application audits to validate accuracy, completeness, and timeliness of processing. Auditors will want to make sure that there are effective controls to verify that all inputs received from upstream or sending applications and transmitted to downstream applications are processed as scheduled. If a processing schedule calls for daily transmissions, how do you know that the right transmissions are received, that there was not a duplicate transmission or that a transmission was not skipped? How do you know that all output that was supposed to be generated, was generated, and successfully passed to subsequent applications for timely processing?

There should be a formal schedule as to when input is to be received from the applications sending you data and when your output is to be transmitted to downstream applications for further processing. In order to ensure completeness of processing, the sending application program should generate a header record on all files that contain a transmission number, date of transmission, record count, and dollar amount. Each time the sending application program transmits a file they should be incrementing the transmission number. The receiving application program needs to verify the sequence number by adding one to the last transmission received to see if it agrees with the new sequence number. If the transmission number received is one greater than then the number expected, a transmission was probably skipped or if it one less, a red flag should be raised indicating a duplicate transmission is about to be processed. If the sequence number has been properly incremented and correctly indicates the next transmission, that is still no assurance that you have received the right transmission. You could have received the same data if the sending application duplicated their processing with the same data, although they ran another cycle. The transmission sequence number would have been incremented correctly but you would not be aware of receiving duplicate processed records. The additional control of checking and validating not only record counts but also dollar amounts should be a warning of potential duplicate data. If you rely just on your balancing routines and just check record counts, that will not suffice, as there might be two consecutive transmissions with the same record counts—this is not a guarantee. However, using the dollar counts as well as record counts, transmission dates, and sequence numbers should be helpful in avoiding duplicates from being processed. If the same record counts and dollar amounts are received, you probably received a duplicate transmission and it should be flagged. This is an excellent example of preventive controls.

Output control is designed to ensure that all output is generated that is supposed to be generated and that it is distributed to the right organization. You should be generating a header record on all output that will be read and validated by the downstream receiving application. Your header record should have the same information as we discussed before: transmission number, date of transmission, record counts, and dollar counts. In this case, your application becomes the sending application and the application that is receiving the transmission should balance to your output total. A schedule log should fulfill this requirement.

When you are undergoing an application audit, auditors will want to know what controls exist to ensure that all interfaces where received and successfully transmitted as scheduled. If you receive data, there should be messages sent back to the sending application that the interface files were received and data successfully processed. If you send data to other application programs, you should likely receive confirmation that the files and data that you sent were successfully received. This documentation should be retained so that an audit trail of successful confirmation can be demonstrated, if and when asked.

Editing and Auditing Data

This textbook describes timeliness and completeness of processing but we also need controls that will address accuracy. We need effective auditing of data established to check for valid data. We do not want to accept any data for processing that doesn't meet designed criteria. We want to prevent erroneous or incomplete data from entering applications as soon as possible. When data is to be used for processing it should be edited for validity as soon as possible. The earlier in the program, where editing occurs, the better. It is important that rejected records appear on error reports generated to allow someone to work the errors for resubmission. As an example, if social security numbers are to be entered on all employee input records and there are alpha characters, blanks, or ten digit social security numbers entered, those errors should be identified as soon as possible, rejected and submitted when corrected. Another example is to check for reasonableness. Programs could be auditing for what makes sense and what does not. If we know that employees are paid commissions on their sales every quarter and we notice that one salesman's commissions are doubling every quarter, we should become skeptical of its validity and question it. The program should flag this as suspicious activity and there should be a procedure for someone, at the right level of management, to follow up for reasonableness. Effective editing is a desirable preventive control. Edits are important in processing data and functions within most, if not all, programs. Failure to edit and audit data as it enters a program could result in erroneous and premature acceptance that can cause processing difficulties downstream.

Error Handling

Let's further examine the situation above when we discussed program edits and audits. Again, records that are rejected must appear on error reports to allow someone to work the errors for correction and submission. If an auditor is reviewing application controls, they will most likely look for error correction procedures and controls to ensure that error records are recycled until corrected and aged so that there is control on how long they have been recycled. Timeliness objectives for working all error messages should be documented and corrective actions should be monitored. All uncorrected errors and rejects should be aged and reports generated that reflect these conditions and escalated and reviewed with executive management, when necessary.

You will need to demonstrate to an auditor that errors are worked, corrected, and resubmitted for processing as soon as possible and within the time frame specified in the error correction procedures. Failure to correct errors timely and resubmit them for processing could be detrimental to a company's financial picture. Documenting procedures for handling errors is just the first step. It is critical that you execute these procedures and can show an auditor that your procedures are effective and that their execution is being monitored. Procedures without timely execution can result in significant problems. When I was an auditor, I encountered the following scenario that is summarized below.

Personal experience 12.2

I conducted a billing audit at a remote site for our company. When I arrived at the audit location, I reviewed their billing process and asked the audit client to provide me with their error handling procedures. I was shown an error handling procedure that was well documented, indicating what to do when errors could be generated from the billing application. The procedures identified the types of edits and audits that were in place, what error messages could look like and who was assigned to make the corrections. This was a good start from an auditor's perspective since not every department that I audited had documented their error handling procedures. I was encouraged. I asked the manager if I could see examples of the errors that were generated in the last cycle. He led me to a room and showed me boxes and boxes where the error messages were stored and had not been corrected. Being blown away by the number of boxes, I asked him how long they were sitting there without being corrected. The length of time was significant and I asked why they were not corrected and resubmitted. He informed me that management and key personnel had changed numerous times over the last couple of years and when the responsible party who was assigned to correcting the errors left their job rather abruptly, no one picked up the slack and made any corrections and resubmissions. I discovered that the process for review, correction and resubmission was not documented so no one else knew what had to be done. Since this was a billing application, there was a significant delay in revenue being billed. A delayed billing of hundreds of thousands of dollars resulted. This unfortunately resulted in an unsatisfactory audit that could have been avoided.

Balancing/Database Reconciliation

There are times that auditors will ask questions on application balancing and/or database reconciliation. You need to be prepared to answer these audit questions. Regardless of your audit concern, you need to ensure that you are executing balancing and reconciliation controls—it is just good common sense and good business prudence.

When referring to application balancing, you need to focus on the balancing that takes place within an application to provide for the integrity of processing. Balancing an application can sometimes be simple, but not always. The objective is to be able to demonstrate that all records that were processed needed to be processed, no more and no less. Balancing usually involves two items. One is a record count and the other is a dollar count. Both should be used with one reinforcing the other, generating a greater level of comfort.

Let us look at an order entry application that has a large number of programs and is processing 120,000 records with $1.3 million being in a particular cycle. Control reports that can be used for balancing should be generated at the end of the processing for each application program. You should expect that the output record count from the first order entry program (program one) is the same record count that is being passed to the next order entry program (program two). What you need to realize is that the output from one program should always be equal to the input count to the next program. So if 120,000 records are sent from program one, then 120,00 records should be received by program two. If not, then you probably lost records during the transmission.

What would you expect to see on the order entry's balancing report for program one? Would it show 120,000 records in and 120,000 records out to indicate that no records have been erroneously dropped or added during the processing? It is not that simple. There might have been 120,000 input records and 118,500 output records. How is this possible? Realize that you could have 1500 records rejected in program one because of data processing errors in this scenario or a combination of 1000 records rejected and 500 records bypassed because criteria were not met for continued processing (e.g. reasonableness checks). In this case, your report should indicate 120,000 records read in, 1000 records rejected, 500 records bypassed and 118,500 records generated as output. Record input totals to an application program should equal records rejected plus records bypassed plus records outputted. Now what if you had 122,000 output records? Could this be valid? Yes, this is a possibility—there could have been an explosion of records. Your specifications for the program might require the generation of additional records under various conditions. The 2000 additional records need to be explained. You need to show how many records were inputted, how many were rejected, how many were bypassed, and now how many were exploded, in addition to just showing the output total. As the permutations and combinations of processing scenarios increases, balancing will likely become more difficult. As programs are processing their data, balancing may not be straightforward. What records go into a program may not be the same number coming out. In any event, all variances need to be explained (Figs. 12.1, 12.2, 12.3, and 12.4).

If you are updating databases during application processing, you will need to conduct reconciliations to confirm integrity. The total records started with should agree with the final record count from the previous processing cycle. You would then take into consideration records added and records subtracted to your number and that should reconcile to your closing record total. The closing number will then be recycled and become the starting number for the next cycle.

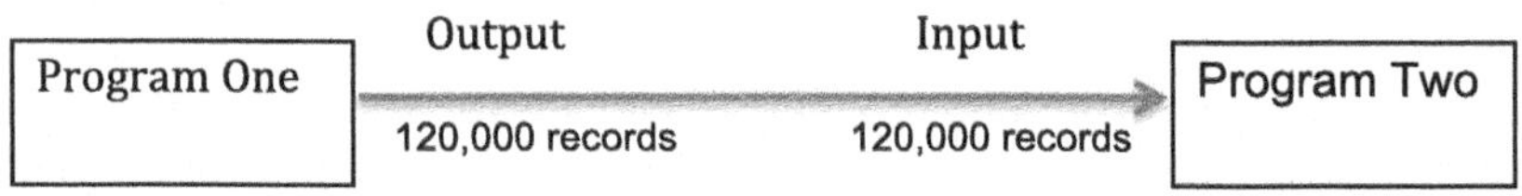

Fig. 12.1 Balancing records between programs

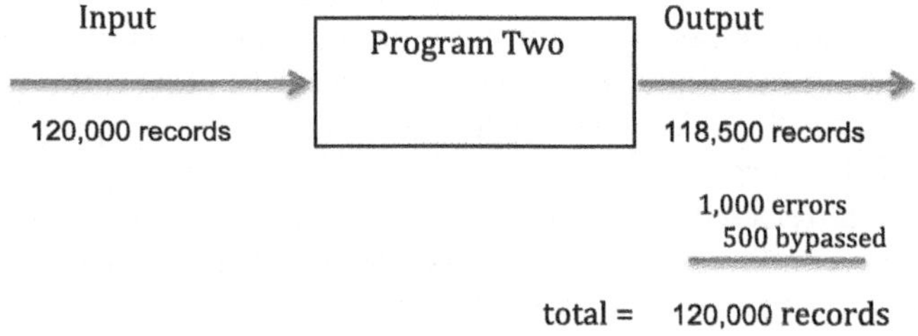

Fig. 12.2 Balancing records bypassed

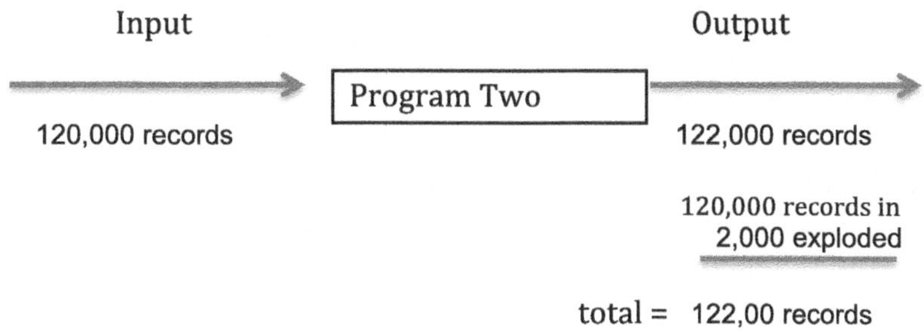

Fig. 12.3 Balancing records exploded

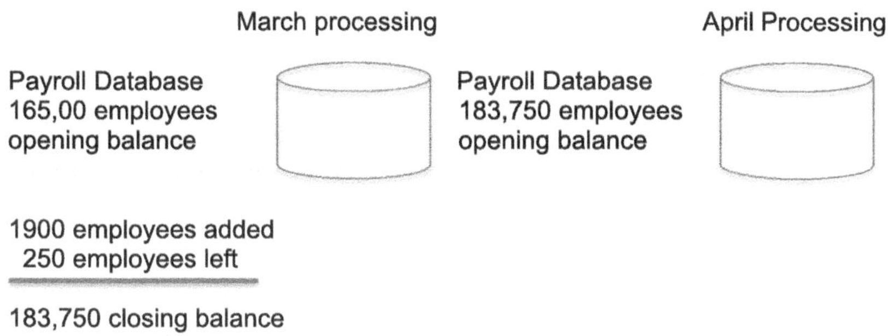

Fig. 12.4 Database reconciliation

Application Monitoring

This is an area where auditors can spend a significant amount of time reviewing and it can involve the operations department and the programming department as well as the business process owner. Some indications of when an application can have problems occur when it frequently aborts; when the application is in an endless loop and continues to process without concluding; when the amount of time it processes is unacceptable even though it eventually ends; the amount of computer storage needed for its processing grows exponentially with each run and is excessive, negatively impacting other processing; the calculations are continuously erroneous; and not all expected outputs are generated each cycle.

The procedure for application monitoring should be well documented. The procedure will need to address various questions that an auditor can ask. For example:

- Who is monitoring the running of the application?
- Is it the operations staff, end user, developer, process owner, or all of them?
- When there is an incident, where is it recorded?
- What types of incidents are recorded?
- Who decides if corrective action is needed?
- Who is responsible for resolution?
- Where is the action recorded that resolved the problem?

If the application that you are responsible for is being audited, then here is a dialog between you and the auditor that can take place and hopefully can prepare you on what to expect:

Auditor: Who is monitoring your applications to ensure that they are operating as intended?

Audit client: Monitoring is performed by the operations department for mainframe applications and by end users for distributed processing applications, which are run on various servers throughout the country.

Auditor: Can you show me the documented procedure that discusses application monitoring?

Audit client: Sure (the audit client shows the auditor the procedure)

Auditor: I see that it states that incidents causing the application to abort are entered into a log by operations for follow-up resolution by the appropriate party. Who is the appropriate party?

Audit client: If it is an operational error, for example, a database cannot be read, job control language problem, or insufficient space allocated, then the operations department will address the problem. If it is a programming error then the programming department will be notified.

Auditor: Is the resolution recorded?

Audit client: Yes, there is a problem ticket entered into a log that is continuously updated from entry through resolution indicating who worked on the problem, when they worked on it, what action was taken, and the date that it was resolved.

Auditor: And if the application does not abort, is other monitoring performed?

Audit client: Yes, there are various error messages generated during the running of applications that require action to be taken.

Auditor: I would like to see these error messages for your application. Can you provide me with a listing for the last year?

Audit client: We don't keep the error messages for more than two months. The volume is prohibitive. We have error messages for the last two months that are contained in several boxes. Do you want to see them all?

Auditor: Why are there so many? Is the application a problem?

Audit client: They are really not all error messages. Nearly ninety percent are warning messages.

Auditor: What kind of warnings?

Audit client: There is a message if space is a potential problem and then there is a message for every interface received for totals generated that did not balance.

Audit client: It sounds as if this application has serious problems. Just show me these error messages for the last month and indicate which messages you needed to take action on based on your application monitoring procedure.

The Next day:

Auditor: OK. 'Do you have evidence that interfaces were eventually balanced?

Audit client: OK, here they are.

Auditor: This will do. Now demonstrate that if action was necessary, that it was taken.

Audit client: I can show you that if there were error messages, they were initialed when resolved with a resolution date. This would include processing edit messages, duplicate record messages, etc.

Auditor: OK. But what about all interfaces where there were balancing issues? Do you have evidence that was eventually balanced?

Audit client: We resolve out of balance issues but we don't keep records.

Auditor: Then there is no audit trail of action taken?

Audit client: That's right.

As you can see there are many questions that can be asked when it comes to application monitoring. This is just a sample. And the auditor can take two different approaches going in two different directions, The auditor can start with the error messages in error logs that indicate resolution to see the origin of the errors, or he or she can start with error messages on a given day to see if the errors were resolved. Some auditors will take both approaches, which is called either a front-to-back or back-to-front audit.

Backup and Restart Procedures

Even though backup and restart procedures are not an area that you think an auditor will examine, you need to be prepared as a process owner to answer any questions that an auditor has, and you should get support from the IT community, if necessary. The auditor can ask you if there are any procedures to effectively back up and restore data in case of application failure. We are not talking about business continuity in case of a disaster at the site where your application is running and data is stored so processing can take place at another location (this has been addressed separately), but if the application aborts in the middle of its processing. This is a recovery control in the midst of an application running and is suddenly terminated. The application needs to have controls to continue processing, in this case, with saved data.

The auditors could also attempt to ascertain whether or not there are documented restart procedures. You will be dependent on receiving answers on restart from the programming community. Coding, within a program, when required, will address restart instructions. This might involve taking checkpoints at various stages while a program is running that is used for backup purposes. This is usually meaningful for programs that run for a long time. You do not want to have to start the program running from the beginning again—you can save hours of processing time if you can just continue processing from the point at which the program aborted or from a checkpoint where data was saved. The checkpoint might have been taken half way through the processing or at another point in the processing.

The restart or recovery procedure should ensure that no data would be lost, erroneously processed, or processed twice because of failure. The failure may be the result of application flaws or hardware problems. The auditor when reviewing backup and restart procedures will, in all likelihood, in addition for asking for documented procedures, ask for computer logs. They will want to see if the procedures were ever tested, how frequently they were tested, or if the restart procedures were actually used during production cycles. They might also inquire that if recovery was necessary, was it successful. Another question could be how long did it take to recover and was all data restored? The auditor no doubt will ask if they are doing a thorough analysis, ask for a log of application failures and determine if the cause of application failures was known and what corrective action was taken.

Summary

Auditors will hold you accountable, as the process owner, to answer questions on application controls even if your staff was not directly responsible for writing the application code. You will need to work closely with your IT organization and ensure their cooperation in support of any audit. You may be the business process owner or application owner who is being audited but either way, whoever the audit client is, he or she will be held accountable and needs to be audit ready. If you are the accounts payable owner or inventory management owner or any other business process owner, you probably developed some application controls with your IT personnel. However, you need to understand the controls, be able to explain the controls and demonstrate effective execution either by yourself, or with the assistance of supporting organizations. The intent of this chapter was to introduce you to or reinforce your understanding of various application controls.

The success of the programming effort of all applications is dependent on a project manager. The project manager is responsible to ensure that new applications are developed on time, within budget while meeting all requirements. Project managers are assigned responsibility to ensure that the quality of what is delivered meets expectations of the end users and process owners. This will involve overseeing the following tasks: making sure that there is a project plan during all phases of development; tracking coding and testing activities from start to completion; establishing and meeting metrics; validating quality of the completed application output; effectively managing risk management, change management and all work efforts; and obtaining customer sign-offs before promotion to production. This list is not all-inclusive. One of the more important tasks that need to be added is that the project manager is responsible for the design and implementation of effective application controls before applications are migrated into a production environment. Inserting controls after applications are already in production can be too late in the game. To use an old adage, the horse can already be out of the barn by the time that you realize that the barn door was not locked.

Specific application controls consist of input/output and interface controls; application editing and auditing; error handling; balancing and database reconciliation; application monitoring; and backup and recovery procedures.

Input, output, and interface controls should be established for an application to validate completeness of processing. There should be transmission controls to verify that all records and dollars received from an upstream application are received and processed, and transmitted to a downstream application. There should be controls to avoid duplicate and/or omitted processing. Important preventive controls are editing and auditing controls that check on the validity of data to prevent erroneous, incomplete, or unreasonable data from being processed. Error handling should ensure that there are documented procedures that address the accuracy of processing and the timely correction and resubmission of erroneous or rejected records. Balancing focuses on a programs input record count being equal to the output record count from the previous program. Balancing should also ensure that all records processed by an application program are accounted for—records and dollars read into a program should equal records and dollars output plus records rejected plus records exploded. With regard to database reconciliation, the database closing balance should be reconciled to its opening balance plus records added minus records subtracted.

Application monitoring is another basic detective control. If an application is not working satisfactorily, aborting regularly, or not being able to process accurately due to software or hardware issues, the issues need to be recorded in a log, assigned to an individual for resolution and tracked until closure. With regard to backup and restart procedures, programs that process for extended periods of time should have checkpoints where if there is an incident when a program aborts, the data already processed has been saved and the program can restart from the point where it aborted or at one of the checkpoints taken during application processing.

Guidelines

1. If your applications are audited, solicit help from your IT department.
2. Ensure that application controls are documented either by yourself or by IT. This would apply to applications in the development stage or if the applications are running, in production.
3. Meet with your IT manager before the auditors arrive to review controls.
4. If you feel that controls are missing or weak, document any corrective actions that you plan to take. It is always beneficial to be able to

demonstrate to auditors that you were aware of certain issues before the auditors arrived and have resolution plans. It will be a plus not only if you can demonstrate to them that you were aware of the issues before the audit started but you have documented planned corrective action that is being tracked that you can show them.
5. A risk assessment would be helpful if application controls are weak or missing. We will talk about risk assessments later with evidence of review by executive management.
6. Make sure that if errors or issues logs are used that they are available to show the auditors.

Chapter 12 Exercises

1. You are the purchasing manager in your company. You have just been promoted to your managerial position 3 months ago. The auditors sent you an announcement letter two weeks ago that they are going to conduct an audit of the purchasing application beginning August 1st. You are a bit nervous since you know that the purchase application that was installed six months ago was late in meeting its targeted scheduled date, was over budget and the end users are not happy with its processing. They claim that there are too many errors and too many requirements that are not being met. To make matters worse, many of the programs within the application are aborting frequently and the executives are distressed. That is one of the reasons why they removed the previous manager and selected you to be the new process owner. The audit is to begin next week. What steps do you take to ensure audit readiness? Do you ask the auditors for a delay since you are a relatively new owner? List five actions that you will take.
2. You are an IT manager and have been asked to develop and install a new payroll system within the next 18 months. You have received the requirements for the new system and they have been approved with an initial budget. You have three programmers in your department and one is a recent college graduate. You need to do whatever it takes to meet the target date for installation. What action do you take? List what you would do with regard to application controls.

Chapter 12 Questions

Please select the best answer to the following questions:

1. You are a billing manager and just received word that internal audit will be conducting an audit of your application next month. What action do you take:

   A. You inform the auditors that they should audit the IT manager who developed and is maintaining the application.
   B. You ask the auditors for a postponement since your senior staff member is planning to be out for 4 weeks attending education classes.
   C. You contact your IT department and ask them to participate in the audit and give you whatever support they can.
   D. You know your application has control issues and you ask the auditors if they can possibly audit another application.

2. Which of these statements is true?

   A. You cannot validate that you received the right transmission for processing from the sending program in an upstream application just by checking the totals and sequence number in a header record.
   B. If the sequence number on a file transmission you receive is one greater than the previous transmission number, then you are guaranteed that you are processing the correct records.
   C. Just checking the dollar total on a header record and agreeing with it will ensure you that you are processing the right data.
   D. You could have a problem even when a program sends you a transmission with a sequence number one greater than the previous sequence number on the last transmission and the record count agrees with what you received. You should also check the dollar total.

3. Effective editing should be:

   A. detective control
   B. preventive control
   C. deterrent control
   D. reporting control

4. An example of an auditing control for reasonability control is:

   A. checking to see if a required zip code field has been filled
   B. checking to see if record counts received on a file agree with record counts on what was sent
   C. checking to see if there are no duplicate records received on a transmission
   D. checking to see if social security numbers do not contain nine zeroes

5. An error handling procedure should include:

   A. the corrective action that is planned to be taken for each error
   B. an indication of who was responsible for correcting any error
   C. the date as to when the error was resolved
   D. all of the above

6. When balancing a program, which statement is correct?

   A. The input record count to a program should always equal the output.
   B. The output record count on a file from a program sending records should always be equal to the record count to a program receiving the same file.
   C. Databases do not have to be reconciled
   D. All of the above are true

7. When an application is being monitored, an individual is looking to see:

   A. if the data is being edited
   B. if there is an application owner
   C. if the application programs are running to completion
   D. if there is adequate separation of duties

8. Are backup and restart procedures usually expected to be found in all programs?

   A. yes
   B. no

9. All business process owners are also application owners.

    A. true
    B. false

10. Who is in the best position to design application controls?

    A. the application owner
    B. the application owner working with IT
    C. IT
    D. the audit staff

CHAPTER 13

Recent Challenges

> Our greatest weakness lies in giving up. The most certain way to succeed is always to try just one more time. —Thomas Edison

There are evolving audit challenges today that as business professionals, you should be aware of and ready to address from an audit readiness perspective. Because these challenges are new and present us with a need to change our thinking, we need to understand them and change out thinking to ensure control and prepare for audits. Not only will the auditors, but perhaps more importantly, corporate executives, employees, shareholders, stockholders, and investors will be expecting us to be ready to face these challenges. In this chapter, we will be looking at spreadsheet controls, cloud computing, outsourcing controls, and cyber security.

Spreadsheet Controls

As more and more individuals are becoming better educated and more sophisticated with their knowledge of Lotus 1–2–3, Microsoft Excel, and other software, so has executive alacrity extended to use spreadsheets to provide data to drive business decisions. The executives want the data quickly and without dependency on elaborate and expensive systems to generate the reports that they wish to see and when they want to see them. As a result, the use of macros and multiple linked spreadsheets has become more apparent than ever before. There are few corporations

E. Danter, *Audit Defense*, Palgrave Studies in Accounting and Finance Practice, https://doi.org/10.1007/978-3-030-92466-9_13

where spreadsheets are not used on a daily basis. Spreadsheet users have increased significantly over the years and the need for tighter controls has never been greater. Spreadsheet applications, or single programs, provide information used by management to make decisions, which materially affect the successful operation of a business enterprise.

Simple calculations present the risk of misstatements and arriving at wrong conclusions—the calculations need to be accurate. The use of spreadsheets and specific lack of controls have become contributing factors in reporting errors in numerous companies.

According to research, the percentage of all spreadsheets that suffer from a least one major user error is very high, averaging close to 50 percent. As a business professional, subjected to an audit, don't be surprised if you hear the following questions from an auditor regarding the risk of using a spreadsheet:

- Is the spreadsheet used for personal or business use?
- What is the knowledge of the individual building the spreadsheet?
- Is the spreadsheet properly classified?
- Where is the spreadsheet stored and who has access to it?
- How often is the spreadsheet updated and by whom?

The following are primary areas of concern with the use of spreadsheets:

- Input errors with cut and paste mistakes, inaccurate references, or just careless data entry with rounding errors or incomplete data
- Logic errors with wrong formulas or calculations being used
- Spreadsheet layout errors with wrong cells, wrong headings, cell ranges, or functionality not meeting original specifications

These are pro-active measures that can be taken:

- *Take inventory of spreadsheets.*
  Each spreadsheet should be inventoried with an owner identified and a description of the purpose of the spreadsheet.
- *Identify all users.*
  All users should be identified along with their access authority. Update authority should be limited to a minimum number of individuals, preferably just one person and a backup, who need to

generate a spreadsheet. Read access should be restricted to those with a business need.

- *Document desk procedures.*
  Each owner of the spreadsheet should document the desk procedure used to generate the spreadsheet. This would include defining where the input is coming from, detailing when and how the data is used including the formulas and external links, defining how it is stored, explaining how it is accessed, defining how it is backed up and retrieved, and describing who uses the output and for what purpose.
- *Include spreadsheet generation in existing controlled applications.*
  Explore the possibility of including the process and procedure for the generation of the spreadsheet in an existing application, rather than it being generated and maintained on its own. This should enhance security and data integrity.
- *Ensure adequate separation of duties.*
  You do not want one person generating the spreadsheet, having access to the spreadsheet, and disseminating it for business purposes without at least another individual involved to independently verify the calculations and numbers being generated.
- *Validate all output.*
  Spreadsheet results need to be manually checked against the original data to reduce dependency on output derived from the formulas being used, since the formulas might be in error. Verification of testing steps should be done on a frequent basis to ensure that processing is still valid and that formulas have not been erroneously changed.
- *Use a change management system.*
  A change management system should be used throughout the life cycle identifying and tracking changes to formulas and data, ensuring that all changes are appropriately authorized and that an audit trail is maintained for all changes.
- *Utilize a standard software methodology.*
  Apply standard software development methodology including: gathering of requirements; designing the spreadsheet; testing the calculations; and employing library control.
- *Rely on version control.*

Utilize version control to ensure that the latest version is being used and that only one person can update the spreadsheet at a time in a controlled environment.

- *Schedule independent reviews.*
  Generate a higher comfort level by having independent reviews of logic and results verified. These reviews should be documented.
- *Establish backup procedure.*
  Ensure that the spreadsheets are backed up on a regular basis and can be easily retrieved if needed.
- *Establish balancing and reconciliation.*
  Balancing and reconciliation procedures should ensure that all input is completely and accurately processed when data is obtained and output totals can be accounted for.

Here are some examples of control issues with the use of Spreadsheets to demonstrate the reality of this problem—be careful:

- There was a $24 million clerical error on a spreadsheet at TransAlta in June, 2003.
  The mistake resulted in TransAlta, a large Canadian power generator, buying more US power transmission hedging contracts in May at higher prices than it should have. The error was a cut and paste error in an Excel spreadsheet.
  Corrective action: Have another employee double-check the documentation.
- Fannie Mae discovered a $1.3 billion honest spreadsheet mistake in October 2003.
  Fannie Mae, which finances home mortgages, discovered a enormous $1.136 billion error in total shareholder equity. Mistakes were made in a spreadsheet used in the implementation of a new accounting standard.
  Corrective action: It's best to have a financial peer review the documentation.
- The University of Toledo lost $2.4 million in projected revenue in May 2004.
  The University of Toledo officials discovered an internal budgeting error that meant that they will have $2.4 million less revenue to work

with than anticipated. The mistake was a typo in a formula that led officials to overestimate enrollment and therefore projected revenue. Corrective action: Have another employee double-check the documentation.

- Kodak adds $9 million to Loss in November 2005.
  A severance-related error stemmed from miscalculating severance pay accrued by one employee.
  The $11 million severance error was traced to a faulty spreadsheet. There were too many zeros added to the employee's accrued severance.
  Corrective action: Improve controls with additional review.
- In 2012, London Olympics were publicly embarrassed by a simple Excel typo on a spreadsheet.
  The London 2012 Sumer Olympics organizing committee had 10,000 tickets to sell for the synchronized swimming event. Unfortunately, an employee missed a single key stroke and entered the number 20,000 into the spreadsheet instead of 10,000, as a result, the committee vastly oversold tickets to the event and were forced to admit its carelessness and make amends to thousands of ticket holders.
  Corrective action: All significant spreadsheet entries should be independently checked.

Cloud Computing

Cloud computing is one of our more challenging areas of ensuring control today, as more and more companies are transgressing toward the utilization of cloud computing.

But what is cloud computing and what are the new control challenges that have surfaced resulting from its popularity and growth?

Cloud computing is made up of two "ends," a front end and a back end. The front end is what the client sees and the back end is made up of data servers and storage systems.

Cloud computing enables convenient, on-demand network access to a shared pool of computing resources (e.g. networks, servers, storage, applications, and services), rapidly provisioned and released with minimal management or provider interaction—it is like a utility. Just as enterprises pay for electricity, gas, and water they use, they now have the option of paying for IT services on a consumption basis paying for only what they use.

Cloud computing exhibits these five characteristics.[1]

- *On Demand Self-Service*
  You can provision computing capabilities, such as storage, as needed automatically without requiring human intervention with each service's provider.
- *Broad Network Access*
  Capabilities should be accessible from any device as long as internet connectivity is available.
- *Resource Pooling*
  Provider's computing resources are pooled to serve multiple customers.
- *Rapid Elasticity*
  To the consumer, the capabilities available for provisioning often appear to be unlimited and can be purchased in any quantity at any time.
- *Measured Service*
  Cloud systems automatically control and optimize resource usage by leveraging metering capabilities.

The following are the benefits of cloud computing and some of the reasons why many corporations have headed in this direction:

- Cost savings is a major reason used for cloud computing.
- Since data for multiple customers are stored in one place, algorithms and statistics improve as the customer base enlarges. This allows for improving analytics benefitting all companies using the system.
- The cloud makes a monitoring system more manageable.
- The cloud allows improved monitoring for compliance, fraud, and independent audit with a significant potential savings impact.

Engaging in a relationship with a third party will mean that the business is not only using the services and technology of the cloud provider, but also

[1] Cloud Computing basics extracted from the second edition "IT Auditing—Using Controls to Protect Information Assets" by Chris Davis and Mike Schiller.

must deal with the way the provider runs its organization, the architecture the provider has in place, and the provider's organizational culture and policies.

As a client, you must always make sure that you have a good understanding of the requirements around data, access management, and operational use before moving any sensitive information to the Cloud, or integrating Cloud-based services into critical processes. You must also make sure that you plan and manage any data, applications or systems, which are moved into the Cloud throughout their entire life cycle.

As a process owner, whether you are an IT manager or not, you need to be aware of and concerned by the following risks that are associated with cloud computing. An auditor can be concerned with these risks as well and ask you what you are doing to address the risks.

Risks and Guidance

- Enterprises need to be particular in choosing a provider. Sustainability is of particular importance to ensure that services will be available and data can be tracked.
- Third party access to sensitive information creates a risk of compromise to confidential information. In cloud computing, this can cause a significant threat to ensuring the protection of intellectual property (IP) and trade secrets.
- The cloud provider often takes responsibility for information handling, which is a critical part of the business. Failure to perform to agreed-upon service levels can impact not only confidentiality, but also availability, impacting business operations.
- The dynamic nature of cloud computing may result in confusion as to where information actually resides.
- Compliance to regulations and laws in different geographic regions can be a challenge for enterprises. How do you tailor agreements with a cloud provider to make sure there is compliance with local requirements? Proper legal advice should be obtained to ensure that the contract specifies the areas where the cloud provider is responsible and liable for ramifications arising from potential issues.
- Public clouds allow high-availability systems to be developed at service levels often impossible to create in private networks, except at extraordinary costs. There is a potential for commingling of information assets with other cloud customers including competitors. This is a very serious concern.

- Due to the dynamic nature of the cloud, information may not be immediately located in the event of a disaster. Business continuity and disaster recovery plans must be well documented and tested. The cloud provider must understand the role it plays in terms of backups, incident response and recovery. Recovery time objectives should be stated in the contract. You should ask the cloud provider what the recovery times are and how frequently were the objectives met.
- Privacy has become of primary importance to enterprise customers and unauthorized access to data in the cloud is an overriding concern. When embarking on an agreement with a cloud provider, an enterprise must conduct an inventory of its information assets and ensure that they are properly classified and labeled. This helps to determine: What should be specified when drafting a service level agreement; any need for encryption of data being transmitted or stored; and controls for sensitive information. Information protection will evolve as a result of a strong comprehensive Document of Understanding (DOU) that is supported by an equally strong and comprehensive assurance process. Unauthorized access to data in the cloud is a risk that must be understood by you and the cloud provider and you will need to feel comfortable that the cloud provider has adequately addressed this concern and has suitable controls in place.
- Clear expectations regarding the handling, usage, storage, and availability of information must be articulated in the DOU. Additionally, requirements for business continuity and disaster recovery will need to be communicated in the agreement. You are entrusting the cloud provider to adequately address these risks as custodian of your critical and sensitive data.
- As enterprises look to the cloud to provide IT services that have been traditionally managed internally, they will need to make some changes to help ensure that (1) they continue to meet performance objectives, that (2) technology and business objectives are strategically aligned, and (3) that risks are managed.
- Access to data will now be shared not dedicated. You need to ensure adequate protection of data that, in a cloud, will now reside over one or more data sets.

You will need to be prepared for questions that an auditor might ask. You may need to refer to your (DOU) with the cloud provider or ask the cloud provider directly, regardless of any audit, to get the answers to the following questions that are needed:

- What are controls over cloud computing?
- Are existing policies structured to support cloud-based operations?
- What are the required skill sets and does the service provider posses these skills or is a third party necessary?
- What are the metrics that are in place?
- Are the metrics being met?
- How do you address deviations or missed metrics?
- How are identity and authentication to systems and data managed?
- How is access restricted just to data that is authorized?
- How is audit logging addressed?
- How are logging issues communicated in a timey fashion?
- What education is required for users, and is it being supplied?
- Is penetration testing being conducted and by whom?
- What are policies that are followed in a multi-tenancy environment?
- What are contractual requirements?

Note: It is important to note that some corporations use a Document of Understanding (DOU), or Memorandum of Understanding (MOU) to describe agreed to services and roles and responsibilities between an enterprise and an *external* service provider. Many of these corporations will use a Service Level Agreement (SLA) to define the services and roles and responsibilities between departments *within* an enterprise. Corporations can use either vehicle—it is their call. Both are contracts—the only difference that I am aware of is that the DOU or MOU is a *legal* contract.

Outsourcing Controls

First we need to define outsourcing as its usage has grown exponentially over the last few decades. The decision to outsource operations is usually based on a desire to reduce costs and to allow a company to focus on its core competencies. Outsourcing can mean having another company provide application development support, storing computer equipment on a co-location data center, providing tax or financial services, to having a company run their IT operations. This also includes the use of cloud computing services that we previously discussed.

The review of the adequacy of controls in an outsourcing environment is usually conducted by a completely independent external auditing organization and not by your internal audit function.

To understand the challenges with outsourcing processing, let's start with a case study.

Case Study on Outsourcing

You are the payroll manager in your company. You decided last year to outsource your semi-monthly payroll processing to the ABC company that specializes in providing payroll services. The majority of personnel in your company are paid semi-monthly with the senior executive being paid monthly. You decided to continue to have your IT department process monthly payroll in your company but to outsource the semi-monthly processing. This decision was made so your company could reduce costs and focus on its core manufacturing business. You were made aware that payroll processing is frequently outsourced by many enterprises so you were not too concerned when you hired the ABC company to process your payroll.

Your outside auditing firm has arrived to conduct an audit of your payroll process. You explain to them that most your processing has been contracted to the ABC company. You are a global company and compliance with payroll regulations (e.g. taxing) are complicated among the various worldwide locations. You tell your outside auditing firm that because of the challenges you face, you are grateful that ABC has the expertise needed to handle the job effectively. However, your auditing firm stills hold you accountable for the accuracy of the payroll processing and asks you to answer a number of questions about the ABC company. You tell them that you can't answer most of their questions because the ABC company has payroll responsibilities and they should ask the ABC company. Your external auditing firm asks you, "since ABC is providing a payroll service shouldn't you know if they have effective internal controls in their organization"? You are asked that since Sarbanes Oxley considers audits reports on service organizations to be very important, if you know if any independent reputable third party reviewed the effectiveness of ABC's internal controls. You are asked if you know if they are compliant with applicable regulations. You are asked if you were aware of or had seen a Service Organization Control Report (SOC) report being generated by an independent auditing firm on ABC's controls. You answer that you do not know. Your outside auditing firm asks you, (1) "If ABC is processing your payroll, wouldn't it benefit you to know their control posture"? (2) "Why did you hire them?" (3) "Has your payroll processing been accurate and timely over the last year?" You admit that there have been some payroll payment problems but you never inquired of ABC if there was a favorable SOC report generated by an audit firm.

One of the benefits of SOC reports is that it is an authoritative guidance that allows service providers to disclose their control activities and processes to their customers and their customers' auditors using a uniform reporting format.

An independent outside auditor should have conducted a SOC audit at the ABC company. If they conducted such an audit, there responsibilities would have been to:

- determine if controls at ABC were documented
- find out whether the description of controls fairly presented the relevant aspects of controls in operation as of the date of the report
- learn whether the controls were suitably designed to achieve the specified control objectives
- ascertain whether the controls that were tested were operating with sufficient effectiveness to provide reasonable assurance that control objectives were achieved.

An outside independent auditing firm will render its opinion on the control posture in the SOC report conclusion. There is no "pass" or "fail" conclusion as with traditional IT audits. The language of the opinion generally follows explicit guidelines as determined by the AICPA. These opinions usually address these four questions:

1. Did the service organization's description of controls fairly represent the organizations controls as of a specific date?
2. Were the controls suitably designed to achieve the control objectives?
3. Were the organization's controls placed in operation as of a specific date?

4. Were the controls that were tested operating with sufficient effectiveness to provide reasonable assurance that objectives were met, during the period specified?

The conclusion will either be a "qualified" report, in which case there were concerns that will prevent the auditing firm from rendering a favorable report, or an "unqualified" report, which is certainly more desirable.

A SOC report could benefit both the outsourcing company (client) and the service provider to whom the processes are outsourced to.

Client benefits are:

- A SOC report without qualification should provide a higher comfort level to your CEO and executives as to the effectiveness of the service organization's controls, making their own SOX certification easier and attestation by external auditors more likely.
- Client organizations that obtain a report from their service organization (and they should ask for a report) receive valuable information detailing the design of the service organization's controls, a statement on their effectiveness as concluded by an independent firm's assessment.
- A qualified report will identify shortcomings to help the service organization improve controls that can be monitored in the future.

A service provider can also benefit. They can benefit if they receive an "unqualified" opinion by an independent firm that can result in the service organization standing above its peers. This can position them in obtaining additional contracts.

Note: Before the report being referred to as a SOC Report, it was known as a SAS70 Report. The SAS70 standard was designed to assist CPAs reporting on controls at a service organization that affected user entities' financial statements, not for reporting on all system controls. SAS70 was misused and was used as a framework for all control assessments. As a result, the AICPA replaced SAS70 reports with SOC reports that review effectiveness of all service organization processing, not just those controls directly impacting financial statements.

Health Insurance Portability and Accountability Act (HIPAA)

Another audit challenge, that you should be aware of and where you should have established and executed effective controls, is compliance to HIPAA. What we are referring to is a set of U.S. national standards for the protection of certain health information that has been in effect since 1996. The U.S. Department of Health and Human Services (HSS) issued the Privacy Rule to implement HIPAA requirements.

The Privacy Rule standards address the use and disclosure of an individual's health information called protected health information (PHI) by organizations referred to as covered entities. The term, covered entity applies to any entity that provides treatment, payment and operations in health care (e.g. hospitals, doctors, dentists, healthcare providers) and business associates who are performing processes in support of a covered entity (e.g. actuarial, accounting, consulting, financial services). The business associates need to have access to patient information in order to be required meet HIPAA compliance. You may or may not be a covered entity or applicable business associate, but if you are, you need to be compliant and audit ready.

Internal audit plays a role in HIPAA compliance by reviewing operations with the goal of identifying potential security violations. It is important to note that companies that deal with protected health information must have network and process security measures in place and follow them to ensure HIPAA compliance.

The Privacy Rule pertains to all PHI including paper and electronic usage. A Security Rule specifically pertains to Electronic Protected Health Information (EPHI). It lays out three types of security standards for compliance: administrative, physical, and technical. If you are dealing with the protection of health information you need to put the following policies, procedures safeguards in place:

Administrative safeguards:

- Covered entities must adopt written privacy policies and designate a privacy officer to develop and implement procedures.
- The policies and procedures must reference management oversight.
- Procedures should identify employees or classes of employees who will have access to EPHI and access should be restricted.

- Procedures must address authorization, establishment, modification and termination (similar to control procedures that you should be familiar with by now).
- Entities must show that they have an ongoing training program for handling PHI.
- Covered entities that out-source some of their business processes to a third party must ensure that the third party is HIPAA compliant.
- Covered entities are responsible for backups and disaster recovery.

Physical safeguards:

- Controls must address the introduction and removal of hardware and software from the network.
- Access to equipment containing health information should be carefully controlled and monitored.
- Access to hardware and software must be limited to authorized personnel.
- Required access controls consist of facility security plans, maintenance records, visitor sign-ins, and escorts throughout secured facilities.
- Policies should address proper workstation use.
- If contractors are used, they too must be trained on physical access responsibilities.

Technical safeguards:

- Information housing PHI must be protected from intrusion.
- Encryption must be used for information flowing over open networks.
- Each covered entity is responsible for ensuring that the data within its systems has not been changed or erased in an unauthorized manner.
- Data corroboration, including the use of double keying, message authentication, and digital signature, may be used to ensure data integrity.
- Covered entities must authenticate entities they communicate with by password systems, two–three way handshakes, or telephone call back.

Summary

There are recent control challenges that are addressed in this chapter. These are spreadsheet controls, controls for cloud computing, outsourcing controls, and safeguard controls for health information.

Spreadsheets are widely used throughout many companies but there is a high percentage of errors due to manual dependencies. Management relies on the accuracy of the information that they see on the spreadsheets so you need to reduce the risk of misstatements and management drawing wrong conclusions that are used to drive business decisions. There are input errors, logic errors, wrong cells, wrong headings, incorrect cell ranges, and careless data entry just to name a few of the problems. You need to take pro-active steps to address these and other concerns with the use of spreadsheets. These pro-active steps include: taking inventory of spreadsheets, identifying all users, documenting desk procedures, ensuring separation of duties, validating all output, schedule independent reviews, establishing balancing and reconciliation procedures, and establishing backup procedures.

A cloud computing system is made up of a front end, the side that the client sees, and a back end, made up of data servers and storage systems. The cloud allows improved monitoring for compliance, fraud, and independent audit with a significant potential savings impact. However, the risks need to be known and successfully addressed. Some of the risks are: (1) ability to choose a provider who can provide sustainability, (2) confusion as to where information actually resides and speed of recoverability, (3) risk of compromise due to third party access to sensitive data and protection of intellectual property, (4) failure to perform to agreed-upon service levels, (5) potential for commingling of information assets, (6) compliance to regulations and laws in different geographic regions, (7) information not being immediately located in the event of a disaster, (8) adequate encryption, classification and labeling of data, and (9) unauthorized access to protect privacy since data is now shared.

If you are outsourcing any of your processes you need to inquire if the service provider's controls have been independently reviewed by an outside audit firm and the results shared with you. The outsourcing control report is called a SOC report. The audit by an outside auditing firm and the issuance of a SOC report is not mandatory but it is beneficial to both the provider of service and the client. Remember, as a process owner, you are still accountable for the accuracy of your processing whether or not you have contracted processing responsibility to a third party.

There are US standards for privacy and the security of health information for any individual. These standards are contained in the Health Insurance Portability and Accountability Act (HIPAA). These security standards for compliance to HIPAA include administrative, physical, and technical standards.

Guidelines

1. Take pro-active control measures when using spreadsheets that include: documenting desk procedures; training backup personnel; ensuring that formulas, cells, calculations, and output are independently reviewed; have independent reviews of the formulas used for calculations; and securing the spreadsheets but have them readily accessible if needed.
2. Ensure that you have a SLA or DOU in place with your cloud computer service provider. Review and monitor responsibilities for the control and the security of your data per the SLA or DOU. Frequently monitor compliance to the agreement or contract.
3. Ensure that your data residing in the cloud is not comingled and can be readily accessed when needed.
4. If you are processing health information for individuals then make sure that you have control procedures established that are being effectively executed to provide HIPAA compliance.

Chapter 13 Exercises

1. Your executive wants you to gather and report on certain data that will help him propose plans to arrive at strategic business direction. He needs to have this information as soon as possible to review with his bosses, the CFO and CEO, so prudent decisions can be made. He cannot wait for system generated reports and wants you to be able to establish a procedure to generate a spreadsheet with the information he needs. What control measures do you consider?
2. Your company is looking to reduce costs and is looking at outsourcing some of its processes. They ask you to put together a DOU for a service provider. What do you include in the DOU?

Chapter 13 Questions

Please choose the best answer for each of the questions that follow:

1. All users of spreadsheets should have both read and update access.

   A. true
   B. false

2. Which are primary areas of concerns when using spreadsheets?

   A. input errors with cut and paste mistakes
   B. logic errors with wrong formulas
   C. logic errors with wrong cell ranges
   D. all of the above

3. Version control should be used when using spreadsheets to:

   A. ensure that spreadsheets are backed up on a regular basis
   B. make sure that all input is completely and accurately processed
   C. ensure that only one person can update the spreadsheet at a time
   D. help identify the access authority of all users

4. Corporations utilize cloud computing because benefits could include:

   A. a better chance of compliance to regulations and laws
   B. savings in cost because you only pay for services needed
   C. protection of data is easier for a provider of service than for you
   D. data can be more easily located in case of a disaster

5. The review of the adequacy of controls in an outsourcing environment is usually conducted by:

   A. the audit committee
   B. the internal audit organization
   C. a completely independent external auditing firm
   D. the CIO

6. A review of the controls of an outsourcing provider of service is called:

   A. a Service Organization Control Report

B. a Service Outsourcing Control Report
C. an Assurance Control Report
D. a Systematic Overview of Controls Report

7. Who can benefit from an outsourcing control report?

A. the service provider
B. the client
C. both the service provider and the client
D. neither the service provider nor the client

8. Which is more of a desirable outsourcing report?

A. a qualified report
B. an unqualified report

9. HIPAA stands for:

A. Health Insurance Protection and Accountability Act
B. Health Information Protection and Accountability Act
C. Health Information Portability and Accountability Act
D. Health Insurance Portability and Accountability Act

10. If contractors are used by a hospital to process PHI they do not have to be trained on physical access responsibilities

A. true
B. false

Reference

Davis Chris, Schiller Mike (2011) IT Auditing—Using Controls to Protect Information Assets, 2nd edn.

PART III

Pro-active Measures

By failing to prepare, you are preparing to fail
—Benjamin Franklin

After learning about the audit process and expanding your understanding of effective controls that auditors will be searching for, as discussed in Parts I and II, it is essential that you know what are some pro-active steps that you can take and put this knowledge to use in defending yourself against any audit (internal or external). Any fear of audits that you harbor might not disappear but should diminish if you are audit ready—fortify yourself with the activities outlined in this part.

Being audit ready and preparing yourself to be in a position to defend against an internal or external audit require you to take pro-active measures. These steps should enhance your optimism for success. If you don't take any action you are on a track toward failure. One of the worse decisions that you can make is to do nothing, assume all is well, and have an illusion of control.

The results of audits can be a total surprise to your executives. They can be blindsided if they are presented with unsatisfactory audits if you had previously told them that they were audit ready. How many times have audit clients and a company's chief executives been caught totally unprepared? You don't want to be called in by your CEO to explain what happened. You cannot just try to excuse yourself by saying that you were unprepared—it might be too late and you may not survive. You need to take preemptive action so that this does not happen. But what can you do to avoid this surprised audit result in the future? The answer is to establish a program that will guide you along a path with an ultimate goal of achieving audit readiness. You cannot afford to parade around wearing the emperor's clothes, naked and thinking that you are attired in the most magnificent clothes. You need to have a program in place, effectively being executed, to help you and your staff know when your controls are missing or inadequate. You need to have a well-controlled environment. You and other process owners who are also potential audit clients need to take pro-active measures to achieve this objective. You can no longer trust your staff if they tell you that everything is all right—you need to verify. Suffering from illusions of control can be dangerous and disastrous.

There are various activities that you should initiate before audits are conducted to determine if there are, in fact, adequate controls established. These actions will first include identifying what your existing exposures and issues are and then understanding the risks involved in order to help you decide on the necessity of corrective action or to accept risks of not taking any corrective action. You should also gain awareness and increase your comfort level with all testing that was taken for applications developed and installed in support of your process. These activities are pro-active in nature and can play an important role in identifying where controls are inadequate, weak, or non-existent. You want to accomplish this prior to audits being conducted—you do not want the auditors identifying where your control exposures exist, either in design or execution, rather than yourself. There is no need to rely on the auditors to recommend corrective actions before you take action. Taking pro-active steps should help you to stay ahead of the curve and have a positive effect during an audit.

You should not wait for audit reports to be written and distributed before action is taken. You and your staff should be involved in pro-active activities and attempt to identify as many issues and needed controls as they can *before* the CEO is told, as a result of an audit, that you have serious control issues and exposures.

It is important to identify areas in your processes where controls are lacking or where controls are weak in order to understand where and what controls need to be designed into your processes. The pro-active approaches that I discuss can help achieve this. This chapter will be the initial step in helping you to understand, where and when controls are needed.

There are too many managers and staffs who are re-active rather than pro-active when it comes to improving their control postures. They wait for a situation to arise resulting in possible audit failure or delayed, lost or erroneous processing occurring before they take any corrective action—it is often too late then. They need to identify and get out in front of any exposure that could have a negative impact on their audit position and eventually be detrimental to their revenue picture. If you are a potential audit client, you need to take preventive measures in order for you to first recognize control concerns and then you need to take corrective action to avoid any further issue. Don't just sit on the track, even if you do not see a train approaching. It can come at any time—be ready and don't get run over.

Therefore too many examples and skills which are [illegible] preparation when it comes to important [illegible] posture. [illegible] [illegible] to [illegible] [illegible] or [illegible]

CHAPTER 14

Identification of Exposures and Issues

Even if you are on the right track, you'll get run over if you just sit there.
—Will Rogers

created by Bia Sous

E. Danter, *Audit Defense*, Palgrave Studies in Accounting and Finance Practice, https://doi.org/10.1007/978-3-030-92466-9_14

Before you identify your exposures, you should understand the following relationships between your process and procedures and then between your procedures and controls.

Processes, Procedures, and Control Documentation

One of the first objectives that auditors have when they arrive to conduct an audit is to understand the processes, procedures, and controls. This will apply to any business process audit. If it is an IT audit, in addition to learning about the process, they will want to be made aware of the applications that support the process and will probably expect to review application documentation, as well. There are auditing standards and audit processes that are followed by audit organizations but the approach is not an exact science and the audit technique they follow will vary from audit to audit and among audit departments. As an audit client, you need to be audit ready for as many paths that the audit could possibly take. There are some elements of the audit process that are a given, some even a certitude, and others that are variables. Auditors requesting to look at your process documentation is almost inevitable (Fig. 14.1).

Be cognizant of the following:

- At the top level you have processes that should be documented.
- The processes will indicate what is to be done.
- Underneath the processes, procedures should be documented.
- The procedures should specify how things are to done, by whom and when they should be done.
- Processes without procedures are incomplete and auditors will expect procedures to be documented as well as processes.
- Sometimes there are high level procedures followed by detailed procedures.
- Below the detailed procedures are even more detailed "desk procedures", which indicate the specific tasks an individual needs to take to execute the procedure. Desk procedures are important if someone goes on vacation, takes ill, or is terminated. Auditors will not always review "desk procedures" but it is to your advantage to have them documented, available, and ready to use if necessary.

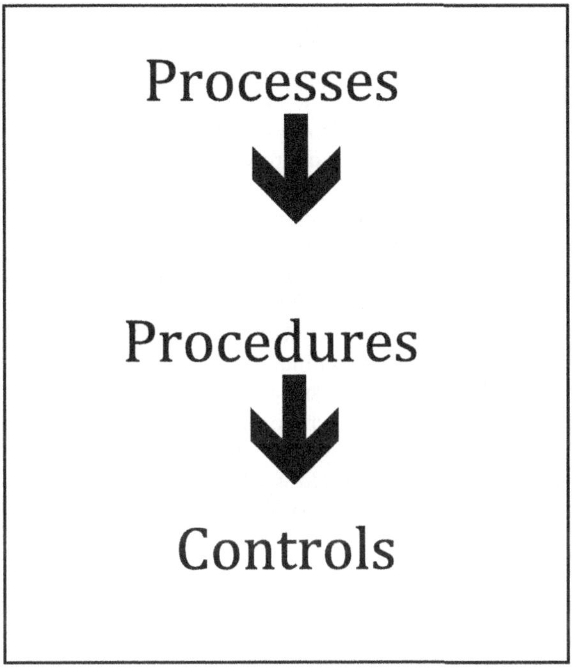

Fig. 14.1 Processes, procedures, and control documentation

Below is a case study that demonstrates what you could be faced with if desk procedures have not been documented.

Case Study on Desk Procedures

Brian Worsey is being audited and the auditor asks him to explain his process. Brian verbally takes her through the complicated process that involves running the accounts receivables application, a stream of fifteen programs, with numerous backups, interfaces, special overrides, unique job streams at the end of every month, etc. The auditor then asks Brian how long Brian has had his job and Brian replies, "twenty years". As a matter of fact he is planning to retire within the next six months because of poor health. The next day the auditor comes back to continue his review of Brian's processes but Brian has been taken to the hospital. Meanwhile, the previous night there was a problem during the A/R processing run. The accounts receivables input could not be read and no one knew what to do. There were no instructions on what to do in this situation and how to recover. They wanted to call the accounts receivables senior executive but he was out of town and Brian never wrote down whom to call in an emergency. There is a scramble now to continue the run.

Fortunately, Brian is recovering in the hospital but unfortunately, much of what Brian does is not documented. He never found enough time to sit down and document his process. The department is in chaos. Brian knows every step of what he does but now someone else needs to step in and take over his responsibilities. The auditor asks if she could come back, perhaps next week. She is told that it will not be problem and she says that she understands that continuing to run the business comes before the audit at this time. The next day she makes the following entry in her notes. "There is no existing operational process documentation for the company's accounts receivables system. The lack of process documentation or a documented run book caused a 24 hour delay in processing and a delay of recording $5 million in receivables".

Processes

A business process is a set of repetitive functions executed to result in predefined output. Every process should have a business process owner who is responsible for documenting the process. Documenting each process, describing how the process works, and its procedures, is an excellent vehicle for identifying where potential exposures exist and if controls need to be developed. If controls are documented, they can be evaluated to determine their adequacy and if they need to be enhanced and or modified. Unfortunately, controls can be missing from procedural documentation. In many cases, they were never documented because they are non-existent. Controls are frequently an afterthought and are usually not paid nearly as enough attention to as they should, until it is discovered that they are missing. It is important to realize that it is much more costly to design and implement controls after processes and procedures have been designed and deployed, than early on in the development stage. The earlier process documentation is reviewed in its life cycle for adequate controls, the more likely potential weaknesses can be identified. Early identification can result in corrective action being taken early and lessen the likelihood of erroneous processing or uncontrolled activity.

Process Narratives

Process documentation frequently consists of process narratives that describe the process in detail. Process narratives should include the following elements:

1. *Process name*—This is simply the process name that is generally recognized and associated with the process throughout the company (e.g. purchasing, order entry).
2. *Process owner*—This is the individual who has been assigned business ownership and who is responsible for the effectiveness and efficiency of the operations supporting the process, the adequacy of control, the timeliness of processing, the quality of output, the accuracy of results as well as application security for the various applications supporting the business process.
3. *Process objective*—The objective of the process, it's purpose, should be described.
4. *Process scope*—It is important to identify the scope of the process so there is little or no confusion as to when and where it starts and ends. When a company's business process descriptions are reviewed in totality and connected together, there should be a comfort level that business entities and business disciplines have been described and that none have been omitted. Processes should flow smoothly, one into the other and should be interwoven to cover the business.
5. *Roles and responsibilities*—This process element addresses the roles and responsibilities of different organizations involved in executing the process. This may include operational personnel, IT personnel, HR personnel, financial organizations, managerial roles, staff roles, executive responsibilities, user responsibilities, etc.
6. *Process description*—This is a detailed description of the process that should be augmented by the process flow that will be discussed next. The description should address who is responsible for the process, what the process involves, when it is executed and where it takes place. Do not try to answer the question of how it is implemented. This will be discussed later under procedures.

7. *Input*—There should be a separate section in the process narrative that identifies all inputs (data and/or files) and their sources. It would be helpful if there were a description as to what processing is to take place with all inputs identified and when the inputs are to be received.
8. *Output*—Process outputs also need to be described. You should identify each output (data and/or files), when it is generated, its purpose, its classification, and its destination.
9. *Key events*—Identify what are considered to be the key events associated with the process. For example: What triggers the process? How do know that the process was effectively executed?
10. *Control points*—You will need to discuss control points in the process. You should indicate where they are as well as their function. We will discuss control points in more detail, later.
11. *Business rules*—Every process should comply with business rules. You need to identify what these rules are.
12. *Dependencies and relationships*—There will be dependencies and relationships that will need to be effectively executed for this process to be reliable and efficient. Each dependency should be identified. Dependencies can be communications equipment, personnel, the latest hardware, the latest software, expertise, experience, networks, successful interfaces with other processes, etc.
13. *Process measurements*—You should describe measurements that you have in place so that management can assess the effectiveness, timeliness, and quality of processing. Process owners and users usually define measurements. You should also state how often your process is to be evaluated and by whom.
14. *Process improvement plans*—You should describe any immediate or long range plans to improve the process.

This list is not all-inclusive but it should give you a foundation for a process narrative. In addition to process narratives, what is very helpful is using a process flow diagram that will help you identify where controls need to be placed within your process.

Process Flow Diagrams and Control Points

A process owner can also find it beneficial to create a process flow as part of any process documentation. There are various techniques that can be used that will identify where controls should exist. These controls, indicated on the flow chart, should map to the discussion of controls in the process narrative. A control point is a time within a process where checking can be done to validate that the process is being effectively executed. Control points are also called exposure points. Exposure can exist whenever data is:

- Collected
- Transcribed
- Processed
- Transmitted
- Stored

Auditors will be focusing on control points in an attempt to give themselves a comfort level as to how well processes are monitored. Following is a simplified flow diagram with control points for an "Issues Management Process" that adheres to the discussion above. It is followed by a process narrative. The type of flow diagram used is an example of what is referred to as a "swim lane" flow diagram. Swim lanes indicate the organizations responsible for the function performed, the chronological sequence of events, and a dependency relationship. You are not obligated to use swim lanes or the process narrative format. This is only one example of what can be used. Most processes within the company will no doubt be much more complex and elaborate (Fig. 14.2).

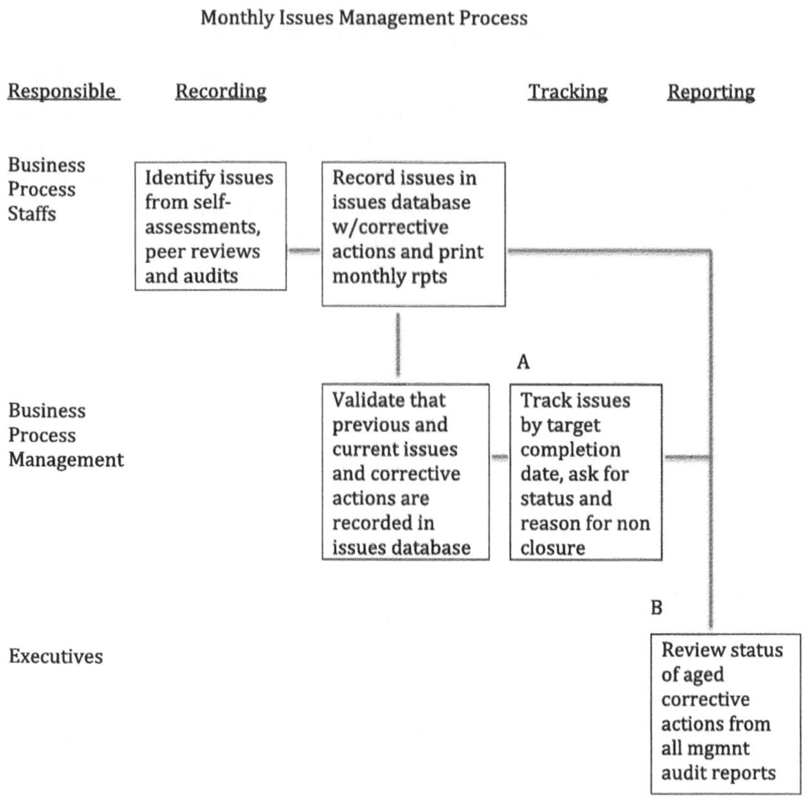

Fig. 14.2 Process issues management frequency: monthly

Narrative of Issues Management Flow Diagram with Control Points

Process Name	Issues Management
Process Owner	Allison Brig
Process Objective	The objective of this process is to identify and effectively manage control issues emerging from reviews or audits, ensuring that they receive adequate focus, attention, and resources necessary for timely resolution. The process addresses recording, tracking, and reporting of issues
Process staff personnel	1. Identify issues through management reviews, self-assessments, and audits

(continued)

(continued)

	2. Record issues and corrective action plans with target implementation dates in an issues tracking database
Process management	1. Identify all issues as a result of past and current audits and reviews
	2. Track corrective action target dates for completion and report status to the process executives
Executives	Review corrective action plans to see if target dates have been met, and if not, ask for an explanation
Process Description	Issues that arise as a result of self-assessments, audits, or reviews that cannot be resolved within forty-eight hours should be recorded in an issues tracking database. They need to be tracked with corrective action plans and reported to executive management until corrective action plans are implemented. Issues that can be resolved in less than forty-eight hours need not be formally tracked in an issues database
Input	1. Self-assessment issues
	2. Audit report issues
	3. Peer review issues
	4. Issues raised by any manager
Output	1. Issues recorded in the issues database
	2. Corrective actions recorded in the issues database
Key Events	1. Identify issues
	2. Record issues in issues tracking database
	3. Track issues and corrective action plans in issues tracking database
	4. Report issues to executives
	5. Executives review aged issues
Control Points	A. Generation of status reports to track/record issues
	B. Review by executives
Business Rules	Corporation policies, standards, and guidelines
Dependencies	There is a dependency that all issues that are identified will be recorded promptly into the issues database
Measurements	Objectives will be established for the percentage of corrective action plans to be resolved by scheduled target dates and measurements will be generated quarterly to track attainment of these objectives
Improvement Plans	Process improvement plans will be established once the process is implemented and in place for six months. We will be looking at how the process can be improved with regard to timeliness, accuracy of processing and quality of output

Personal Experience 14.1

In my three plus years that I spent in corporate internal audit I was involved either as the lead auditor or team member where close to 20 audits resulted in failures when they involved IT. This was because I had 12 years experience in developing and maintaining systems and knew where many of the skeletons were. Many of the same issues were repetitive and were occurring over and over again. Executive management decided that the best thing that I could do was to educate the process owners and stop faulting them. To my knowledge, for the first time in the history of corporate audit within our company, a moratorium was declared. I was told not to conduct any more audits but to take two auditors with me to a primary company processing site that was in trouble with failed audit after failed audit. We were located at the site for six months, flying home on the weekends. We interviewed and educated more than 70 process owners and key staff. We helped them flow each of their processes, identifying, all inputs, outputs, processing, error procedures, controls, etc. At times it was like pulling teeth as many of them had not thought about their systems at this level, could not explain the processing, and could not answer our questions. We pulled in IT personnel that included programmers, designers, and operational personnel along with any other personnel from any organization that their systems were dependent upon. As a result of this effort, frustrating at times but certainly rewarding, processing was understood better than it had been and control deficiencies were addressed.

Procedures

Having process documentation without procedures is analogous to purchasing a new car without an owner's manual. You may know that the process is that you want to change a tire, but you may need a step-by-step procedure if you never changed a tire before. Processes tell you *what, when,* and *where* but not *who* and *how*. Procedures describe "how" to get from point "A" to point "B" and can usually be broken down into two levels. There are general procedures, sometimes referred to as "high level" procedures and then "detailed" procedures. High level procedures will inform the reader of the various tasks needed to execute a process while detailed procedures will describe how each step is to be accomplished and by whom. Depending on the process that is documented, it may be sufficient to document high level procedures without requiring detailed procedures. The more elaborate the process, the greater the need for more detailed procedures. Auditors will ask for process flows, will most likely discuss process controls with you and will also probably ask for procedures. The may or may not. "peel the onion" down to detail procedures but detailed procedures can be very helpful and beneficial in changing environments where there is frequent turnover of process personnel. Let's look at the relatively simple process that we previously discussed on "Issues Management" and see what might be considered the supporting high level procedure and a more detailed procedure.

For "Issues Management" the high level procedure might be:

1. Conduct self-assessments, audits, and peer reviews.
2. Record issues and corrective action plans in an Issues tracking database.
3. Generate reports to see if issues have been closed.
4. Report corrective action status to executive management.
5. Executive management ensures aged issues are closed.
6. Implement process improvements if deemed necessary.

A more detailed procedure might be:

1. Process managers prepare self-assessments for their departments
2. Self-assessments are distributed by the process management to their staffs twice a year to be completed.
3. Staffs complete the self-assessments.
4. Process management asks other managers to conduct peer reviews to validate the self-assessment responses.
5. Process managers review completion of self-assessments, ensuring that all "YES" answers explain how testing was achieved and all "N/A" answers are explained as to why they were designated as "N/A".
6. Management compiles all of the issues and now has their staffs enter issues with corrective action plans into the "Issues Tracking Database".
7. A monthly report is generated by IT for all issues.
8. Management reviews the report to see if all issues have a corrective action plan with a responsible party for resolution.

9. If an issue does not have a corrective plan, management asks his staff why there is no corrective action plan.
10. If the staff indicates that the issue does not need a corrective action plan, management asks if a formal risk assessment was performed.
11. Management asks if there was evidence that the risk assessments were reviewed and accepted or rejected.
12. Management reviews the issues report to see if there are indications as to which corrective were completed, when they were completed, and which corrective actions are past due.
13. Management asks IT to run another report that shows the aging of open corrective actions by 30, 60, 90, or greater than 90 days.
14. Management confronts their staff as to why corrective actions that are aged for extended times have not been resolved.
15. Quarterly, the process management needs to review the aged corrective actions that are past due greater than 90 days with their executive and discuss what happened and how they can be closed.

As basic as this example is, the purpose is to give you an idea of what a high level procedure might be as opposed to a detailed procedure. There is another level below detailed procedures called "desk procedures". Auditors might ask to see desk procedures but as indicated earlier, many audits might not get down to that level.

In the Issues Management process, an illustration of an extract from a desk procedure might be:

> To support the Issues Management process please distribute the self-assessment on May 1st and November 1st to the following managers: Juan Morales, Heather Black, Cory Blake, Ilya Sani, and Gregory Baines and ask them to return the completed self-assessments within 14 days. As they are received, file the completed self-assessments in your file for completed assessments.

High level procedures are the link between the process that defines *what* and *why*, with the high level procedure that focuses on *how*. The more detailed procedure will focus on *who* and *when*. Desk procedures are the procedures needed by each individual to complete their tasks. Desk procedures should be detailed enough so that if someone leaves their job unexpectedly, someone else can step in as soon as possible and follow the detailed procedure step by step until the task responsibilities are completed. It describes each and every step required to be fulfilled, peeling back the *who* from an organizational level to an individual level and the *how* from a general to a detailed step-by-step description of their actions. Depending on the process that is documented, it may be sufficient to document high level procedures without detailed procedures, or detailed procedures without desk procedures. However, you should be very careful to document as much as you think is necessary, not just from an audit perspective but from a business perspective as well. You need to decide not only what the audit exposure could be but what missing documentation can be detrimental to your business. I included another personal experience below that I had that demonstrates the value and necessity for desk procedures.

Personal Experience 14.2

I was working in the business controls department. My manager was responsible to generate very sensitive spreadsheet reports, which the executives depended upon to help them to make valid and quick business decisions. These decisions were based on the numbers and statistics that my manager generated on her spreadsheet that she prepared for them. Complicated calculations were needed to produce the spreadsheet as a result of data that was inputted from various departments. The spreadsheet was very sensitive and my manager kept it in her locked desk at the end of the day. And then it happened—she took ill and one day was unable to come into the office. Unfortunately, as you probably guessed, this was the day of the month when the senior executives needed this spreadsheet. They called me to see if I could generate the spreadsheet for them. My first obstacle was not being able to get into my manager's desk to retrieve the spreadsheet that she was working on. She never left me the key to her desk and no one else had access. Even if I could open the drawer in her desk and pull out the spreadsheet to work on, I did not understand how to generate the report. She never documented any desk procedures that described each task that was needed to generate the spreadsheet. There was no one else who could help. I called her and told her that the senior executives were waiting for the spreadsheet and inquired f there was anything that I could do that day. They were upset that the spreadsheet was not available and that no one else could generate it. My manager said that the executives would just have to wait for her to return to the office, which should be the next day, hopefully. We had no choice. The situation could

> have been avoided if she had desk procedures documented and had made arrangements for me to back her up. Unable to find someone who could open her desk and retrieve the spreadsheet was also a problem that needed to be resolved and was—lessons learned that will not be forgotten.

Self-Assessments

There are various techniques that can be used to identify control exposures. It can start with a self-assessment. No one is better able to assess his or her control exposures than a first line manager and their key staff. They are the ones who day in and day out execute required process activities and are in the best position to identify potential issues, shortcomings, or control concerns. Early warnings can be identified in self-assessment questionnaires and can play a major role in establishing corrective actions, if done honestly and thoroughly. Unfortunately, there are at least three major concerns that can negate their potential benefits. These are:

- Self-assessments are thought by many managers to function as report cards and no one wants to report failing grades.
- Self-assessments are thought to be a nuisance and are not taken seriously.
- Self-assessment questions are too general or vague and leave open many different interpretations of the questions.

If managers are asked to assess their control posture, they will possibly believe that if they bring forward issues, they are informing executive management of their own failures. As a result, they can be discouraged from completing self-assessments. Why should they admit that they are not prepared and that they have process, procedure, and/or control weaknesses? It makes little sense to many. The only exception and different perspective to this reluctance would be the situation where a new manager is involved. Someone who has recently taken over a new department will want to know where his or her process weaknesses are so that corrective actions can be established to address the concerns. After all, they are the new player and have been hired to evaluate their department and make necessary improvements. In order to be successful when they move into their new position, they need to know where any vulnerabilities exist in their processes. They can accomplish this task by first asking their staff to honestly complete self-assessments and make suggestions for improvement. Another option that new managers have is to go one step further and ask for their departments to be independently audited so they would know how much work will be needed to establish a well-controlled environment. This is a strategic move for new managers and one where most new managers will be hesitant. No one welcomes the idea of auditors coming in assessing their processes. This is true even though auditors will not necessarily blame them for current problems if they are on the job for a short period of time, but there are no guarantees and there probably would be some hesitancy. Another possibility is if self-assessments were executed and if exposures were identified, then auditors would probably expect to see corrective action plans documented and underway, if possible.

New managers will also have a chance to get their departments in shape. Realize, however, that they will probably get only one chance from the auditors and their management will not blame them for their predecessor's shortcomings. New managers need to encourage their employees to make suggestions and assure them that they will not be held responsible for exposures that are identified. The operative word here is suggestions that new managers should welcome. They could use the suggestions to focus the department's attention and effort on addressing the exposures identified and putting plans in place to resolve as many issues as possible.

Now let's get back to the process manager and fear of reprisal. It is a challenge, a difficult undertaking, sometimes even a very daunting uphill battle, to get an honest appraisal. Managers need to be told and need to believe that there will be no repercussions and that they are starting with a clean slate—a difficult sale. They need to be apprised that it will be in their best interest if they find their own problems and clean their own dirty laundry as opposed to having an illusion of control and for someone else to discover and reveal their control exposures. Every effort needs to be taken to get the right message communicated to management and their staff for self-assessments to be effective. Regrettably, too many times self-assessments indicate that all is rosy and peachy or they identify only minor issues. An audit then takes place and the auditors arrive at a different conclusion, identifying major control exposures. Your executives can query you at this time and ask how this happened.

The second problem with self-assessments is that in addition to fear of reprisal is that not everyone takes these seriously enough. They are thought to be a nuisance and are really just a formality, a requirement that needs to be fulfilled but with no real value. There is an objective by many managers to complete the assessments as quickly as possible so that they and their staffs can get back to work and concentrate on their real jobs. This mentality needs to be addressed—having better controls in place will allow managers to do their job better. Managers need to be aware of the benefits. The best way to accomplish this is with education and a demonstration that more efficient processes with tighter controls will eventually reduce resources, administrative costs, and increase integrity, leading to greater customer satisfaction. This is a daunting task but needs to be a tops-down approach from executive managers to the first line managers and key staff.

Still another problem exists when managers and their staffs answer "not applicable" to self-assessment questions when they think that the questions do not apply to their organization or just that they do not understand the question. And it is not too infrequent that there are questions that have been answered "yes" when they should have been answered "no" or vice versa, primarily because they were misunderstood and rather then get clarification, the intent is to move the assessments along as quickly as possible and avoid trouble. It is up to the individuals who design the assessments to deliver quality assessments that have clear instructions, well worded and are understandable. This is key. Self-assessments are only valuable when there was a sincere effort and time was taken in developing the right questions.

The intention here is to design a general self-assessment that will satisfy questions from all organizations and then to modify the basic self-assessment with unique control questions that might apply to a specific organization. Executive management could solicit key managers to help design a generic self-assessment. This committee of managers could propose their ideas for discussion and determine what questions would make the best sense. They should strive toward wording the questions simply and concisely, hopefully avoiding misinterpretations. Once there is agreement on the general questionnaire, each manager would then have the option of adding their own questions or in modifying the questions so that it would help them address their own unique environment.

Let's take a look at the mechanics of completing an assessment. Managers will be asked and they can ask help from their key staff members to answer questions either by "yes" the control is in place, "no" the control is not in place or "N/A" if the control is not applicable. If "N/A" is used, the manager needs to explain why it is "N/A". A valid reason for a "N/A" response might be if you are a database administrative manager and you are asked if you add comments to source code documentation when application code changes are made. Since your department does not code application changes, the answer is "N/A". In addition, it is essential that managers indicate how they can verify that controls are in place. For instance, if they answer "yes" to the question, "Is there adequate separation of duties", they need to explain how separation of duties is accomplished within their departments. If managers are not completing self-assessments themselves, but their staffs complete the assessments, management will still be held accountable for the answers. All self-assessments should be signed and dated by the manager of the department when the self-assessments are completed.

An example of a very simple self-assessment questionnaire is indicated in Fig. 14.3.

It would be in the best interest of a company to have individuals who have participated in numerous audits before to develop or to be members of the committee developing the self-assessment questionnaire. They should be able to anticipate some of the questions that auditors will ask. It certainly would help in knowing what questions an auditor will ask and then ask yourself the same questions and answer them before the auditor asks. Questions asked throughout this textbook could be candidates for inclusion in self-assessments. Do not hesitate to include them. Other questions can be derived from the material that is spread out among the various chapters and they too should be considered for self-assessment questionnaires. It is important to realize that the completion of the self-assessment, if done well, will not only help you to prepare for audits, but can identify potential control exposures within your process. This is an opportunity to do more than just prepare for an audit, but to improve your process—take advantage.

Now as a process owner, how do you know how you should respond to the questions? One way, if you are uncomfortable with just asking your staff for answers, is to conduct reviews before answering the questions, especially in answering those questions that focus on execution. These reviews should be independent and not conducted by members of your department. The reviews can be conducted by peer managers and their staffs.

Control Question	YES/NO/NA No or NA-please explain	Yes- How was it tested? How can it be demonstrated?
Is your process adequately documented and key activities and controls identified?		
Can you demonstrate an up-to-date overall process flow and narrative for your process?		
Are control measurements established to ascertain whether key control points are functioning properly and if the process is effectively being executed?		
Does the flow with a narrative address inputs, outputs, interfaces, dependencies, process objective, responsibilities, process description, key events and control points?		
Is there a plan to review processes to see where they can be improved?		
Are measurements reviewed with management on a timely basis and are appropriate actions taken to correct process weaknesses?		

Fig. 14.3 Self-assessment

Peer Reviews

Peer reviews require you to have good working relationships with your peer managers—you can help each other by supporting each other. There are managers in your company who, when asked, will probably tell you that they have documented procedures and controls. And if they were asked if they were executing the procedures, they could easily say "yes". However, one of the best ways to know if procedures and controls are actually being executed is by scheduling independent reviews. This is where you can help each other, by conducting independent reviews for other departments. The reviews need to be independent because there are very few of your staff, who will admit that procedures and controls are not working. After all, it is their responsibility to ensure effective execution. They will be ashamed, reticent, and reluctant to tell you otherwise and will also be too close to the actual procedures to see clearly if the execution is working effectively. Being too close to day-to-day operations can cloud one's judgment. As we have heard many times in audit conversations, "trust, but verify".

Before you invite your peer managers to conduct an independent review of the answers indicated in your self-assessment questionnaires, it might be a good idea to offer your services to independently review any assessment that they might have within their own departments. They can help you and you can help them. You can help critique each other's operation.

Peer reviews should be conducted whenever self-assessments are completed and the results documented and compared with previous assessments to determine if the same problems that are identified now were previously identified, and if there were any, if they still exist. You never know how the questionnaires were previously reviewed. Maybe the personnel who completed the assessments were not adequately trained or the questions were vague and still are. This is all the more reason to conduct current reviews of self-assessment questionnaires and the answers given.

One more suggestion for the self-assessment completion process is for managers to have every member of their departments participate in the peer reviews. In this way, not only will it be a learning experience for the members in the department, but everyone's process execution will be independently evaluated. No one should feel that they have been singled out for a peer review because their work is being questioned. Education is important and all employees need to know the benefits and rationale for peer reviews.

Previous Audits

One of the first requests that auditors frequently have, when they arrive at a site, is to ask to review audit reports from previous audits. As an audit client, you need to be prepared if this situation arises. Now you might ask, shouldn't the audit staff have copies of any previous audits? That will assume that either the same internal auditors who are currently performing the audit, that is under way, are the auditors who conducted the last audit or are members of the same audit department. If they were the same auditors or members of the same internal audit organization, they should have a copy. Realize however, that even if the auditors have a copy, they can ask you if you have one in your files to see what action, if any, you took on the exposures and if you are tracking status on any issue that was identified. Auditors can ask you whatever they want to, within reason—it is their audit and their prerogative.

Now what if there were previous audits conducted by your external audit firm? Either way, internal or external audits, you should have a copy and if your internal audit organization asked for a copy or copies from previous audits, you will be compelled to share those audit reports, internal or external, with them. What would they be looking for?

To emphasize, they will be looking to see if previous concerns reported were resolved. And if they were not, they will want to know why not. They will not just ask you if there was resolution but will ask you to provide them with documented evidence. They will want to see, proof, proof, proof.

First, be aware of the fact that audits are usually conducted every year or even on a less frequent basis if: the audit was not critical; audit resource is limited; or if there were no previous serious issues cited before. However, if there were serious issues reported before, a follow-up audit to see if issues were or are being resolved could be scheduled and conducted on a more frequent basis (e.g. semi- annually, quarterly). Issues are followed up to determine if they have been adequately addressed. Again, if the exposures were not significant enough, then the normal audit cycle will prevail, but don't count on it. Once again, what do we mean by normal cycle? Some companies will have critical processes audited between 2 and 5 years, depending on the size of their audit staffs and what they can reasonably cover with limited resources. If it is a not a critical process and there were a few serious concerns or none reported in the last audit, then there might even be a 5 year gap or more between audits of the same process. Why is this important? The time period between audits can be a particularly significant factor between audits—many events can occur that can affect the degree of focus on resolving previous audit findings.

Executive management can change and they might shift priority of work as to what should be worked on; the company might have been bordering on bankruptcy over the last year; or the company might have merged twice in the last three years and might have been absorbed by larger enterprises that shifted focus. These and other reasons for previous audit concerns falling through the cracks might be valid business explanations. However, the seriousness of the exposures that were identified in previous audit concerns will be a determining factor in auditors accepting or rejecting the explanations. Try to convince the auditors, if you can, if there are extenuating circumstances, to mitigate or eliminate any concerns that they still might have with previous issues reported. What would help you, if issues have not been resolved, is to have a documented risk assessment available enlightening the auditors of the fact that the risks are known and reviewed by management. Risk assessments will be covered in more detail in the next chapter. Whatever the justification you have for the auditors, it better be good and be able to stand up to audit scrutiny.

I ran into a situation when I was conducting an audit that I will summarize in the personal experience below.

Personal Experience 14.3

I was assigned to conduct an audit of a billing process that I had not audited before and was not sure if it was previously audited. I asked the audit interface whether there were any previous audits on this process. He informed me that there was an internal audit about five years ago. To his recollection, there were none since then. He was not aware of any external audit but told me he would check and get back to me. I asked him for a copy of the last internal audit report that he had. We probably had a copy of this internal audit report back in our offices but I asked him for it because I wanted to see if they had a copy and if they were working on it. They did have it and he gave me a copy. I read the audit report

> and it was apparent that although there were no "show stoppers" or very significant issues raised, there were exposures that if not addressed, could lead to serious problems. This report and its findings could save me a lot of time. I asked him if the recommendations were responded to and he said yes, He showed me the reply to the audit report, after I asked him. Many of the recommendations had target dates for resolution. I asked him if the exposures were resolved and he said he did not know. I asked him if there was evidence of corrective actions resolving the concerns—he said no. I asked him what happened and why they were still unresolved. He said that there were numerous process owner changes over the last few years and that previous audit corrective actions fell off the radar. I wrote this up in my audit report and stated that previous audit exposures were not resolved and had resulted in large amount of delayed billings and lost revenue because of inadequate controls in the process. They already had an "unsat" audit with little audit work on my part.

Summary

If you are going to be audited, you should be pro-active and take measures to achieve an audit ready posture. As an audit client, you cannot just sit back and do nothing and hope for the best—complacency is not an option. You should not suffer from a false sense of comfort. Know your weaknesses and potential exposures and address them before audit informs you and your management that there are serious exposures. From the two previous sections in this textbook, you hopefully have a strong foundation for what controls are in the range of possibilities. I cannot stress enough the necessity and value add in establishing and executing pro-active measures.

The very first activity that you should pursue is to make sure that your process, procedures and controls are documented. This should involve the use of flow diagrams, process narratives, and the identification of what and where your control points are. You should understand where the data comes from that is input to your process and how it is processed. You should be able to answer the following questions: (1) How do you validate completeness and accuracy of processing? (2) How do you ensure processing timeliness? (3) What errors could occur? (4) What is your output and where does it go? (5) Do you know your dependencies?

(6) Are you aware of the metrics that measure processing effectiveness? (7) Are you knowledgeable of the roles and responsibilities of all parties involved in your process (e.g. other departments)? You need to understand the value and differences between high level, detailed, and desk procedure and to verify that all documentation exists and is available.

In addition to documentation of your process, procedures, and controls you should ask your staff to complete self-assessments. They need to be honest and complete the assessments without fear of reprisals. The assessments should indicate why and what evidence there is if they answered "yes". They also need to explain N/A responses as well. There should be independent reviews of the self-assessments by other organizations. These peer reviews should precede any audit that was announced and that you might be aware of heading your way.

One last point needs to be mentioned when summarizing this chapter. You need to thoroughly review any previous audit of your process. Verify that all exposures were addressed either with corrective actions or risk assessments (risk assessments will be discussed in the next chapter). If auditors find previous issues that were not addressed, it could lead to an unsatisfactory audit. One of the first tasks that you should accomplish before the auditors arrive is to schedule a review of previous audit concerns and resolution.

Guidelines

1. Document your process, procedures, and controls, if you have not already done so.
2. Use flow charts and narratives to ensure that you capture all inputs, processing, and outputs.
3. Ask your IT organization to help you with this effort if they were involved in designing, coding, implementing, or maintaining the applications and programs supporting your process.
4. Review any previous audits conducted and ensure that there is closure for all exposures cited. If the exposures are still open, have available either evidence of corrective actions, or documented risk assessments and executive acceptance.
5. Identify where you believe that controls should be placed that will ensure the timeliness, accuracy, and completeness of processing.
6. Identify all controls that are preventive, detective, deterrent, reporting, or self-correcting.

7. If controls have not been established, define target dates, and assign individuals to work on them. Document any plans in detail and have them ready for any audit.
8. If controls are already imbedded in your process then validate that they are effectively being executed.
9. Assign key staff personnel to complete self-assessments. Advise them to be honest and that there will be no negative consequences as long as they are honest.
10. Instruct your staff when completing self-assessments to explain their answers, citing evidence when necessary.
11. If self-assessments have not been used before and you are not sure of the questions to use then ask for advice from other management who might have conducted self-assessments before. Also see if your company has a template for a self-assessment that you can use and modify for your department.
12. Ask your peer managers to provide you with an independent review of your self-assessments.

Chapter 14 Exercises

1. You are the purchasing manager in your company and you have just received an announcement letter from your internal audit organization that they will be arriving at our site at the begging of next month, which is two weeks away, to conduct an audit of the purchasing process. You are a fairly new manager and have been at your job, responsible for the purchasing process, for only three months. You replaced the previous manager who was dismissed and prosecuted because of fraudulent activity. You want to take pro-active steps to be ready and demonstrate to your executives that they picked the right person to head the department now. Explain in detail 5 actions that you can take.
2. How do you prioritize your pro-active activities? What do you do if you cannot compete all of the pro-active activities that you had planned before an announced audit commences? If you are not comfortable that you will have a successful audit then what are your options? And what do you tell your executives regarding your audit readiness? Will you tell them you will pass or fail? And what is this decision based on?

3. Explain the difference between regular procedures and desk procedures.

Chapter 14 Questions

Please choose the best answer for the questions below:

1. The type of documentation that tells you how things are to be done and by whom is called:

   A. Process documentation
   B. Procedure documentation
   C. Desk Procedure documentation
   D. Application documentation

2. If you have process narratives describing your process, you do not need process flow diagrams.

   A. true
   B. false

3. A control point on a process flow is:

   A. a time within a process that checking can be done to validate that a process is working correctly
   B. not associated with time but more with budgetary capabilities
   C. a time in a process where you believe audit will ask questions
   D. where you believe independent reviews should be conducted

4. A flow diagram that indicates the organizations responsible for functions performed, and the chronological sequence of events is referred to as:

   A. an organizational flow diagram
   B. a functional flow diagram
   C. a chronological flow diagram
   D. a swim lane diagram

5. Elements usually found in a process narrative are:

   A. process description, responsibilities of process management, input and output
   B. control points, process description, measurements

C. key events, process objective, dependencies
D. all of the above

6. The responsible party for completing a self-assessment is:

A. the audit committee
B. the internal audit staff
C. the legal department
D. the process owner

7. One of the more common reasons why self-assessments are not always reliable is that:

A. they are too ambiguous
B. there is fear of reprisal when they are completed if issues are identified
C. there is not enough time so the self-assessments are rushed
D. too many people participate in answering questions

8. If N/A is used on a self-assessment:

A. independent management needs to sign off on the assessment
B. it can not be used on two consecutive assessments
C. a reason must be stated why N/A was chosen
D. all of the above

9. When looking at previous audits before a current audit begins, you:

A. should be looking to see what the previous issues were and evaluate the actions that were taken
B. should primarily be concerned as to when it was conducted
C. should ensure that you have risk assessments documented for all issues identified
D. should ask the internal audit department if they have a copy

10. What is the best reason for conducting a self-assessment?

A. You will have evidence to show internal audit that you take controls seriously.
B. You are complying with company policies, completing self-assessments as quickly as possible so you can focus on your daily tasks and essential business.

C. You can see what potential issues you have and address them before audit identifies them while improving the accuracy and effectiveness of your processing.
D. You can identify your employees who have issues and take disciplinary action.

CHAPTER 15

Risk Management

Never was anything great achieved without danger. —Niccolo Machiavelli

created by Sora Shimazaki

E. Danter, *Audit Defense*, Palgrave Studies in Accounting and Finance Practice, https://doi.org/10.1007/978-3-030-92466-9_15

What this photo attempts to show is that all risks need to be assessed by weighing the risk of an identified exposure against the cost of adequately addressing it. There needs to be a balance.

Risk Management might actually play more of a pivotal role in surviving an audit than most audit clients could imagine. If you have an effective, robust risk management process established and you can demonstrate that it is effectively working, you could survive an audit that otherwise might be a disaster. To further emphasis this point, let's review the following case study:

Case Study on Risk Management

Mia and Shawn were auditing an accounts payable system and numerous concerns and potentially significant exposures surfaced during their fieldwork. Some of the issues were even repetitive from the last audit that was done two years ago. The auditors were in the process of writing fact sheets and needed to verify the findings with the audit client manager, the accounts payable manager, and his staff before migrating the issues to the final report. In discussing the findings with the auditors, the accounts payable manager explained to Mia and Shawn that his team was aware of most of the issues cited before the audit began. Naturally, the auditors wanted to see evidence. The auditors also wanted to know that if most of the issues were previously known, why weren't they resolved. The auditors were told that many of the issues were currently being addressed with corrective action plans being worked on but were still open. There were also issues that the accounts payables manager and his executive manager felt did not justify more resource for resolution. The auditors wanted to know what evidence existed to support these statements. The manager told them that a risk assessment was prepared that stated these risks—they were analyzed and reviewed and that the actions decided on were approved. The auditors wanted to know who approved the risk assessments, when it was written, and if they could get a copy. They were told that the risk assessment was prepared three months prior to the audit and signed off by executive management. A copy was handed over to the auditors. After the risk assessment was reviewed and the auditors felt that it was complete and thorough, they felt that they had to add, at the suggestion of the audit client, words to the final report reflecting the existence of the risk assessment and its approval. This modification, that was not initially planned, changed the complexion of the audit. When the final audit report was written and distributed, it gave credit to the audit client for the prior awareness of almost all of the issues from the previous audit and actions that were taken. There were very few issues that were uncovered during the current audit. The audit report, instead of appearing as an unsatisfactory audit to the reader, now appeared as a satisfactory audit. The auditors had little choice but to give credit where credit was due.

If there were any issues identified in any internal or external audit, peer review, self-assessment, or discovered by a manager, executive, committee, department, or any individual within the company, the exposures need to be evaluated and their impact properly and timely assessed. Any known business risk to a company needs to be sufficiently addressed to decide on the best decision to address both the current risk and the elimination or lessening of any future risk to the company. The vehicle to best address this task is a Risk Management Process that needs to be established and documented and used by every department within the company to assess known risks and aid in deciding appropriate action to take (Exhibit 15.1).

Issues Management Process

We talked about issues and the recording of issues under operational controls. It was here that we recorded and tracked software and hardware issues. Systems going down, networks failing, application aborting, or any other incident that occurred while applications or systems were operational, required that these incidents be logged and tracked until closure.

Now let's look at process issues management. Again we are talking about issues that were identified during audits, reviews, self-assessments, or individual management or staff personnel. These are process exposures. Each process issue identified from the sources mentioned above needs to be carefully scrutinized and validated. What is perceived and what was identified as an issue may not be a valid issue and there might not even be an exposure. There may be controls that were not revealed or uncovered but that may negate the exposure that is thought to exist. There also may be mitigating controls that were not identified that could eliminate or reduce the likelihood of occurrence or business impact. It is important that line management validate each exposure and certify its authenticity.

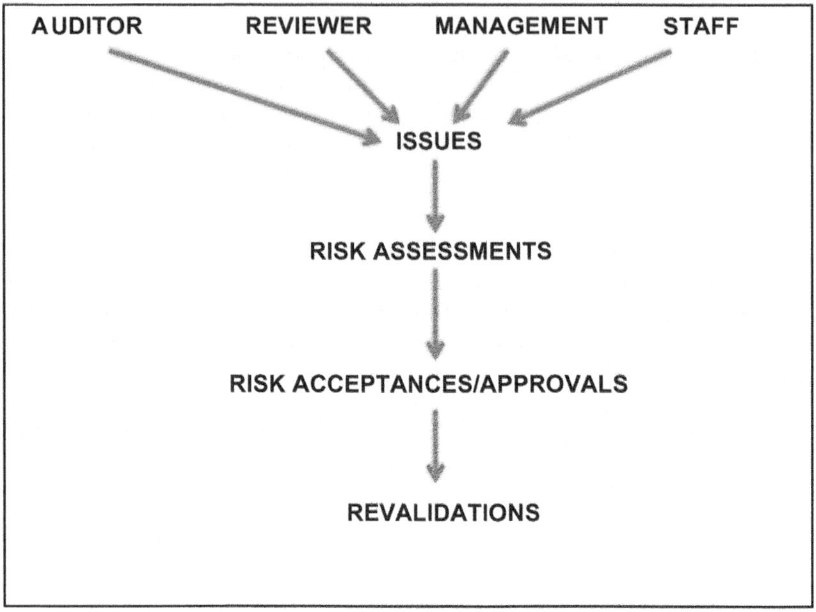

Exhibit 15.1 Risk management process

Once issues are validated, they need to be documented and recorded in an issues log. A centralized database is frequently used to record and track all process issues. All issues need to be recorded with indications as to when and where they were identified, brief descriptions of the issues, owners of the issues, corrective actions planned, target dates for resolution and status. Access to the issues tracking database needs to be protected. Only authorized individuals should have access to this database, as it probably will contain proprietary and/or confidential information. Another item that needs to be considered is who should have read access and who should have update capability to the database. Update capability should be very restrictive and should be given only to owners of the issues. Reports can be generated from this database for further review. Business process owners should scrutinize these reports on a frequent basis (Exhibit 15.2).

Exhibit 15.2 Example of a process issues log

Issue number	*Owner*	*Issue description*	*Date identified*	*Source (e.g. audit)*	*Individual responsible for resolving*	*Target date*	*Status*
1	Lynn Wake	SoD-same individual receiving and recording payments	Sept 23, 2020	Audit	Lynn Wake	Dec 15, 2020	Closed
2	Lynn Wake	No error correction process	June 23, 2020	Peer review	Edgar White	Nov 20, 2020	Still open
3	Lynn Wake	No documented controls	Aug 28, 2020	Self-Assessment	Alyson Reyes	Dec 15, 2020	Closed
4	Lynn Wake	No data classification	June 23, 2020	Peer review	Ethan Volpe	Jan 15, 2021	Closed
5	Jorge Pelez	Code changes made without authorization	Sept 23, 2020	Audit	Jorge Perez	Jan 30 2021	Closed
6	Lynn Wake	Outdated SLAs	Sept 23, 2020	Audit	Jessica Gray	Dec 15, 2020	Still open
7	Mike Dolt	SOD—person taking inventory, also signs off	Nov 24, 2020	Self-Assessment	Mike Dolt	Dec 15, 2020	Closed
8	Lynn Wake	No disaster recovery plan	July 26, 2020	Peer review	Bala Patel	Nov 30, 2020	Still Open
9	Lynn Wake	Unauthorized Access to Confidential Data	Sept 23, 2020	Audit	Bob Green	Dec 20, 2020	Closed

Risk Assessment Process

Once issues have been validated and recorded in the issues database, the associated business risk needs to be assessed before further action is decided. The process of assessing risks requires insight and a business acumen that will result in good judgment.

There should be a formal business risk management process established and documented in each company that is serious about their control posture and in preparing for audits. The risk management process should include an issues log, risk assessment form, risk acceptance requirements, and risk validation instructions.

Not all issues that are recorded in the issues log will necessarily require that a risk assessment be performed. The company should state, in its risk management process, when a risk assessment is required. The criteria might be if an issue is open for 30 days, 45 days, 60 days, etc.

The risk assessment is owned by the business process manager. It is the process owner or a key staff member in their department who prepares a risk assessment form following the company's formal risk assessment process.

Organizations usually choose one of these five choices when managing risk:

- Avoid Risk—Abandon a business practice to eliminate risk. If the risk is significant and it is too costly or is not essential for your business, then perhaps you can eliminate the activity where the risk exists. For example, a vendor from whom you are buying raw material, for your manufacturing enterprise, is delivering defective goods, ten to fifteen percent of the time when quarterly purchases are made. You can avoid this risk of receiving inferior quality by replacing this vendor.
- Reduce Risk—Reduce the probability of the risk occurring. If you have a manual order entry process that is filled with errors, reduce the risk by perhaps automating the process.
- Accept Risk—Accept the risk and continue with business as usual. Your monthly reconciliation of your general ledger indicated discrepancies, once over the last twelve months. There was no problem the other eleven months. It was always accurate in the past years and you feel this could have been a fluke. You accept the risk because the probability of occurrence is very low.
- Transfer Risk—Mitigate the risk by shifting risk to another entity. Your payroll processing over the last year has been very late and inaccurate. You are losing faith in your IT department and employees are getting very upset and expressing their frustration. You transfer the risk by outsourcing your payroll processing.
- Risk Sharing—Combine risk assumption and risk sharing with another entity. You are the billing manager in a manufacturing

company. Too many of your invoices are wrong, and the customers are complaining of being overcharged. You realize that there is a large amount of erroneous data being transmitted to your department from the order entry department and also that your edits could be improved because you are not capturing all the erroneous data. The company's revenue is suffering. Processing controls need to be enhanced in both the order entry application and the billing application. The risk is shared.

Note: Risk management is generally most effective when all risks and solutions are considered instead of examining each one separately. This is known as enterprise risk management (ERM).

Risk Assessment Owner

The risk assessment process should start with identifying the appropriate manager who owns the risk. The owner of the risk is usually the owner of the process where the exposure was found and the risk exists. It is the owner who should prepare a formal risk assessment form and retain documentation. Auditors will look favorably at owners who can demonstrate that they are using a documented formal risk management process and that execution can be demonstrated showing that they are aware of exposures, have assessed the risks, and have established appropriate action with appropriate executive management approval.

Risk Assessment Form

The risk owner should prepare a risk assessment form. There should be a documented procedure on when and how to complete a risk assessment form. The form should contain the following elements:

- Definition of the problem
- Quantification of the exposure
- Development of alternatives
- Calculation of the financial impact for each alternative
- Selection of optimum solution
- Documentation of the decision
- Categorization of the risk

- Approval of the decision
- Revalidation of the risk and decision

Definition of the problem—state the exposure that was identified and indicate where it was discovered (e.g. audit, peer review, self-assessment). Quantification of the exposure—the owner should consider:

- Impact in slowing the business down—some issues will be catastrophic and could cause a process to come to a halt (e.g. no disaster plan), while other issues could result in a small delay (e.g. balancing problem) or some in no delay (e.g. outdated SLA)
- Potential or actual dollar lost—how much revenue has been lost or could be lost
- Cost of recovery—how much will it cost the company to recover any loss due to risk
- Time to recover—how long will it take to recover from loss due to issue
- Possibility of fraud—determine if issue could lead to fraud (e.g. SoD issues)
- Probability of occurrence—how likely is it that the issue will occur
- Criticality to the business—determine if the exposure and incident occurring is critical to the business
- Cost of alternative—estimate cost of alternatives

Develop alternative solution—the alternative solutions should either result in (1) continuing with the business as usual, (2) enhancing controls that are already in place, or (3) introducing new controls in the process. Calculate financial impact for each alternative—the cost associated with each alternative needs to be estimated.
Select optimum solution—the decision should be based on what is best for the company and the financial impact of each alternative.
Document decision—the rationale for the decision should be documented.
Categorize the risk—high, medium, or low risk based on cost of tangible or intangible losses to the company.
Approval of decision—the risk assessment and decision made should be approved by another level of management in addition to the owner.

Revalidation of the risk assessment and solution—all risks need to be revalidated according to the company's risk management process.

An example of a risk assessment form follows. Your company may use a different format, or you have the option of establishing a format on your own. You can use the example as a guide but whatever format you decide to use, remember to have a retention requirement documented and adhere to it so that you can show the risk assessment form to an auditor. You can show it to them whether they ask for it or not—it just might save you from an unsatisfactory audit report (Exhibit 15.3).

Risk Owner - Al Hendley Date – May 3, 2021

Issue – A separation of duties exposure was identified in the internal audit of the accounts receivable process that was completed on February 3, 2021. Sara Coble was assigned the task of receiving checks from customers but is also the individual who was responsible for depositing the checks with the local bank. Because of a lack of adequate separation of duties there is an exposure to fraudulent activity occurring.

Quantification of the exposure – The potential of actual dollar loss is significant as we are a multi million dollar corporation. We received an average of two hundred thousand dollars a month over the last 18 months from our customers. Sara was one of three accounts receivable staff who is responsible for receiving checks but the only one who also has authority to deposit the checks. She deposits the checks for all three accounts receivable staff members. She processes approximately seventy five thousand dollars a month. She has been working in our company for a year and has had these two functions for the last three months. I realize that there is a possibility of fraud, although there has never been any problems for as long as she has been responsible for both functions.

Alternative solutions – There are two al ternatives. The first is to hire an additional person to deposit the checks. The second solution is to have one of the other individuals, who receives the checks, deposit Sara's checks. She in turn would continue to deposit checks for the other staff members but the functions would be segregated. No individual would deposit the checks that they personally receive.

Exhibit 15.3 Example of a risk assessment form

Financial impact of alternatives – The first alternative of hiring an additional person whose function it would be to deposit the checks would cost the firm an additional annual salary of $75,000 to $100,000. There would be no additional financial impact to the second alternative.

Solution – I, along with my director's concurrence, decided to go with the second alternative and segregate functions without hiring additional individuals. We are in the process of training the other accounts receivable individuals and establishing effective governance controls.

Categorizing the risk – The risk would be a medium risk right now. Although we do not have a preventive control, we are monitoring Sara's activities.

We are targeted to have both preventive and detective controls in place by August 1, 2022 and we will revalidate the risk after the solution is in place.

Manager of Accounts Receivable ____________________ Date_________

CFO ____ Date __________

Exhibit 15.3 (continued)

Risk Acceptance

All risks need to be approved by at least two levels of management. The reason for this is that if only one level of management approves the risk and signs off on the decision then there is a possibility that they are directly complicit in the exposure. They could even log the issue as being closed in the issues log, when it is still open.

Risk Revalidation

It is necessary to evaluate all risk assessments on at least an annual basis. Your company might decide to conduct revalidations more frequently for high risks—it could depend on how significant the risk is and if you can wait a full year for revalidation. The risk assessment process established for your company should indicate the time interval required for revalidation. Revalidation is necessary, as there might be changes in the environment, company's position, economic situations, etc., during the interim from the last revalidation that was done until the next scheduled revalidation. The changes in the environment might have an impact on the decision that was made when previously evaluating the risk and actions. The original risk assessment decision may no longer be valid, hence the need for revalidation and if there are extenuating circumstance then a reassessment as soon as possible. If a major event takes place, such as a merger, acquisition, or litigation, I would recommend a reassessment of all high risks within days. Time could be of the essence and its criticality could mean that time should not be wasted.

Summary

Risk assessments play a significant role in achieving a satisfactory audit report as opposed to an unsatisfactory audit. Its importance should not be understated as it could have a negative impact on your career. Having a risk assessment process that is well documented and being able to demonstrate its effective execution could possibly be the deciding factor in passing or failing an audit. Auditors will probably look more favorably at you, and give you credit, if you can convince them that you are successfully managing the risks associated with your identified exposures. These issues are exposures identified as the result of audits, self-assessments, or peer reviews.

All issues need to be recorded and tracked until closure is achieved. Management should address the risks associated with these issues by adhering to the company's risk assessment process. The foundation of the risk management process is the utilization of a risk assessment form where the risk is analyzed for: a quantification of the exposure, evaluating alternatives to address the risk, reviewing the financial impact of each alternative, and a selection of an optimum solution. The risk assessment should be approved by at least two levels of management and be revalidated at least annually.

Risks can either be: accepted where nothing is done and business continues as usual; avoided/eliminated; or mitigated.

Guidelines

1. Verify that all issues from internal audits, external audits, peer reviews, self-assessments, management, and staff control concerns are recorded in an issues log.
2. Validate that the company has a documented risk management process.
3. Check to see if the risk management process has an assessment requirement if an issue is open for an extended period of time (e.g. 30 days, 45 days).

4. Complete the company's risk assessment form to assess all identified issues that are required to be assessed. Risk assessments will be needed for any issue that is open for longer than the time period limit.
5. If the company does not have a required risk assessment form then establish your own form to assess the risk.
6. Make sure that your risk assessment form includes identification of the risk, origin, owner of the risk, quantification of the exposure, alternative solutions, financial impact of alternatives, solution chosen, etc.
7. Once you and your staff have completed the risk assessment form, select the optimum solution.
8. Sign off and date the form.
9. Have your executive manager review, approve and sign the risk assessment form.
10. Retain the form and make sure that it is readily available so that you are in a position to be able to discuss it with an auditor, if necessary; that you have assessed the risk and have the required approvals.
11. Revalidate the risk assessment at least annually or more frequently if required by your company's risk management process, or if needed.
12. Change the original decision, if necessary, due to any environment or business change.
13. Approve the revalidation and obtain your manager's approval as well.

Chapter 15 Exercises

1. You are the payroll manager and have recently been audited. The auditors indicated that taxes being calculated on monthly checks were not accurate. The issue was entered on the issues log but has not been resolved for 47 days. The reason being is that the state tax laws have changed in three states in question and that the programs are still being tested with the new tax laws. You want to follow your company's risk management process and complete a risk assessment form. What specific information and rationale do you indicate on the form for the decision made?
2. You are the purchasing manager for your company and a self-assessment indicated that you are not exercising competitive bidding

for all of your vendors. The concern was entered in the issues log and has been open for 4 months. What action do you plan to take if you are not going to competitively bid all of your vendors in the future?

Chapter 15 Questions

1. After conducting a risk assessment, companies will be choosing to:

   A. Reduce or mitigate the probability of a risk occurring
   B. Avoid or eliminate the risk by abandoning the business practice
   C. Accept the risk and continue with business as usual
   D. Any of the above

2. A risk assessment form needs to be used for every issue on the issues log.

   A. true
   B. false

3. In selecting an optimum solution when completing a risk assessment form, the decision should be primarily be based on:

   A. the past history
   B. cost vs financial impact to the business
   C. time to recover
   D. opinion of the audit committee

4. How many levels of management should approve a risk assessment?

   A. just the process owner is sufficient
   B. just the process owner's manager signature is needed
   C. it doesn't matter which one
   D. both should approve

5. The risk assessment form needs to be revalidated:

   A. every 6 months
   B. annually
   C. at least annually or sooner depending on the risk
   D. auditors will not look for a revalidation

6. If a serious issue has been discovered in a previous audit and the auditors recommended corrective action, the audit client will have no choice other than to establish a corrective action plan.

   A. true
   B. false

7. If a risk assessment is revalidated, the result might be to change the decision based on:

   A. the business changing
   B. technology changing
   C. budget increases
   D. any of the above

CHAPTER 16

Testing

When you're testing to see how deep the water is, never use two feet.—Ben Franklin

If you are an Information Technology (IT) manager or any other process owner who is, or will become an audit client, you need to be involved with application testing. Systems and supporting applications are designed and developed at the request of process owners. The timeliness, accuracy and quality of application processing and subsequent satisfaction of end users will depend on the thoroughness of testing. As a process owner, even though IT may be performing a service for you, you will be involved in many phases of the testing and auditors will hold you accountable if the testing is not satisfactory and if the process is not performing as required. Before a new system becomes operational and runs in a production environment, it should be subjected to rigorous testing. As a process owner you will need to exercise a governance role in assuring the system application's processing is complete and effectual. This task is not limited just to new systems or application programs being developed—it is also true for modifications made to existing programs. You want to ensure that thorough testing is conducted for any new change requirement (large or small) that is specified in a service request.

The phases of testing that are reviewed in this chapter are: unit testing, integration testing, system testing, regression testing, parallel testing, pilot

E. Danter, *Audit Defense*, Palgrave Studies in Accounting and Finance Practice, https://doi.org/10.1007/978-3-030-92466-9_16

testing, and user acceptance testing. We will also be discussing test plans, test cases, and test results (Exhibit 16.1).

Exhibit 16.1 Testing sequence

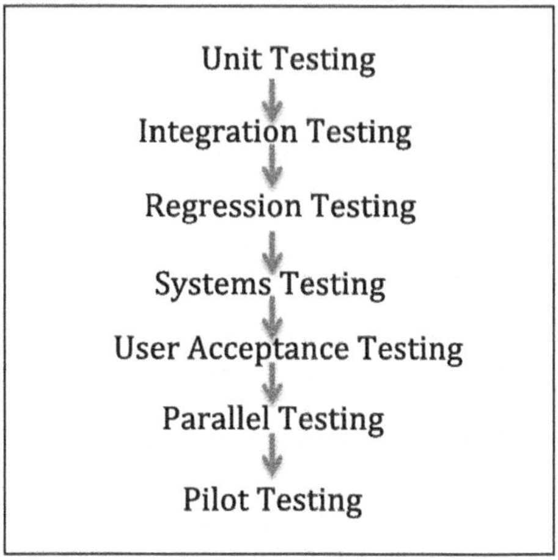

Unit Testing

After specifications and requirements for a new system are generated by process owners and given to the IT department, a design is undertaken. When the design is completed, the programming staff will be given the task to start coding. Each programmer will be generating code. When he or she believes that the coding is complete and satisfies requirements, they will test the code to validate that it is processing data correctly, satisfying expectations. The test data is created entirely by the programmer who is testing their program. The same process would be followed if a service request asked for a modification to an existing program. Unit testing is the first critical plateau. It is the bedrock for a program that can continue a journey down the road through more extensive testing that will lead to the program eventually being migrated, when ready, into a production environment. If you have issues with unit test results, it will delay additional testing until the problems are resolved. Unit testing must be successful to proceed (Exhibit 16.2).

Exhibit 16.2 Unit testing flow

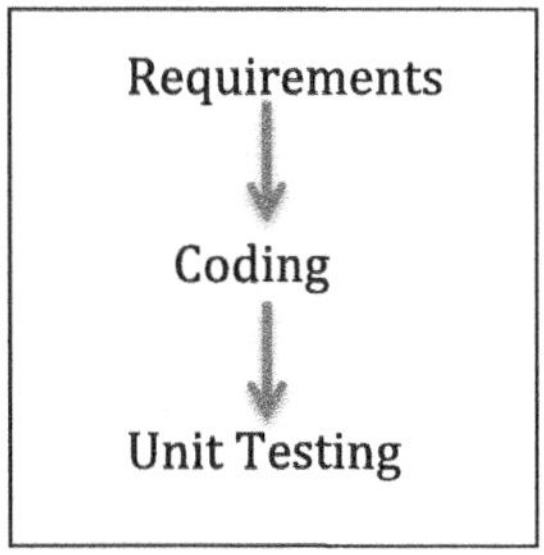

Integration Testing

Integration testing is the testing of a stream of programs to see if they work together and if the output of one program is acceptable to another. Programs might work if they are run singularly, but it is essential to verify that the output of one program can be successfully inputted to the next program. The test data used in the integration testing is usually the same test data that is used in the unit testing. If a program has a successful unit test, it does not necessarily mean that its output is in the correct format and that it can be accepted by the next program, sometimes referred to as a downstream program (Exhibit 16.3).

Exhibit 16.3 Integration test flow

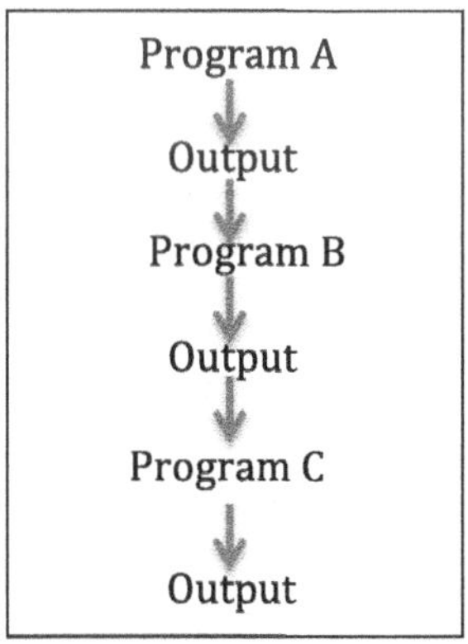

Regression Testing

Regression testing is the validation that the program still works as it did before, outside the parameters of the new change. Sometimes when a program is modified and there is new code, it works fine satisfying the new requirements. However, it is necessary to ensure that the logic that was working before to satisfy previous requirements, still works as it should— we don't want to take a step backwards. For example, if a new vendor (Mr. Smith) is added to a payables file and a program is changed to pay him correctly based on his invoice, he hopefully should be paid correctly based on the testing. However, a previous vendor (Ms. Jones), who was paid successfully in the past, all of a sudden is not being paid correctly now. This is why we schedule regression testing- we want to make sure everything else is still working correctly as it was before.

Systems Testing

Systems testing is the validation that the change works in a production environment as well as a test environment. There are times when a program is changed in an application it works fine in a test or development environment but does not work when the program is moved into the production environment. There could be some other factors that were not considered (e.g. hardware, software, or network differences).

User Acceptance Testing

User acceptance testing is usually conducted by the application process owner using test data that he or she created. There are times however, when user test data is designed and created in concert with the programming department. There are no solid rules but the final decision on who should be involved in creating the test data belongs with the application process owner.

Parallel Testing

Parallel testing involves a test stream of programs running in parallel with a production run to see if the same results are achieved. You want to run a new stream of programs to ensure that you get exactly the same results as you did before, outside of the new changes, which are based on new requirements. You will not replace the old programs with the new programs until you are comfortable that the two processing streams create the same output. Parallel testing is mostly used when there is a major or minor enhancement to an existing application rather than when there is a total new application replacement. The output, for the latter, is more likely expected to be different and the same results not expected as in a parallel run with existing production processing.

Pilot Testing

Pilot testing takes place in a production environment. It is run for a selected sample size for a specific period of time, maybe for two or three weeks or one or two months. It is usually done for large projects because the risk is greater and more difficult to recover if you need to. This is usually done to ensure that it works on a smaller sample size before it is rolled out to run in production for everyone. For example, if it is a new payroll program you might select 1–3 states to run it in first before you use the new program throughout the entire country. If it is successful in the pilot, you can then install it nationally. If it is unsuccessful on the smaller pilot sample you might need to back it out and make adjustments. You are hedging your bets because of the risk being so great. Less harm will be done if there are issues in a pilot test than if the new program was rolled out across the country and issues surfaced.

Test Plans

Auditors will ask you if you can show them test plans that you have for the testing that was done. The test plans should indicate which type of the above testing was planned. For small coding changes you might have just planed unit testing (e.g. one line of coding). For larger coding projects you might have selected to conduct more testing that would have included integration testing, system testing, regression testing, and parallel testing. For a very large project the test plan might have included pilot testing. The auditors should not have a problem with the level of testing you decided as long as you can explain your rationale. This can certainly be true if they found processing errors—they might go back to review test plans to see if they were sufficient, missing, or inadequate . An emergency code change is the one exception. There will not be any test plans expected by an auditor for emergencies due to time constraints and a minimum of time allocated for establishing test plans.

Test Cases

Test cases refer to what is actually used for testing. The test plans might require unit through pilot testing, however, the auditors might not ask you to show them the test cases that were used. They will probably not ask to see the cases because the volume can be voluminous and all test cases are usually not retained. However, they might ask you who prepared the test cases and how many were there. Be prepared to answer at least these questions and show them the test plans, if asked.

Test Results

If there are concerns that auditors have with processing errors, they might believe that testing was not adequate and might want to see the results of the actual testing that was conducted. You should have test results to show the auditors. It will not be as voluminous as test cases, which could be boxes, so you should have something to show that indicates what was tested and the results. This might be just a summary of the test results. The important point is that you are able to show them not only that the testing was sufficient and that there were enough test cases, but that the results were reviewed and satisfactory. There should be documentation that indicates both reviews and independent approvals/sign-offs.

Case Study for Testing

You are the manager of the account payable system. You are being audited. The auditor notices that you are running behind schedule in having a new payables system ready for production. It was supposed to go live and promoted into production on April 12th. It is now July 20th and the target date has been moved three times. The latest date for promotion is September 15th. The auditor asks what the reason for the delays are and you tell him that the testing has not been completed. He asks to see the original test plans and target dates and he asks where the problems are. You tell him, right now, in parallel testing. The test results are not in synch with the production run. He then asks what the plans are to correct the problem and deliver the new system. He asks that you show him all the other testing that was done before parallel testing to see if they were approved and on time. Be ready.

Summary

Answering an auditor's questions about testing will require a joint effort by the process owner and IT. Whether the auditors are looking at testing for a new application system or reviewing the testing for a modification to an existing application program, both the process owner and IT will need to join forces to respond to the many questions that could surface. It does not matter if the audit client is IT management or the business process owner, both will play a role. The business process owner will have written specification for a new application system or he or she will have generated a service request (SR) or change request (CR) for a coding change to an existing application program.

The IT department will be conducting unit test with data that they create. If integration testing, system testing, and regression testing follow, they will determine if the subsequent program(s) work with data passed, if the new program(s) works in a system environment or if previous requirements are still being satisfied. This testing will also be done with data that IT created. Parallel testing and pilot testing, if required for large products, will depend on production data as well as test data. User acceptance testing will depend on test data that the business owner generated to assure that all requirements have been tested and not rely strictly on IT test data. It is possible that the business process owner might ask IT for assistance in generating user acceptance test data and it can be a synergistic effort.

Test plans are generated for all of the test scenarios with one exception. The one exception will be for emergency changes where there is little or no time to generate test plans. Auditors might ask to see test plans for all testing other than for emergency changes.

Generally, all test results should be reviewed and approved by the IT organization and the business process owner should approve user acceptance testing, pilot testing, and parallel testing. This might vary within different enterprises. Again, the auditors might ask to review test sign-off requirements found in testing procedural documentation. You should retain evidence of all test results for a period of time, established by your organization. The period of time required for retention of test results should be documented in the testing procedures for your organization.

Guidelines

1. Have your organization' test procedures readily available.
2. Ensure that there is synergy between IT and the business process owner (if not an IT audit) in combining efforts for audit defense. Both organizations should be on board as soon as an audit is announced.
3. Be able to demonstrate the various test scenarios that took place and be able to explain the rationale for the various testing (unit testing through pilot testing) that was selected to be done. This should depend on the size of the effort and risk.
4. Have all test plans, and test results available for review for a period of time designated by your organizations.
5. Be able to demonstrate that there was approval of test results from management (business process owner and or IT management) on all testing.

Chapter 16 Exercises

1. You are the billing process owner and you were responsible for signing off on a new billing system that was promoted three months ago. The new system keeps aborting and billing has been delayed for all three months that the new system has been in production. Revenue was delayed for more than 15 million dollars. The auditor wants to know what testing was done. What do you tell her?
2. You are the payroll manager and the CIO has been paid late the last three months. The internal audit staff has been commissioned to find out why. You tell the auditors, who are quizzing you, that the program terminated unexpectedly for the executive payroll processing for the last 3 months. You tell the auditors that there were emergency changes that were necessary to be made in the middle of the night on these three occasions and they took an

average of 36 hours to restore the system. The coding problems were different on all three occasions. The auditor then asks you what testing was done to prevent these coding errors from occurring. What do you tell him?

Chapter 16 Questions

Please select the best answer to the questions below:

1. Unit testing is done by either the business process owner or IT.

   A. true
   B. false

2. The testing that involves the business process owner doing the testing is referred to as:

   A. Integration testing
   B. System testing
   C. User acceptance testing
   D. Pilot testing

3. Pilot testing is:

   A. testing to see if the program still performs its functions as it did before
   B. testing with a small sample before rolling it out
   C. testing to see if it works in a stream of programs
   D. testing to see if it runs in a production environment

4. Regression testing means:

   A. testing to see if the program works in a production environment
   B. testing to see if the program still performs its functions as it did before
   C. testing to see if the business owner can test the program as well as IT
   D. none of the above

5. Parallel testing is done:

   A. to see if the program can run in a production environment
   B. to see if the program works with a stream of programs

C. to see if the program can run on two test systems at the same time with same results
D. none of the above

6. User acceptance testing requires end users to approve the test results.

A. true
B. false

7. Test results need to be signed off by the business process owner.

A. true
B. false

8. Test plans specifying the types of testing to be performed is decided by:

A. the business process owner
B. IT
C. depending of the type of testing, either by IT or the business process owner
D. Internal Audit

9. Test cases are needed for all changes with the exception of:

A. large projects
B. small enhancements
C. emergencies
D. legal changes

10. When reviewing testing, auditors will presumably ask to see:

A. test plans for all projects, and enhancements/modifications except for emergencies
B. test results, test cases
C. test cases, test plans
D. approvals for all testing before migration to production

PART IV

Mock Audits

For what one has to learn to do, we learn by doing.—Aristotle

You should have acquired enough knowledge after the first three parts to help prepare you to defend against an audit. You should now be familiar with the audit process, educated on controls, and understand what proactive measures you can take in achieving audit readiness. The intent of this part is to re-enforce Aristotle's quote above. I believe that you can learn only so much from reading, being lectured to, and from a textbook. These are good beginnings and a strong foundation but you need to get over the finish line. You cannot afford to stumble and collapse during the event. You cannot afford to fall short. One of the successful approaches to prepare you for an audit is for you to actually conduct an audit. This is what Part IV is all about. You will further your education by actually preparing for and engaging in a mock audit. The result will be that you will limit surprises that you could encounter and prevent unnecessary exposures, resulting in stronger controls and successful audits.

You will be role playing in class and hopefully experiencing what you will be up against during an actual audit. The simulation of audit activities should make you aware of the depth of audit challenges. I agree completely with Aristotle's quote that the best way to learn is by doing.

In addition to being an excellent vehicle for learning, this should be one of the most rewarding, beneficial, and enjoyable segments of this class.

We will start with how you prepare for the mock audit, then discuss roles and expectations during the audit, followed by writing audit reports, and finally presenting the final audit report to executive management.

CHAPTER 17

Preparation for Mock Audits

The class should be split as evenly as possible with half of the students being auditors and the other half of the class being audit clients. You will then switch roles. Your instructor will choose the participants for each group and the processes to be audited. If you were an auditor for one exercise, you should participate as an audit client in the next exercise and vice versa. Everyone should get an opportunity to portray both auditor and audit client.

To effectively play the roles of auditor or audit client and get the most out of this exercise, you need to totally involve yourself in whatever role you are playing at the time. Try to imagine the questions that you will be asked and the answers that you will receive. Anticipation will make you more effective in your role. Think of an audit as a chess game although it is much more serious than a game. The stakes are a lot higher. In a chess game, if you are aware of and can anticipate the moves that your opponent will make, you will be in a much better position to defend against their attack—you just don't want to wing it and hope for the best. The same will be true if and when you are faced with an actual audit.

E. Danter, *Audit Defense*, Palgrave Studies in Accounting and Finance Practice, https://doi.org/10.1007/978-3-030-92466-9_17

Auditor's Preparation (If You Are Assigned to This Role)

The instructor will ask for one of the students to volunteer to be the lead auditor, if there are no volunteers then the instructor can choose a lead auditor. The individual who will be the lead auditor will assign various functions to be audited by the other students role playing as auditors. For example, one auditor can be assigned to look at separation of duties, another could look at application balancing, another could look at completion of processing, another at accuracy of processing, and another at previous audit issues, etc.

During an actual audit, the lead audit will author the announcement letter and send it to the audit client. However, during the mock audit, each student will prepare an announcement letter.

Audit Client's Preparation (If You Are Assigned to This Role)

If you are an audit client, during the mock audit, you will also need to prepare for the audit. You will begin by assuming that you have received an announcement letter informing you that the audit will be commencing shortly. You start by assigning someone to act as the audit interface. This individual during an actual audit will need to (1) look for office space for the auditors, (2) arrange for equipment and supplies that the auditors asked for and might need, (3) retrieve and have any material that will be needed for the kickoff meeting (e.g. org chart), (4) verify who will be needed to participate in the audit and ensure that they are available, and (5) make sure that self-assessments and previous audits are reviewed for any open issues before the auditors arrive and (6) set up a log to keep track of audit requests. The individual who is assigned as the audit interface should fulfill this assignment during this exercise as best that he or she can. They will also be responsible to set up interview meetings, status meetings, etc., that are requested by the auditors. He or she will be the main interface with the lead auditor.

The audit client also needs to assign roles to other members of the audit client's team who will not necessarily be members of his or her staff but who can role play as other department heads who need to be available to answer any audit questions that might impact their organization. These are individuals that the audit client feels can be of assistance during the audit. For example, one individual that the audit client can ask to be in attendance during the audit is the IT manager, another the HR manager, another a member of the legal department, etc. During the mock audit, as audit client manager, you can assign roles as you like.

The pre-planning session will be followed by each auditor undertaking the following activities: (1) writing the announcement letter (each student will fulfill this activity where they are the lead auditor), (2) gathering documentation and preparing for a kickoff meeting with the rest of the audit team, (3) participating in a kickoff meeting, (4) conducting interviews, (5) writing fact sheets or finding sheets, (6) writing a final audit report, and (7) presenting the final audit report to a business executive.

Note: During the mock audits, neither will the auditors nor audit client prepare for or participate in simulated status meetings.

Summary

When preparing for the mock audits students who are playing the role of auditor manager will assign a lead auditor who will be the main interface with the audit client. In an actual audit the audit manager, lead auditor, and the other auditors decide on what process to audit based on the internal audit department's procedure for selecting the next audit or on a business need that the executives decide on. The internal audit process may require that every process be audited at least every five years, provided that IA has the audit resources. The business need that dictates the next audit may be based on audits that have had evidence of fraud or have a high risk of possible fraud, critical or financial processes or repeating an audit for a process that has recently failed with significant exposures.

For the mock audit, the professor will decide on the process to be audited. The individual, who was selected to be the lead auditor, will assign functions that the other auditors will review. For example, he or she might assign various auditors to look at access security, separation of duties, accuracy of processing, completeness of processing, etc.

The student who is the audit client manager will also select other students to fulfill other roles during the mock audit. These students can be members of his or her staff responsible for different tasks or role-play as managers or staff of other supporting departments who are supporting the audit client.

Each auditor will participate in audit functions from writing the announcement letter, to interviewing the audit clients, to writing and presenting a final audit report to an executive.

Guidelines for the Mock Audit Preparation

1. Instructors will split all of the students into two groups for the first audit. One group will portray the role of auditor and the other group, the audit client. They will then switch roles where they will participate in a second audit.
2. Audit managers will assign a lead auditor.
3. The instructors will decide on what processes to audit for the mock audit exercises.
4. The lead auditor will decide on the functions that each auditor will review during the audit.
5. The audit client will choose an audit interface who will manage the mock audit and be the main interface to the auditors.

CHAPTER 18

Mock Audit Fieldwork

Writing Announcement Letters[1]

Students who are role playing as auditors will assume that they are all lead auditors and will compose announcement letters. They should use the samples of the announcement letters below to write their own announcement letters. (Please insert your own words in place of the italicized words you see). There is an example of a formal letter and the other is an interoffice memo. The announcement letter from internal audit can use either method. Students can get ideas from each of the letters and, if they wish, combine the elements from each of the letters into their own letter (Exhibit 18.1).

[1] Adapted from the ninth edition "Auditing & Assurance Services A Systematic Approach" (pages 73–75) by William Messier, Steven Glover, and Douglass Prawitt.

E. Danter, *Audit Defense*, Palgrave Studies in Accounting and Finance Practice, https://doi.org/10.1007/978-3-030-92466-9_18

Exhibit 18.1 Example I (Financial statement audit)

(Date)

(Name, Title)
(Street Address)
(City, Postal Code)

Dear (*Audit Client name*):

The internal audit team is planning its audit of (*Audit Process*). The objectives of this audit will be to review:

- Reliability and integrity of Financial and Operational Information.
- Compliance with laws, regulations, and contracts.
- Safeguarding of assets.
- Effectiveness and efficiency of operations.
- Following up on recommendations in prior audit reports.

The proposed timetable for this audit is as follows:

Start Date in the field (xx-xx-xx).
Estimated weeks to complete (*Number of weeks*).

The audit team will include the following members:

(*Name*)—Lead Auditor.
(*Name*)—Staff Auditor.
(*Name*)—Staff Auditor.

At the beginning of our audit, we would like the opportunity to meet with you to discuss our audit objectives and solicit your input. Our goal is to perform an effective and efficient audit. We will need your staff to provide us with the following documents and schedules before the audit commences:

- All applicable federal and state laws, regulations, and guidelines.
- Any company memorandums or directives.
- Current organization chart.
- Applicable budget goals and objectives.
- Financial statements for the audit period.
- A copy of the previous audit for the (*Audit process*).

Before the audit team leaves the client site at the end of the fieldwork phase, a meeting will be held with you to discuss preliminary findings raised, any outstanding information and the next steps in the audit. The draft audit report will be completed by the audit staff and reviewed with the audit manager. You will then be presented with the draft audit report. Once you approve the draft, the report will be finalized and presented in a final audit meeting to the CFO for sign-off. You will be expected to provide a response all recommendations in the final report within two weeks.

Our mission is to help you achieve your department's objective by providing you with information about the effectiveness of internal control and recommending courses of actions, which improve performance.

If you have any questions about this year's audit, please do not hesitate to call me at xxx-xxx-xxxx or email me at xxxxxxxxxx.

Sincerely
(*name of lead auditor*).
cc: (*name of audit manager*)—Audit manager
cc: (*name of CFO*)—CFO

Exhibit 18.2 Example II (another financial statement audit)
INTERNAL AUDIT OFFICE

Memorandum

To: (*Name of Audit Client*)

From: (*Name of Lead Auditor*) —Lead internal auditor
Subject: Audit of (*insert process*)

Internal Audit will be performing an audit of (process name), which is scheduled to begin on (date). We tentatively plan to complete our fieldwork by (date), our audit scope will cover the period (date) to (date), and may be changed after the survey is completed. The general objectives of this audit will be to evaluate compliance with organization policies and procedures; laws, regulations, and guidelines. We will also evaluate internal controls. This audit will focus on applicable financial and performance issues (Exhibit 18.2).

The scope of the audit will be the examination of: occurrence, to determine if all recorded transactions and events have occurred and pertain to the entity; completeness, to see whether all transactions and events that occurred during the period have been recorded; authorization, to determine if all transactions have been properly authorized; accuracy, to validate whether amounts and other data relating to recorded transactions and events have been recorded appropriately; cutoff periods, to determine if transactions and events have been recorded in the correct accounting period; and classification, to determine whether transactions and events have been recorded in the proper accounts. The audit will also examine and verify that there are adequate separation of duties controls within the (name of process).

The purpose of this audit is to review and evaluate:

- Reliability and integrity of Financial and Operational Information.
- Compliance with laws, regulations, and contracts with any internal or external organizations.
- Safeguarding of assets.
- Effectiveness and efficiency of operations.
- Following up on recommendations included in prior audit reports.

To assist us with this audit, we would like to obtain some documentation prior to the start of fieldwork. Please provide the following documentation:

- All applicable federal or state laws, regulations, and guidelines.
- Any company policy memorandums or directives.
- A copy of your operating procedures manual.
- Current organization chart.
- Applicable budget goals and objections.
- Financial statements for the audit period.

Please feel free to designate a key member of your staff whom the auditors may contact when requesting data. In addition, please arrange workspaces for the auditors.

The audit team will include the following members:

(*name*)—Lead auditor.
(*name)*—Staff auditor.
(*name*)—Staff auditor.
(*name*)—Staff auditor.

Please do not hesitate to call me at xxx-xxx-xxx or email me at xxxxxxxxxx, if you have any questions.

Sincerely.
(*name of lead auditor*)
cc: (*name of audit manager*)—audit manager
cc: (*name of CFO*)—CFO

Exhibit 18.3 Example III (information systems audit)

To: (*Audit client name*) (Date)
From: (*Lead auditor name*)

Subject: Audit of (*name of system (e.g. billing system)*)

Internal audit is planning an audit of the (*name of system*) covering the period from September 1, 2019 to March 1, 2020 (Exhibit 18.3).

Scope: The functions that we will be auditing are project management; accuracy, completeness, and timeliness of processing; risk and issues management; library control; access management; database reconciliation; change management; testing; customer satisfaction; requirements; balancing; documentation; separation of duties; and error processing. If necessary, the scope will be expanded if other issues surface during the audit.

The objectives of this audit are to determine if there are any control exposures that might infringe on the (*name of system*) processing timely, thoroughly, and accurately; effective project management to ensure that the system was developed within budget; that the system is meeting design requirements; and that the (*name of system*) is satisfying both customer and end user expectations.

The audit will start on November 15, 2020, and is targeted to be completed on December 15, 2020.

The audit team will consist of:

(*name of lead auditor*)—lead auditor
(*name of staff auditor*)—staff auditor
(*name of staff auditor*)—staff auditor
(*name of staff auditor*)—staff auditor
(*name of staff auditor*)—staff auditor.

Prior to our arriving to commence the audit on November 15, please prepare the following documentation: organization chart, mission of department, functions of individuals within the department, any procedure documentation and a copy of the last audit.

Please assign one of your staff members as an audit interface that we can coordinate our requests and responses with.

Please contact me on xxx-xxx-xxxx or email me at xxxxxxx, if you have any questions or concerns pertaining to this audit.

Sincerely,
(*lead auditor's name*)
cc: (*audit manager's name*)—Audit manager
cc: (*IT director's name*)—IT director

After each student writes an announcement letter as lead auditor, they will present the letter to the audit client.

Kickoff Meeting

Both audit and audit client teams will prepare for kickoff meetings. They should bring the following material to the meetings and present the following to those present:

Lead Auditor and other auditors working as a team:

- A brief overview of the audit organization.
- The names of the auditors participating in the audit.
- The name of the lead auditor (introducing himself or herself).

- The mission of the audit staff.
- The audit reporting structure.
- Protocol of the audit (what is expected as far as proper decorum). For example, all issues that are raised should be brought to the attention of the lead auditor with any escalation of issues being addressed by the audit manager or the audit client's manager.
- The audit process—beginning with the announcement letter, followed by interviews after the kickoff meeting, requests for documentation or meetings made to an audit interface, findings or fact sheets written and reviewed, draft report written and reviewed, final meeting with executives, sign-off and distribution.
- Status meeting schedule—this is proposed by the lead auditor and needs to agreed to by the audit client.
- Expectations of turnaround on requests.
- Audit report distribution.

Audit Client and his or her team:

- A high level view of the organization's mission.
- Key functions of the department.
- The audit client's organization.
- Name of audit interface.
- Any material or documentation previously requested in the announcement letter or later that is available.

Conducting Interviews

This is an important phase of the mock audit and should be very educational. Its intent is to prepare you for an actual audit interview where many, many questions will be asked and the answers are extremely important. By looking at and examining the procedures and control documentation prior to, during, or after the interviews and the interview itself, the auditor will have formulated his or her concerns. It is from the basis of these concerns that the auditors should be writing fact or findings sheets, reviewing their concerns and issues with the audit client and their staffs, ironing out all differences, making enhancements to the fact sheets, if needed, and then using the fact sheets to produce a draft and then a final audit report. You can then understand the importance of these interviews. Again there are do's and don'ts that should be adhered to when being interviewed. I will be redundant because of their significance and repeat them here as many were previously addressed.

Auditors will most likely conduct numerous interviews at any time. The audit's success or failure will rely heavily on the interview process, the importance of which needs to be understood. As a rule, auditors should only be given what they ask for. Too much information can get you into trouble. On the other hand, if you have information that was not asked for, that could turn perspectives around and could possibly be of help, you should bring that forward. Be careful—this is a slippery slope. Only offer information that was not asked for if it could help. What is meant by that is if you never established a specific control that could mitigate an exposure that the auditor believes exists but there is an auxiliary or secondary control that accomplished the same task, then share that control with the auditor. For example, during an interview the auditor might ask you if you have documented evidence that shows that you review issues in the issues log. Wrong answer would be if you say "No, but I don't think that it was ever done before." The auditor never asked if was done before so you gave him more information—end result was that it magnified his concern. However, you could answer "No, I have no documented evidence but executive management reviews the issues log every quarter and there are documented minutes covering a discussion of reviewing the issues log." This was not asked by the auditor but mitigates the risk. Be careful. You need to be assured that you have documented minutes from a meeting where the issues log was discussed, as this will probably be the next audit request.

Now let's focus on the mock audit and role playing. The student, playing the part of auditor, in the mock audit should concentrate on:

- asking questions pertaining to the documented procedures (pretending that he or she looked at them).
- pretending to match the documented procedures to the procedures that you are told by the audit client individual interviewed, that they follow, looking for discrepancies.

- inquiring about control points, asking how the processes are controlled.
- asking questions pertaining to separation of duties.

Examples of auditor's interview questions are:

- How long have you worked in this position?
- How did you learn to complete the process?
- How many other people execute the same functions?
- Can you explain the procedure that you follow?
- Is the procedure documented?
- Has the job changed over the last year?
- What controls are in place?
- How do you or your manager make sure that the controls are executed?
- Do you have evidence?
- Is there separation of duties?
- What metrics are there?
- What issues have you noticed?
- How would you improve the process?

Now let's look at the audit client and what is expected of them during the mock audit. The student, role playing as manager or staff person, being interviewed can take liberties in deviating from what he or she should say to the auditor and have some fun. Normally, during an actual audit, the audit client should:

- never lie to the auditor
- if they don't know the answer to a question say that they do not know and will get back to the auditor after more research
- talk to the facts only and not give an opinion.

However, during the mock audit exercise, the individual being interviewed can choose to, and should at times, make up answers that violate the above. In other words, make up answers that avoid the questions, make no sense or blame others. This happens in actual interviews so it would be of interest to simulate how the auditor would respond. Have some fun. The other option that the individual has who is being interviewed is to respond back with an answer that makes sense. You can use the material and information on controls that you learned during the class. You were educated and hopefully gained knowledge—you can use it.

You can and should be honest at times and fabricate your answers at other times. It is your choice on how to answer the auditor's questions. This should give the auditor, during the exercise a feeling that you have a well controlled environment or that you have numerous control issues, which will cause the auditor to have little faith in what you tell them.

When the two groups split into auditors and audit clients, the auditors will conduct the interviews utilizing the following questionnaire format that they have prepared before class (Exhibit 18.4).

Exhibit 18.4 Interview question format

Auditor's name ________________________________

Process Being Audited ________________________________
(e.g. project management, requirements, disbursing payments)

Audit Question	Answer

Your professor will decide on how many questions that you will need to ask. The procedure that you should follow as an auditor is to come to class with your questionnaire that will contain the specific number of original questions that you are told to use. For example, this can be 10, 15, or 20 original questions (for our purpose in this textbook, there will be 10 original questions) for the functions that you have been assigned to audit. Based on the answers that you receive in class from the audit client, you will add follow-up questions. To each question that you have, you should add a specific number of follow-up questions. For example, if you have 10 original questions that are numbered 1a, 2a, 3a, etc. You might be asked by your professor to add 4 follow-up questions to each of your original question so your total will be 50 questions. In the questionnaires that follow you should see that the answer to question 1a will lead to question 1b, the answer to question to 1b will lead to question 1c, the answer to question to 1c will lead to the next question, which is 1d, and so on. The same will be true of the next set of questions where the answer to 2a will lead to the question for 2b and the answer to question 2b will lead to question 3a, etc. As stated above, your professor might ask you to add 4 additional follow-up questions to each of the originals or it could be 3 or 5 or whatever is decided.

Let's look at examples of questionnaires that should clarify what needs to be done and how to accomplish the objective. For the purposes of this exercise and for you to get the most benefit, you will see that there will be two sets of answers to basically the same questionnaire. Answers to the questions will be generated by the students (the audit clients). As stated earlier, the answers do not have to be accurate or positive, in all cases, and can be negatively or nonsensically answered. It is interesting to see how those in the auditor's role digest and follow-up depending on what answers they get. What you should realize is that based on the answers that are given by the client, the auditors will reach different conclusions and the flavor of the audit report can turn 180 degrees in a different direction, resulting from different answers to the questions. This could effect the outcome of the final audit report being satisfactory or unsatisfactory or unqualified versus adverse.

Let's take a closer look at an example of questionnaires used during the exercise. The questions and answers are filled in to demonstrate how the answers that are received should lead to the next question. The original questions are highlighted (Exhibits 18.5 and 18.6).

Exhibit 18.5 Example one—auditing the accounts receivable process (version 1)

Name – Name of auditor`
Process Being Audited – Accounts Receivable

Audit Question	Answer
1a. **Do you have documentation of the Accounts Receivable process?**	Yes
1b. Does the documentation include a description of the controls?	No
1c. Why not?	We have been performing A/R functions for 5 years and know what the controls are. They don't have to be documented.
1d. Can you explain to me then what the controls are?	No I can't. As the A/R manager I rely on Diane, as my lead staff person, to reply to control questions.
1e. Can I ask Diane some questions about the controls?	I am afraid not, she has been out on maternity leave for the last month.
1f. That is interesting. With Diane out for a month, who is her backup?	I am afraid that there is no -one.
1g. Why not?	We have been very busy and did not have the time.
2a. **In looking at your documented process I noticed that here are aged unbilled records that appear on an aged report. Is that right?**	I believe so. Diane works that report and no one else has worked it.
2b. Well, in her absence does that mean there is no one working the unbilled A/R report?	Yes, that's right. It will have to wait for her to return.
2c. If you had control documentation, could it be possible for someone to work the A/R aged report so revenue would not be delayed?	I suppose so.
3a. **Who does the write-offs for customers who are not paying their invoices?**	Mat Wright is responsible for the write-offs.
3b. Who approves the write-offs?	Our treasurer approves them.
3c. Can I see the write -offs for the last three months?	No, we only keep them for 1 month
3d. When can I see the write-offs for the last month that you have?	I can show them to you right after this interview.
3e. (After looking at the write-offs) When I looked at the write-offs, I noticed that half of them were not approved by the treasurer but by Matt. Why, and don't you think this is a separation of duties concern?	Not sure why Matt signed. I think the treasurer was o n vacation. I guess it could be a SoD problem but we never thought about it.

(continued)

Exhibit 18.5 (continued)

4a. **Do you have an open order report for customer orders that have not been competed?**	Yes we do.
4b. Can I see the latest copy?	Sure
4c. In looking at the shipping report and comparing it to the open order report, I see shipments that were not billed. They are still on the open order report, why?	I am not sure, we review this report annually.
4d. So the open order report is not compared to a shipment report except on an annul basis?	That's right.
4e. Don't you think there is an exposure to fraud?	Very little. in the last 10 years, we have just a few instances of fraud.
5a. **Is your credit function separate from your billing function**?	No
5b. Why not?	We are saving expense on hiring additional personnel whom we feel aren't needed.
5c. Have you conducted a risk assessment to assess the degree of risk and look for cost effective solutions to mitigate any possible risk?	Yes we have.
5d. Can I see the risk assessment?	Nothingwas documented. It was verbal.
5e. Then how do I know if the risk was approved and who approved it?	You have to trust me in telling you the truth
6a. **Can you tell me who is responsible for cash receipts** ?	Seth Brooks
6b. Can I speak to Seth?	Sure, we wi ll set up an interview
6c. (Meeting with Seth). Hello Seth, can you tell me if you have responsibility for cash receipts?	I do have responsibility.
6d. What other functions do you have responsibility for?	I also have responsibility for the accounts rec eivable function.
6e. (meeting again with manager) – Don't you think that you have a SoD problem with Seth being able to divert cash and him being able to cover up the shortage of cash in the accounts receivable records?	We have never had an instance of fraud over the last 5 years since I have been a manager and Seth has had both functions
7a. **Do you have a procedure to check a customer's credit history?**	Yes
7b. Is the procedure documented?	Yes

(continued)

Exhibit 18.5 (continued)

7c. Can I see a copy of the procedure and customer approval forms for the last 3 months for new customers?	The person who has that documentation is Lynn and she has been in the hospital for 2 weeks.
7d. Does she have a backup?	Not really. She did, but the individual was fired last month for fraud and we have not yet replaced him.
7e. So who is now approving credit for new customers?	I guess no -one
8a. **I noticed that revenue transactions are not properly classified. Do you have a chart of accounts?**	Yes
8b. Can I see it?	Yes
8c. So what do you think the reason is for improper classification?	Must be an application problem in IT since they do the processing. It is their problem.
8d. Do you know if the IT department did enough testing?	I have no idea.
8e. Do you have a SLA with them that defines testin g responsibilities?	I don't know what is in the SLA.
9a. **What control do you have to ensure that if revenue is recorded that goods have been shipped?**	There are monthly customer statements and there would be complaints.
9b. Have there been complaints?	A few
9c. How many is a few in the last 6 months?	Eight, I think
9d. Can you check and show them to me this afternoon?	I can check but they are offsite and it will take 24 hours
9e. Do you have evidence that the complaints have been reviewed?	Good quest ion – I will check
10a. **What control do you have to see if revenue transactions are recorded at the right dollar amount?**	Each sales invoice is checked to see if it agrees with shipping document and customer order for product type and quantity
10b. Can you show me that the accuracy was checked this month?	Absolutely, but the volume is high so I will show you ten that I selected.
10c. I would like to select and sample ten invoices myself, rather than you selecting them for me, and you can show me the ship ping document and customer orders OK?	We will see what we can do
10d. Have you had any discrepancies in your checking?	No
10e. For how long a period of time?	We have only been checking accuracy for the last four months

Exhibit 18.6 Example two—auditing the accounts receivable process (version 2)

Name – name of auditor
Process being audited – Accounts Receivable

Audit Question	Answer
1a. **Do you have documentation of the Accounts Receivable process?**	Yes
1b. Does it include a description of the controls?	Yes
1c. Can I get a copy of the process documentation to review?	Yes, we can get it to you by tomorrow.
1d. Can you explain to me then what the controls are in the meantime?	We have separation of duties, chart of accounts, frequent verification of reports, follow-up on aged A/R, credit authorizations reviews, etc.
1e. Can I see evidence that the controls are being worked?	Yes, but can you be more specific in what you want to see?
2a. **Do you have backup for personnel who are executing the controls and reviewing their effectiveness?**	We have backup for all of our staff.
2b. Can I see a list of your staff personnel and their backups?	I can get that for you this afternoon.
2c. Have all your personnel who review controls and their backups been trained?	Yes
2d. By whom and when?	Either myself or my lead staff person trains them at least annually or sooner, if needed
2e. What documentation to show me that they have been trained?	We have emails going back and forth.
3a. **Who does the write-offs for customers who are not paying their invoices?**	Mat Wright
3b. Who approves the write-offs?	Our treasurer
3c. Can I see the write-offs for the last three months?	There were just four but you can see them
3d. When can I see the four that you have?	By tomorrow
3e. (After looking at the write-offs) When I looked at the write-offs, I noticed that half of them were not approved by the treasurer. Can you tell me why not?	I think the treasurer was on vacation. The signature you see should be the assistant treasurer.

(continued)

Exhibit 18.6 (continued)

4a. **Do you have an open order report for customer orders that have not been competed?**	Yes
4b. Can I see the latest copy?	Sure
4c. In looking at the shipping report and comparing it to the open order report, I see shipments that were not billed. They are still on the open order report, why?	I am not sure, we review this report every two weeks
4d. Can you show me evidence of the last three times that it was reviewed?	Sure, when do want to see them?
4e. Tomorrow?	You will have them
5a. **Is your credit function sepa rate from your billing function?**	Yes, we have a SoD matrix that describes the functions of all my staff.
5b. Can I see it?	Yes
5c. (After reviewing the SoD matrix) I noticed that there are two names here of people who are not on your organization chart , how come?	These individuals left the department last month and we need to update the matrix
5d. How often is the matrix reviewed and updated?	It is reviewed quarterly and updated at that time, if necessary
5e. So these people would have been on the matrix with functions they no longer support until next month?	Actually, they would have been removed next month at the end of the quarter. However, we will change the matrix now. I can also show you evidence of the last review and last update if you want.
6a. **Can you tell me who is responsible for cash receipts?**	Seth Brooks
6b. Can I speak to Seth?	Sure, we will set up an interview
6c. (meeting with Seth). Hello Seth, can you tell me if you have responsibility for cash receipts?	I do
6d. What other functions do you have responsibility for?	I also have responsibility for the accounts receivable function. I am the backup but not the primary person responsible for A/R
6e. (meeting again with manager) – Don't you think that you have a SoD problem here wi th Seth being able to divert cash and he can cover up the shortage of cash in the accounts receivable records, even though he is just the backup?	We have never had an instance of fraud over the last 5 years since I have been a manager. We understand the risk however. We are short handed but we completed a risk assessment and conduct a manual review of all Seth's A/R transactions

(continued)

Exhibit 18.6 (continued)

7a. **Do you have a procedure to check a customer's credit history?**	Yes
7b. Is the procedure documented?	It is almost completed, we have been working on it for 2 months
7c. Can I see a copy of the procedure as it looks right now and customer approval forms for the last 3 months for new customers?	The person who has that documentation is Lynn and she has been in the hospital for 2 weeks
7d. Does she have a backup?	Yes, she does. Ariel is her backup.
7e. So if Ariel is now approving credit for new customers can I see copies of approval for the last three months?	Yes
8a. **I noticed that revenue transactions are not properly classified. Do you have a chart of accounts?**	Yes
8b. Can I see it?	Yes
8c. So what do you think the reason is for improper classification?	It could be an application problem in IT since they do the processing.
8d. Do you know if the IT department did enough testing? Were you involved?	I am hoping they did but apparently something fell through the cracks. We get involved in user acceptance testing but did not see this problem surface
8e. Do you have a SLA with IT that defines testing responsibilities?	I believe testing responsibilities are in the SLA, but I will check
9a. **What control do you have to ensure that if revenue is recorded that goods have been shipped?**	There are monthly customer statements and there would be complaints
9b. Have there been complaints?	A few
9c. How many is a few in the last 6 months?	Three, I believe
9d. Can you check and show them to me this afternoon?	I can check but they are offsite and it will take 24 hours
9e. Do you have evidence that the complaints have been reviewed?	Good question – I will check
10a. **What control do you have to see if revenue transactions are recorded at the right dollar amount?**	Each sales invoice is checked to see if it agrees with shipping document and customer order for product type and quantity
10b. Can you show me that the accuracy was checked this month?	Absolutely, but the volume is high so I will show you ten that I select

(continued)

Exhibit 18.6 (continued)

10c. I would like to sample 10 invoices myself and you can show me the shipping document and customer orders OK?	We will see what we can do
10d. Have you had any discrepancies in your checking?	Yes, just one, but it was corrected
10e. Do you know why and can you show me evidence that the problem was resolved?	It was a program coding error but I believe that it was fixed. I can show you evidence that it was corrected.

As you can see from these two interviews that the auditor keeps asking question after question based on the responses that she received. This is what you should be doing during the mock audit.

You will notice how important the answers are as the auditor will draw different conclusions after each example. The results of the first interview could lead to significant issues and an adverse report. Let's take a closer look to see what issues or exposures that the auditor could have observed and then look at the second interview. Hopefully, you can see how important it is to be prepared for the auditor's questions and in answering them to the best of your ability.

First A/R Interview

- The auditor will have an issue with the answer to question 1b where there is no documentation describing the controls.
- The answer in 1c that they know what the controls are without documentation won't be sufficient. What if key personnel leave the department or get sick?
- Question 2a asks for backup and there is none.
- Answer in 2b is unacceptable that there was no time.
- Answer to question 2d indicates that there is no one working unbilled A/R report—another problem.

- Question 3e and answer indicate a SoD problem. Also the manager should know why Matt signed and if the treasurer was on vacation. Couldn't someone else have signed?
- The answer to 4c is not a good answer. The manager should not have said that the open order report was reviewed annually. He was not asked. Don't volunteer information that could open up more concerns.
- Answer to 5a is a SoD problem with credit function not being separated from billing function.
- Answer to 5d is also a problem. Risk assessment was verbal and there is no documentation to see if it was done or approved.
- Answer to 6e indicates another possible SoD problem with Seth having cash receipts and responsibility for A/R functions.
- Answer 7e is another problem where no one is currently approving credit for new customers.
- Answer to 8c is a big mistake. The manager is blaming IT for improper classification when he should have said he did not know and will check.
- And the answer in 8d where the manager says that he does not know if IT did enough testing could lead to an issue. Is he throwing them under the bus? The A/R manager is accountable to know what testing IT did. IT, in this case, is a service organization and their responsibilities should be detailed in a SLA that the A/R manager should be familiar with. The A/R manager is accountable.
- The answer to 10e could have been "no discrepancies for as long as we have been checking" and then let the auditor ask for how long have they been checking.

Too many issues and exposures revealed in the first interview that will probably end up in final report—it should read like an adverse audit report.

The audit client is much more prepared in the second interview.

Second A/R Interview

- The response to question 1e is interesting. Here, the audit client wants the auditor to be more specific in what the auditor wants to see. This is a good answer as it could avoid confusion.
- The A/R manager's answer in 4c to the discrepancies when the shipping report was compared to the open order report should have been expanded to say that he will check and get back to the auditor.
- Minor issue in SoD matrix (answer to 5c) with regard to people still being on the matrix who should have been removed. This appears to be a timing problem with the update.
- The answer in 6e is good where there is a known risk. Manager indicated a risk assessment with secondary manual control. Here volunteering additional information was a good thing.
- Answer to 8e is also good where A/R manager is not sure what is in the SLA with IT as far as testing responsibilities but indicates that he will check rather than blaming IT.

We can see that this interview went a lot better than the first interview with the audit client being better prepared. The results of this audit will probably be qualified or even unqualified with only minor issues.

Now let's look at an interview being done with the IT manager being the audit client and an interview being conducted on a billing system (Exhibits 18.7 and 18.8).

Exhibit 18.7 Example three—audit of the billing system (version 1)

Name – name of auditor
Process being audited – Billing

Audit Question	Answer
1a. When did the new billing system become operational?	Six weeks ago
1b. Is the system having any problems?	Yes
1c. What kind of problems?	System aborts on the average once a week - application programs or data needs to be fixed
1d. What is the reason?	Looks like testing wasn't sufficient to catch many coding problems or invalid data coming into the system
2a. **What testing was done and where were the problems?**	We started with unit test then did integration system and parallel testing.
2b. Do you have test plans?	A few
2c. Why just a few? What is retention requirement?	We have no retention requirement for test plans .
2d. Do you have any testing procedures?	Some that indicate what testing is planned but that is all.
2e. Do you retain any test cases or test results available for review?	Test cases are too voluminous but we have test results with some approvals
2f. Can you show me the test cases for the last month of unit testing before the system went live?	I suppose so.
3a. **Do you have customer sat issues with the billing system?**	There are no customer sat issues that I know of
3b. How would you know?	I guess they would tell us.
3c. Do you have customer sat surveys?	Yes, but we stopped them two weeks ago.
3d. Why did you stop them?	There were too many problems.
3e. What were problems other than program aborting?	A number of times billing was not accurate, not all requirements were met, and bad data was entered from order entry and could not be billed.
4a. **Did you deliver the new system on time?**	No
4b. How late were you?	Six months
4c. Why were you so late?	There were a number of reasons.

(continued)

Exhibit 18.7 (continued)

4d. What were they?	Requirements kept changing, we understated the work involve, we lost three good programmers, and we had trouble with project management .
4e. What do you think was your biggest problem causing you to be so late?	It was probably poor project management .
5a. **Who was your project manager?**	Kara Jennings
5b. Can you set up an interview with Kara?	We fired her last week .
5c. Who did you replace her with?	Ari Hemhurst
5d. How much experience does Ari have in project management?	This is his first project management assignment .
5e. How much education in project management does he have?	I have no idea .
6a. **Was the billing system delivered over or under budget?**	Way over
6b. How much over budget are we talking about?	Five million dollars
6c. Why so much?	Coding and testing took a lot longer than estimated and we had to hire four additional programmers .
6d. Did you get additional funding without much difficulty?	At first yes, but then it was very difficult
6e. Why were the executives resistant to keep increasing your funds?	They said that they were losing faith in our ability to deliver and wanted to bring in a new staff rather than pouring more money into the project.
7a. **Do you have the new system fully documented?**	No
7b. Why not?	We kept pushing to meet our targeted schedule delivery date and could not take time to fully document.
7c. Do you have controls included in your documented procedures?	No
7d. Why not?	We were g oing to put controls in later in order to meet our delivery schedule .
7e. Do you have adequate controls in the system now even though they are not documented?	We are still working on them and spending most of our time trying to fix the program problems.
8a. **Are there good dat a edits in the system?**	Yes
8b. How do you now that?	A lot of data coming into the system is kicked out as errors because of our edits for validity and reasonableness .

(continued)

Exhibit 18.7 (continued)

8c. Are editing errors that are rejected promptly corrected and entered back into the system?	Not always
8d. Why not?	Our correction procedures are not documented so sometimes no-one knows how to fix the errors and resubmit
8e. How much revenue is being delayed because or billing editing errors not being resubmitted?	Not sure of the exact dollar amount since we don't track it but I would say tens of thousands of dollars.
9a. **Do you have a business continuity plan documented in case of a disaster?**	Yes
9b. Can I see it?	Sure, by tomorrow
9c. Who was involved in putting the plan together?	My department, IT and end –users
9d. Was it ever tested?	Yes it was originally
9e. Was the test successful and can I see the results?	The test was successful but we never documented the results .
10a. **With all your necessary coding changes, do yo u have a documented ch ange management procedure? And if yes, can I see it?**	Yes we do and I get it to you in about an hour.
10b. (after looking at change management procedure) I noticed that business process owner approval is necessary before changes are made, did you get approvals?	No, these were emergencies and there was no time as most of the program aborts took place in the middle of the night.
10c. Then according to your procedure you are suppose to get post approval the next day? Can I see those for the last month?	Sorry. We did not get post approvals because the volume is so high
10d. So programmers are migrating code changes directly into the production library without approvals and not using the test libraries?	That's correct
10e. This appears to be a SoD exposure, do you have you a documented risk assessment and acceptance?	There is no documented risk assessment but we orally accepted the risk. We do not have a risk management process.

Exhibit 18.8 Example four—audit of the billing system (version 2)

Name – name of auditor
Process being audited – Billing

1a. **When did the new billing system become operational?**	Six weeks ago
1b. Is the system having any problems?	Yes, a few
1c. What kind of problems?	Requirements changed and we had to change the program, the program needed to be changed to enhance edits
1d. What were the reasons?	Requirement to include state tax for Florida billings was wrong and had to be replaced. And there was an incident of erroneous data coming in from order entry system that was not edited and should have been .
1e. What testing was done and where were the problems?	We started with unit test then did integration system and parallel testing. Our tests did not work ok because of coding problems. These problems were unexpected.
2a. Do you have test plans?	Yes
2b. Can I see them?	Of course. I will show you our test plans tomorrow.
2c. Do you retain any test cases and are test results available for review?	Test cases are too voluminous to retain them all but we have test results.
2d. Can you show me the test cases and approvals for the last month of unit testing before the system went live?	Sure
2e. (after reviewing test results and approvals) I noticed that the results for two test cases were not approved. Why not?	I am not sure, I wil need to get back to you after I check with my staff
3a. **Do you have customer sat issues with the billing system?**	We have no issues that I know of
3b. How would you know?	We conducted customer sat surveys .
3c. How often were they conducted?	We conducted the surveys every two weeks after we went live .
3d. Do you usually conduct them so regularly?	No, only for new systems. Otherwise we conduct them quarterly .

(continued)

Exhibit 18.8 (continued)

3e.Can I get copies of the surveys?	I will need to check with the customer.
4a. **Did you deliver the new system on time?**	No
4b. How late were you?	Three weeks
4c. Why were you late?	Lead programmer had to be replaced because he got COVID virus .
4d. What did you do?	We brought in a replacement and had to bring the new programmer up to-date with requirements and pro ject schedule .
4e. Where you satisfied with the performance of the new programmer?	Yes, he was very good
5a. **Who was your project manager?**	Kara Jennings
5b. Can you set up an interview with Kara?	Yes, just let us know when would you like to interview her
5c. How much experience does Kara have?	This is her third system where she has been a project manager. Before that she was programming for us for five years.
5d. Were her other systems delivered on time, within budget and did she meet requirements?	They were delivered on time, within budget and met requirements, except one of the systems. It was over budget by $300,000
5e. Why was it over budget?	I believe they had to hire three additional programmers since they underestimated the work needed.
6a. **Was your billing system delivered over or under budget?**	It was a little over budget.
6b. How much over budget are we talking about?	One hundred thousand dollars
6c. Why?	We had to spend additional money to replace project manager who got COVID 19.
6d. Did you get additional funding without much difficulty?	Yes
6e. What are your maintenance expenses?	Very little – one programmer is handling all maintenance activity
7a. **Do you have the new system fully documented?**	Yes
7b. What does your documentation consist of?	Process flow charts and narratives

(continued)

Exhibit 18.8 (continued)

7c. Do you have controls included in your documented procedures?	Yes, we have control points and control descriptions.
7d. Can you share the system documentation with me including controls?	Yes
7e. What are your controls to ensure that only authorized personnel are accessing production libraries and data?	We have adequate separation of duties where business process authorization is needed for programmers to access production libraries and production databases.
8a **Are there good data edits in the system?**	Yes
8b. How do you now that?	A lot of data coming into the system is kicked out as errors because of our edits for validity and reasonableness.
8c. Are editing errors that are rejected promptly cor rected and entered back into the system?	Not always.
8d. Why not?	Our correction procedures are documented but we are still educating our staff on how to and when to resubmit and track corrections.
8e. Is revenue being delayed because billing is not timely for rejected errors?	Probably, but I am not sure how much. I will need to get back to you.
9a. **Do you have a business continuity plan documented in case of a disaster?**	Yes
9b. Can I see it?	Sure, by tomorrow.
9c. Who was involved in putting the plan together?	My department, IT and end–users.
9d. Was it ever tested?	Yes
9e. Was the test successful and can I see the results?	The test was successful and I can show you documentation of test and results by tomorrow.
10a. **Do you have a documented change management procedure? And if yes, can I see it?**	Yes we do and I get it to you in about an hour.
10b. (after looking at the change management procedure) I noticed that business process owner approval is necessary before changes are made, do you al ways get pre-approval?	Yes , except for emergencies. There is no time for pre -approvals as most of the programs abort that emergencies address take place in the middle of the night.

(continued)

Exhibit 18.8 (continued)

10c. Then according to your procedure you are suppose to get post approvals the next day? Can I see those post approvals for the last month?	There were only two. We have one but the other one was not post approved.
10d. Why not?	The manager who was in charge left the company the next day and we never got her approval.
10e. Then do have the approval from an authorized backup for her or if not from her then her manager?	I am afraid not.

As we saw before with the A/R interviews, the auditors ask a lot of questions and you need to be prepared. And again, the wrong answers can lead to trouble. In the IT interviews, the first example of an interview will probably result in an unsatisfactory audit and the second, in a satisfactory audit report.

Let's first take a close look at the first IT interview and see what we can learn.

This system has a lot of problems and the audit client, even after knowing that the auditors would be arriving soon and asking a lot of questions, did little to improve the situation.

First IT Billing System Interview

- Question 2b is the first problem where the auditor sees an issue after ascertaining that there are many operational problems with the Billing system. Here, the audit client responds that there are a few test plans. The audit client could just have answered "yes" and then let the auditor ask if there were test plans for all the testing. He fed the auditor.
- The answer to question 2c where the auditor asks if there are testing procedures again could have been answered with just a "yes" and let the auditor pursue. The answer "some" is another flag for the auditor.
- The answer to 5d is getting the audit client in more trouble. There were numerous problems with choosing Kara Jennings to be the project manager and then she is replaced with Ari Hemhurst who

has no project management experience and the audit client does not even know how much project management education he has. The audit client should have been prepared to answer these questions about project management.

- The answers to questions 7 are just as troubling and a concern to the auditor. The system is not fully documented and controls are not documented. The audit client should have started working on the system documentation, including controls, before the auditor arrived. In that way, he could have said that this was a known problem and that steps were in progress to address the issue and were being worked on.
- The answer to question 8c "are errors promptly corrected and entered back into the system?" is damaging when answered "not always" and then followed up by saying correction procedures are not documented. Again, efforts should have been underway to correct this before the auditors arrived. Even if the procedures were not completed, they could have been plans being executed to correct this problem.
- The answer to question 8e "how much revenue is being delayed?" should have been answered with I don't know, but I will check and get back to you. It is bad enough that the audit client does not know but he should at least let the auditor know that he will find out. This could be a significant problem if there is huge amount of delayed revenue.
- In question 9e, the auditor is asking for results of the business continuity testing. Instead of answering just that the results were successful but never documented, the audit client could have volunteered that the auditor could ask other organizations involved and provide verbal evidence, at least. This could have mitigated any suspicion that the auditor might have had that it was never tested.
- Questions 10e is asking for a documented risk assessment and acceptance. Again, the audit client should have been aware of this exposure and started corrective actions to document.

This interview indicates not only that there were serious issues with developing and installing this system but also that nothing or very little had been done to rectify or resolve the problems.

Now let's examine the second interview.

Second IT Billing System Interview

- Question 2c asks for test cases and the audit client responded that they are not kept because they are too voluminous but then mentioned that they had test results. This is volunteering information that the auditor did not ask for. It opens up an additional request from the auditor to ask to see test results. This is OK if you have the test results, but be careful when volunteering additional information.
- Question 2e is where the auditor is asking why two test results were not approved. The audit client answers as best that he could. He does not make anything up. He tells her that he is not sure but will research and get back. Good approach.
- In question 3e, the auditor is looking for customer sat surveys. The audit client correctly responds that he will check with the customer first to see if they can be shown to the auditor.
- In question 8c, the auditor asks if rejected errors are corrected promptly and entered back into the system. The response was "not always"—a better response might have been "we correct them and re-enter them as quickly as we can" and then let the auditor ask more follow-up questions.
- In question 8e, the auditor is asking if revenue is delayed due to errors not timely being corrected and re-entered promptly. Good answer here in that more research will be done before getting back to the auditor.
- Question 10e is looking for post approval on an emergency change from the manager's backup after the manager left. The answer was that it does not exist. The audit client could have added any auxiliary controls that were exercised. For example, there was a review by others of the actual coding change done later and there was no additional problem identified. This could give the auditor a sense that you did all you could to ensure that the change was good and nothing else was changed at the time of the emergency.

In general, the problems identified in the 2nd interview were a lot less serious and the audit client was better prepared to anticipate the auditor's questions. When the answers were not known the audit client told the auditor that he would get back to her. This was a much better job in making the auditor feel more comfortable with the audit. The first interview will probably lead the auditor to push for an unsatisfactory audit report based on her interview and exposures noted, and the second interview will probably result in a satisfactory audit report with recommendations for improvement.

The interview is one of the most critical elements in the audit and it could mean the difference in the case of a financial statement audit between an unqualified, qualified, or adverse audit report and the difference between a satisfactory or unsatisfactory audit report for an information systems audit.

Plan before the auditors arrive to identify problems as a result of peer reviews or self-assessments and start establishing or enhancing procedures and controls. Being able to anticipate what the auditors will ask for should help you to avoid surprises and to be prepared. And remember, do not leave inexperienced staff alone during the interviews, have someone take notes, and tell your staff never to lie to the auditor. Many an interview session will be, to use a metaphorically used expression, ***showtime***. This is the time where you can either help yourself in succeeding to convince the auditor that you have a well controlled and efficient process or where you will fail to convince the auditor of the former and are yanked off the stage by your executive.

Writing Fact Sheets

During the mock audits, those who are playing the role of auditor, will be writing announcement letters, conducting interviews, writing fact sheets (also called finding sheets), and then writing audit reports and presenting them to the executives. In an actual audit, the issues and exposures cited in the fact sheets will stem from the interviews and the documentation that the auditors reviewed.

However, for the purpose of the mock audit, the fact sheets *will be mutually exclusive* from the interview and you should take the liberty of identifying significant issues for the functions you reviewed. You should be noting only serious issues in detail in the fact sheets. You will need to contrive issues from any notable potential control issues that you learned that could occur from any of the material previously covered during the class. *Do not rely on the interviews for your detail.* I will be discussing the format of the fact sheets below.

Those who are portraying audit clients in the mock audits will carefully review the fact sheets and assume that there are factual errors or misleading statements. You will either sign off on the fact sheets or refuse to sign, due to any misstatements—your call.

These fact sheets play a very important role during the audit since the facts that are stated here, along with the recommendations will most likely be moved into the audit report once the facts are agreed with.

Now let us look at two examples of fact sheets, which auditors could have possibly written, that can help you understand what you might expect to see stated in fact sheets and that could be reflected in final audit reports. One will be on Change Management and the other on Completeness of Cash Receipts (Exhibits 18.9 and 18.10).

Exhibit 18.9 Example of a fact sheet for Change Management

ChangeManagement

Introduction: The Change Management process was reviewed to see if it provides reasonable assurance that changes to application systems (throughout program development, upgrades and maintenance) are authorized, tested and approved prior to being installed in production. The Change Management Process includes recording, tracking and approval from request being submitted to promotion including emergency promotions and version control.

Observations: 1) The Change Management Process is not documented. 2) The activities, roles and responsibilities associated with managing change requests are not clearly defined.

Concerns/Risk: Without a documented process, members of the team may perform the work in an inconsistent or even fraudulent manner, failing to obtain the necessary approvals or apply appropriate controls.

Recommendations: Document details of the Change Management Process that includes 1) all activities to be done to complete a change request 2) roles and responsibilities 3) the required approvals for a change request 4) activities for handling exceptions such as emergency changes

Exhibit 18.10 Example of a fact sheet for Completeness of Cash Receipts

Completeness of Cash Receipts

Introduction: A major misstatement related to the completeness assertion is that cash for checks are lost or stolen before recorded in the cash receipts records. Proper segregation of duties and a lockbox system are strong controls for ensuring that this assertion is met. An additional control is reconciliation of the daily cash receipts with the amounts posted to customers' accounts in the accounts receivable subsidiary ledger.

Observations: 1) We reviewed 50 checks received during the audit period and found 20 (40%) were not properly endorsed. Fifteen were not endorsed and five were endorsed by employees who were not authorized. 2) In addition, there was no documented procedure for the reconciliation of daily cash receipts with posting to accounts receivable subsidiary ledger. 3) We also found that one employee had access to both the cash receipts and accounts receivable records. 4) There was no lockbox.

Concern/Risk: When a lockbox system is not used checks need to be restrictively endorsed when received and a daily cash listing prepared. When an entity does not have adequate separation of duties, an employee has the ability to steal cash and manipulate the accounting records to hide the misstatement.

Recommendations: 1) Establish a lock box system 2) Document a daily reconciliation process of daily cash receipts 3) Establish adequate separation of duties 4) Ensure checks that are received are properly endorsed.

Summary

During the mock audits those students, who are role playing as auditors, will be writing individual announcement letters addressed to the audit clients. They will announce the start date and target end dates of the audit, the audit period and the scope of what the audit will cover. Kickoff meetings will be simulated and they will be followed by interview sessions. The interview sessions are where the importance and challenges of actual audits should become apparent. The auditors will generate questions based on the answers that they receive from the audit client and their staffs. The responses to the auditors can be based on material covered in class or fabricated. What is important is to see how the auditors respond to the answers they receive and to demonstrate the continuous barrage of audit questions that the audit clients will be subjected to.

The interviews will be followed by the writing of finding sheets, or fact sheets, where the auditors will include introductions to the functions reviewed, observations, concerns/risks followed by recommendations. The functions selected for the findings sheets are just for serious issues. During the mock audits, findings sheets should be reviewed by the audit clients. The audit client needs to argue the information in the finding sheets if they are inaccurate or misleading since they are the basis for the audit report.

Guidelines

1. Auditors should use the announcement letter suggestions that are included in this chapter, but they can use their own originality, if they want.
2. When the interviews are conducted, the auditors should bring to class questionnaire formats with a number of original questions. The instructor will decide on the number of original questions that are required. As a result of the interview, the auditors will add follow-up questions.
3. The audit clients will pretend to have documentation to give to the auditors or they will tell the auditors that the documentation or requests asked will be supplied or responded to as soon as possible or that it is not available.
4. The audit clients can provide answers based on accepted and widely known controls that they can pretend to have or they can make up lies or stories and see what the auditor does with the responses. This should not happen in a real audit but unfortunately, it does.

CHAPTER 19

Writing and Presenting Mock Audit Reports

During the mock audits, the auditors after the completion of their field-work will theoretically analyze what they found and write a final audit report. But for the mock audit, the auditors will not be limited to the concerns noted as a result of the interviews. The audit report and interview sessions *are mutually exclusive exercises.* The material in the audit reports is not reflective of the issues and concerns that were noted in the interviews—the issues and exposures do not have to be the same as noted in the interviews. When you write the audit reports you are almost starting from scratch. The only material from any previous exercise that you will use in the audit report wording will come from the fact sheets. We will indicate shortly how you should insert the material from the fact sheets, that you previously wrote, and place the wording directly into the audit reports.

Since the writing of the audit report is the culmination of what you learned during the course, take a great deal of time in putting it together—it should play a significant role in your final grade. Because of its importance, I will repeat much of the wording that is in Chapter 4 describing the format and content of the audit report and then spend time on presenting some examples that hopefully will help you generate your own reports.

During the course of a regular audit, the lead auditor will confer with his or her team, will review all the fact sheets, and put together an audit

E. Danter, *Audit Defense*, Palgrave Studies in Accounting and Finance Practice, https://doi.org/10.1007/978-3-030-92466-9_19

report. The overall audit opinion should be a consensus among the team members. However, for the mock audit exercise, each student, who is an auditor, will be assuming the role of lead auditor—you will be writing your own report. One important point is that the audit reports should be adverse or unsatisfactory reports with numerous material exposures and concerns.

Audit Report Format

You should follow the format below for the audit report or something very close to it:

- Salutation—This indicates who the recipient of the audit report is. It is usually the business process owner or his or her executive. It also includes the name of the process that was audited and an indication of who is sending the report, usually the lead auditor.
- Introduction—The introduction describes the process or processes that were audited, what the purpose of the audit was, when the audit was started, when it was completed, and the names of the auditors who participated in the audit.
- Scope—The scope indicates the functions within the process that were audited and the period of time that the audit covered, from when to when. The period of time is usually six months or one year. For example, from January 1, 2020, to July 1, 2020, or from January 1, 2020, to December 31, 2020.
- Executive Summary—This is the opinion that the audit staff reached, expressed by the lead auditor. It is a summary of major or significant issues written so that executives, who may not choose to read all the detail in the report, can understand the overall control posture of the functions in the process that was audited. The executive summary should be able to stand by itself and identify all of the significant issues with a summary of supporting information. It should describe the major functions in the audit where issues were identified and the relative exposures in each of these areas. Executive might decide to read the details of the report, if they wish, and are not limited by time. However, they should be able to determine if the audit is satisfactory or not, know where exposures exist and what the ramifications and weaknesses are that have a negative impact on the business, just by reading the executive summary.

- Details—The fact sheets that you wrote should be moved, almost verbatim, into the detail section of the audit report. We will assume that agreement was reached on the fact sheets with the audit client and the fact sheet verbiage can be moved into the Details Section of the audit report. This should eliminate or minimize any surprises. The audit clients, after reading and agreeing with the fact sheets, should be aware of what exposures, if any, will appear in the final audit report. If done correctly, each function that was reviewed should have a detail finding, if there was an issue. If no issues were found with a particular function, the auditor should state that there were no exposures in this area. If he or she has not indicated this in the report, you should ask them to include a positive statement to this effect in the report. Each function appearing in the final report, again these are issues, should have a description of the purpose of the function, observations on what exposures were found, what the concern or risk is with the exposure(s) cited, and recommendation(s) as what could be done to address the issue. The recommendations are the auditors' recommendations and do not have to be agreed to by the audit client, although it would be advisable for the auditor to discuss the recommendations with the audit client and their staff before they appear in the final audit report. This should be done in our mock audit exercises.
- Key Controls—The auditor should indicate the controls that were in place and effectively being executed that were good. The audit client would benefit from knowing to continue to execute these controls. The auditors should also state procedures that are well documented, effectively working and well controlled within a process. As an audit client, you should be given credit for what is working well. If the praise is not apparent when the report is written then you should ask the lead auditor to do so. It is the auditor's report so they may agree or not agree. At the very least, you should ask that credit be given when deserved. You have nothing to lose by asking and can benefit, if credit is given.
- Closed Items—If an audit client resolved issues during the course of the audit, they should be given credit. The issues that were closed during the audit can be listed.
- Copies—The audit manager and the audit client's manager should be copied on the report. The common practice is to copy everyone on the report who was copied on the announcement letter.

Examples of Audit Reports[1]

The format of audit reports can vary from company to company. It is the company's decision on what format they will want the audit reports to use. However, the format below is what we use for the mock audit report.

The examples that follow are for audit reports for financial statements and audit reports for information systems. You will notice some differences in the wording between the two, especially with the functions that are indicated in the scope (Exhibit 19.1).

Exhibit 19.1 Example of financial statement audit report

Organization: (insert company name) manufacturing company   Location: Albany, New York

To: Sam Peel, *(insert company name)* Revenue Manager   Date: December 27, 2020

From: Internal Audit

Introduction: *(insert company name)'s* internal audit staff conducted an audit of the Revenue Process at *(insert company name)* in Albany, New York. The company's annual average revenue for the last five years was 130 million dollars. The objective of the audit is to give reliability and creditability to the financial reports that are distributed to shareholders. The audit began on November 1, 2020, and was completed on December 22, 2020. The audit team lead was Michelle Young and the other auditors were Brian Pickett, Liz Maloney, and Eric Lee. We wish to thank Sam Peel, the revenue manager, and his staff for their cooperation and support.

Scope: We conducted our audit in accordance with the standards of the Generally Accepted Auditing Standards. The standards require that we perform an audit to obtain reasonable assurance about whether the financial statements were free of material misstatements and whether effective internal controls over financial reporting were maintained. Our scope included a review of functions that supported the revenue process from

[1] Audit report examples can be found in:

Davis Chris, Schiller Mike (2011) "Auditing—Using Controls to Protect Information Assets"—second edition, pages (52–57).

Messier William, Glover Steven, Prawitt Douglass (2014) "Auditing & Assurance Services: A Systematic Approach"—ninth edition (pages 247–249, 612–619).

September 1, 2019, to August 30, 2020. These functions were order entry, credit authorizations, shipping, billing, cash receipts, accounts receivable, and the general ledger.

Note:
An executive summary, or opinion, is written so that someone who does not have the time or inclination to read all the detail can understand the overall state of controls in the environment. It should be able to stand by itself but not discuss every issue, only significant issues. The executive summary summarizes the observation from the fact sheets that were previously written and will be in the detail of the audit report. The executive summary just highlights the issues from the fact sheets but with enough substance so the reader will know the issues that you found and the concerns.
Example of a poor executive summary: We found that controls were generally well designed and effectively executed under management governance. However, additional management focus is needed in the areas of billing, order entry, cash receipts, segregation of duties, shipping, and accounts receivable.
This is not giving the executives enough information.
A better executive summary would be:

Executive Summary: A material weakness is a deficiency or a combination of deficiencies, in internal controls over financial reporting, such that there is reasonable possibility that a material misstatement of the company's annual or interim financial statements will not be prevented or detected on a timely basis. There were material weaknesses in the areas of (1) billing where we found 30 examples of delayed billings for $128,000 and 15 instances of missed billings of $98,000 during the audit period, (2) order entry where .... (add in observations with numbers and percentages from fact sheets and concern), (3) cash receipts where .....(add in observations with numbers and percentages from fact sheets with concerns), and (4) segregation of duties where we found that one individual had responsibility for shipping and billing. Unauthorized shipments can be made and theft of goods possible (5) shipping where we found 45 unauthorized shipments, (6) accounts receivable where we found... (add in observations with numbers, dollars, and percentages with concerns from the fact sheets). In our opinion, because of the effect of the material weaknesses described above, the revenue department has not maintained effective control over financial reporting as of December 22, 2020.

Response: Mr. Sam Pellet should reply to Ms. Michelle Young on action to each recommendation in this report by March 1, 2021. Please copy Roberta Jones, audit manager and Luis Morales, CFO on your response,

Observations and Recommendations: (Insert the fact sheets detail here).

Key Controls: We found controls in the area of credit authorization and the general ledger to be effective and we had no concerns with these functions (Exhibit 19.2).

Sincerely,

Michelle Young
cc: Roberta Jones
cc: Luis Morales

Exhibit 19.2 Example of information system audit report

Organization: (insert company name) manufacturing company   Location: Albany, New York

To: Jessica Li, IT Development Manager   Date: December 27, 2020
From: Internal Audit

Introduction: *(insert company name)'s* internal audit staff conducted an audit of the new *(insert company name)* Billing System, that is operational in Seattle Washington. The objective of the audit is to review the accuracy and completeness of processing and adequacy of design and execution of controls supporting the billing system. The billing system was installed on September 1, 2016. The audit began on October 9, 2020, and was completed on December 5, 2020. The audit team lead was Juan Diego and the other auditors were Bob Lutz, Andrea Niche, and Ethan Holberg.

Scope: We reviewed the design of controls and effective execution of processes established and maintained in support of the billing system for the period from January 1 to July 30, 2020. These processes included separation of duties, project management, change management, business continuity plans in case of a disaster, user-id administration, privileges users, code testing, risk management, issues management, application controls, requirements processing, library control, data classification and protection, network control, error correction procedures, balancing and reconciliation, and password controls.

Example of a poor executive summary: We found that controls were generally well designed and effectively executed under management governance. However, additional management focus is needed in the areas of separation of duties, user id administration, risk management, and library control.

Again, this is not giving the executives enough information. It does not identify the actual problem or risk. A stronger executive summary would be:

Executive Summary: A number of significant control concerns were found during the functions audited. We found that 18 of 53 program change requests (PCRs) were not properly authorized. 5 of the 18 were authorized by the programmers themselves and 13 had no authorizations. Unauthorized changes could result in fraudulent activity. To add to the risk, we found that 3 of the 5 programmers, supporting the billing system had direct access to update code in the production library. This means that these programmers can alter production code functionality without going through proper testing and approval. Another concern that we observed was that there were 4 out of 6 (66%) monthly out of balance situations between total input and output records processed within the six month audit period. There was also no issues management process to identify the number of issues and to ensure that all issues that surfaced during the audit period were resolved. The development team is planning to develop an action plan to address these concerns. Further details are found in the Observations and Recommendations section below.

Response: Ms. Jessica LI should reply to Mr. Juan Divega by February 28, 2021, on action to each recommendation in this report. Ms. Rita Flynn, the audit manager and Mr. Sang Wing, IT director, should be copied on the response.

Observations and Recommendations: (insert fact sheets) This is detail of all the issues found in the functions audited that should be copied from the fact sheets that you wrote. Again, it is important to indicate your observations or issues you had when you reviewed a particular function, the concern and risk that exists and recommendations made.

Key Controls: *Give the audit client credit for what controls were effective that you noticed in administration controls.*

Closed items: *Indicate any items that were closed during the audit.*

Sincerely,

Jessica Li
cc; Ms. Rita Flynn

cc: Mr. Sang Wing

The example above starts off with a negative statement about controls in the executive summary. When you write your audit reports do not put a positive statement in the beginning of the executive summary. Your report should be a negative report, either an adverse financial statement report or an unsatisfactory information systems report and should read like one.

Presenting the Audit Report

After you have completed your audit report, the next segment of the mock audit exercise will be for the auditors to present their audit reports to the audit client executives. This is a sales pitch but one which needs to be approached carefully. The roles of both the auditor presenting the audit report and both the audit client and the audit client's executive, on the receiving end, need to be understood—jobs and livelihood are at stake.

The Auditor's Role

You will be presenting issues that surfaced during the audit along with recommendations to senior executives within your company. The purpose of your meeting with the executive is to make them aware of the seriousness on the exposures and of the risks involved. You need to understand that the executives should have received a heads-up from their management team and audit client before your meeting with them, but they may not have seen nor read an executive summary. The status reports that they received from their management team probably came from the fact sheets written and status meetings that were held. It is your mission to summarize the issues and concerns, to convince them of the seriousness of the findings, and obtain their sign-off before distributing the report. This will not be an easy task since you will be asking them to sign off with their agreement to the facts stated in unsatisfactory audit reports. The repercussions of them signing off on unsatisfactory audits could lead to a shortening of their careers, financial penalties, or just plain disappointment. They are not going to be eager to sign-off and the strength of your request for sign-off must be compelling. This will not be an easy task notably because of the negative repercussions that could evolve as previously stated but ego could also play a role. These executives will, in many cases, have many more years of experience in the business than you have and might be somewhat unsettled by your belief that you can tell them what they need to do just after just a few weeks of what you learned during an audit. In their eyes, you are probably a novice to them and perhaps not in a position to voice judgment on how they execute their processes.

The Audit Client's Role

You will need to defend yourself to the best of your ability but within reason while treating the auditor with respect and hearing them out. There is a lot of attention that will placed on audit results and questions will be asked by the senior executives in your company (e.g. CFO. CIO), and possibly by the company's audit committee members.

When the auditor is meeting with your senior executive (this role can be played by your instructor) and presenting the final audit report, you should, playing the role of the audit client, be present. The purpose here is to ensure that the issues and concerns cited in the audit report are indeed factual and have been previously reviewed and concurred with. Your senior executive should not agree to sign unless you, the audit client, are comfortable with the accuracy and fairness of the report. This will depend on the interaction with your management team who were there from the start of the audit and a comparison of the final audit report to the fact sheets. The audit results are too important to just sign off and have it distributed without challenging the content, when there is doubt.

If the senior executive and audit client agree with the facts, the senior executive can still refuse to sign-off on the report if he or she disagrees with the overall opinion that the auditors reached. There might be a feeling that the risks are a lot less than what is stated in the auditor's opinion and or a belief that the report, although factual, is not taking into consideration the work that that was done and efforts underway to address known control weaknesses. The image that your organization is in dire straits, on the verge of significant financial consequences, is an opinion that the senior executive and audit client manager might not share. They could also feel that there are functions that are well-controlled and effective process and procedures in place but that your team is not getting credit that is due. Your senior executive can challenge the auditor before he or she signs but be careful here. If there is evidence to support the auditor's findings, they might be on thin ice by refusing to sign. They will need to justify your decision. They will need to review the *facts* with you very carefully. The senior executive can disagree with the facts and refuse to sign if the facts are erroneous or misleading. He or she will have a very difficult time in refusing to sign if they agree with the facts but not the overall opinion and believe that the report is misleading, in their opinion.

Summary

Each auditor will write their own audit report during the mock audit exercise. The audit reports will not be a reflection of what they encountered during their interviews. It will be a totally separate effort collecting issues, concerns, risks, and recommendations that can be extracted from the finding sheets that were composed. The executive summary highlights the significant issues for the executives but gives them enough information with numbers and percentages so they realize the seriousness of the exposures. Each auditor will present their audit report during the mock audit and should be able to convince the senior executive of major risks. The audit client executive (can be a role played by the instructor) will need to rely on their management teams to having agreed with the facts in the report but do not have to necessarily agree with the auditor's opinion. They will need to justify not signing if that is the decision they reach.

Guidelines

1. Auditors should use numbers and percentages in the audit report.
2. Auditors should copy and paste the information from their finding sheets to the audit report placing them under a section titled "Detail" or "Observations and Recommendations."
3. Audit client executives should make sure that their management who are audited (audit clients) are present in the meetings where the auditors are presenting the audit report and asking for sign-off.
4. Senior executives and audit clients should make sure that the audit report is factual and fair before they sign-off. They do not have to sign-off and agree with the recommendations. These are the auditor's recommendations and will be responded to separately.

Conclusion

Utilizing this textbook for your education is not a guarantee that you will pass audits. It is not a panacea. It is a starting step—hopefully a significant step on your journey to success. Use the information detailed along with the exercises and quizzes that are in the textbook and those that your instructors will provide, along with class discussions, to enhance your preparation to be audit ready.

This textbook is divided into four parts. Part I discusses the need for corporate governance, regulations, and control frameworks, that became more essential as a result of the scandals that occurred in the beginning of the twenty-first century. These scandals including Enron, WorldCom, Tyco, HealthSouth, Adelphi, and others were instrumental in increasing the need for corporate governance and increased audit activity. Students should further research these scandals. There are many noteworthy publications that can be researched to obtain more detail and deeper understanding of how they occurred and the repercussions of corporate governance failure. Part I also discusses the audit process from auditors pre-planning their audits through the writing and distribution of the final audit report. Part II will provide the students with insight into the importance and benefits of controls while educating the reader on the types of controls that includes preventive, detective, deterrent, reporting and correcting controls and discusses administrative controls, physical controls, access controls, operational controls, security, and separation of duties. The controls are examined both from a financial statement

E. Danter, *Audit Defense*, Palgrave Studies in Accounting and Finance Practice, https://doi.org/10.1007/978-3-030-92466-9

audit and from an information systems audit perspective. Students should utilize the books and material referenced at the end of each chapter for additional education and further research. Part III describes pro-active measures that audit clients should take in preparation for audits. Audit client should be cognizant of the control issues that exist, understand the risks, and testing that they should apply to validate that controls are effective. Part IV describes mock audits that will help students familiarize themselves with the audit process by actually simulating and participating in an audit.

Be prepared and be audit ready. Internal auditors are well schooled and educated in conducting audits but the establishment of a level playing field, where you, as prospective audit clients, are also educated, is essential and beneficial. Adequate training and preparation should help you to adequately defend yourself and avoid being surprised by an auditor's approach, their questions, the audit process, and of course, the audit result. Take pro-active measures and avoid having an illusion of control. You need to design, install, and be able to demonstrate effective execution of as many required controls, as addressed in this textbook, as possible, *before* audits are announced.

If you can't implement the controls that you feel are needed, at least establish corrective action plans with target dates to resolve identified exposures. Document appropriate risk assessments, when possible, and obtain executive approvals on decisions made and steps taken to eliminate, reduce or accept risks. These actions will help you and best serve your company. There are many benefits from having effective controls in place. And not having them established, and the absence of correction action plans can be disastrous, resulting in unwanted events—be able to defend yourself and avoid disappointing outcomes.

The objective of this textbook was to highlight basic processes, procedures, and controls that you will need to establish in order to achieve success. You should be able to apply the knowledge you obtained on controls and the audit process to prepare for audits while gaining audit experience during the mock audit exercises and role playing. The intent is to first learn and then to apply what you learn. I sincerely hope that the objective was achieved and that your audit challenges will be successfully met.

Index

A
Access to the tape library, 122
Accountability, 27
Accountants, 7
Accounting Separation of Duties, 184
Accounts payable department, 189
Accounts receivable, 186
Accuracy of processing, 136, 213
Adelphi, 12
Adequate control design, 77
Administrative controls, 97
After hour reviews, 128
Aged trial of balance, 185
A Marginal opinion, 75
Analytical procedures, 74
Anderson, Arthur, 11
An Illusion of control, 265
Announcement letter, 31, 33
Annual reviews, 92
Anti-virus programs, 142
Anti-virus software programs, 142
An Unsatisfactory opinion, 75
Application access, 136
Application access controls, 136
Application and system failures, 80
Application audit, 214
Application balancing, 217
Application changes, 154
Application code, 136
Application controls, 207
Application data, 132
Application data, tables, and libraries, 136
Application developers, 131
Application development department, 209
Application development organizations, 211
Application documentation, 252
Application monitoring, 219
Application Owners, 209
Approve access, 106
Approve access to code, 182
Approve access to production data, 182
Approve code promotion to production, 183

E. Danter, *Audit Defense*, Palgrave Studies in Accounting and Finance Practice, https://doi.org/10.1007/978-3-030-92466-9

Approve code promotion to UAT, 183
Approve request to change code, 182
A Satisfactory opinion, 75
Auditability, 80
Audit client(s), v, 1
Audit committee(s), 5, 16
Audit director, 33
Audit findings, 38, 271
Audit interface, 35, 52
Audit interviews, 47
Audit logs, 102
Auditor, v
Auditor-in-charge, 33
Auditors' opinions, 50
Audit process, 36
Audit readiness, 1
Audit ready, vi, 35
Audit ready posture, 272
Audit report
  audit client's manager, 61
  audit manager, 61
  draft of, 63
  executive summary, 60
  favorable comments, 61
  introduction, 60
  issues and concerns, 65
  recommendations, 61
    accept the recommendation, 62
    rationale for rejection, 63
    reject the recommendation, 62
    respond to the recommendation, 63
  salutation, 60
  scope, 60
  sign off on, 64
Audit reports, 270
Audit response, 62
Audit trail, 45, 182
Authorizing and granting access to applications, 138
Authorizing auditor, 76
Automated controls, 97

B

Backup and restart procedures, 222
Back up data, 222
Badge reader(s), 116, 128
Balancing/data base reconciliation, 217
Balancing routines, 214
Billing, 185
"Blanket" SR, 155
Board of Directors, 16
Building access, 116
Business continuity, 164
Business continuity testing, 336
Business need, 108
Business process, 4, 254
Business process owners, 2
Business Recovery and Continuity, 163
Business risks, 84

C

Capital assets, 197
Cash receipts, 185
CEO, 81
CFO, 81
Challenges, viii
Change application code, 183
Change control process, 162
Change management, 154
Change request (CR), 154
Checkpoint, 222
Chief Audit Executive (CAE), 5, 17, 19
CIO, 81
Classification of data, 124
Clean desk reviews, 125
Cloud computing, 227
  broad network access, 232
  measured service, 232

on demand self-service, 232
rapid elasticity, 232
resource pooling, 232
Cloud provider, 233
COBIT 5, 26
COBIT framework, 28
Code migration, 158
Coding error, 140
Collections, 186
Collusion, 174
Combination lock, 123
Commingling of information assets, 233
Committee of Sponsoring Organizations (COSO), 23
Completeness, 80
Completeness of processing, 213, 215
Compliance reviews, 99
Computer crime, 77
Computer network, 140
Computer Operations Department, 209
Computer operators, 120
Computer room control, 119
Computer viruses, 140
Confidential and sensitive financial data, 119
Confidential physical control, 123
Continued business need, 133
Contractors, 120
Control benefits, 79
Control, category
corrective controls, 90
detective controls, 89
deterrent controls, 88
preventive controls, 87
recovery controls, 90
reporting controls, 89
Control challenges, 241
Control environment, 27
Control exposures, 59
Control importance, 76
Control Objectives for Information and Related Technology (COBIT), 24
Control points, 84
Controls, vi
Corporate governance, 4, 9
Corporate scandals, 77
Corrective action plans, 163
Corrective actions, 59
COSO framework, 23
Cost accounting, 195
Cost effectiveness, 85
Covered entities, 239
CPAs, 238
Create/develop UAT data, 183
Credit authorizations, 185
Critical errors, 100
Custody of the securities, 199
Customer expectations, 75
Customer satisfaction, 266
Customer sat surveys, 337
Cyber security, 77, 78, 139, 227

D

Database administrative (DBADM) authority, 134
Database reconciliation, 224
Data integrity, 240
Data tables, 157
Deactivation, 110
Delay in complying, 44
Desk procedures, 252, 262
Destruction of classified information, 125
Detailed procedures, 252
Develop alternative solution, 286
Development library, 157
Director of Internal Audit, 17
Disaster plan(s), 164, 167
Disaster recovery plan, 164
Disbursements, 189

Division of responsibilities, 172
Documentation, 44
Documentation requests, 44
Document Change History, 103
Documented business recovery, 167
Documented restart procedures, 222
Documented service level agreement, 99
Document of Understanding (DOU), 98, 235
Dollar amount, 213
Downstream applications, 213
Downstream program, 295
Duplicate processing, 224
Duplicate transmission, 213

E

Early warning of processing problems, 80
Editing and auditing data, 215
Efficiency, 80
Electronically transmitting confidential data, 125
Electronic Protected Health Information (EPHI), 239
Eliminating exposure, vii
Emergency changes, 154, 160
Employee badges, 116
Employee payments of services and benefits, 193
Encryption guidelines, 125
Encryption of data, 234
Endless loop, 219
End users, 132
End user satisfaction, 80
Enron, 11
Enterprise risk management (ERM), 285
Erroneous activities, 9
Erroneous data, 215, 224
Error correction procedures, 215
Error handling, 215
Error reports, 215
Escorted visitors with a business need, 123
European Court of Auditors, 15
Execute UAT, 183
Execution of controls, 75
Executive approval, 62
Executive manager, 64
Exposures, 47
External audit firms, 10, 31
External audits, 7

F

Fact sheets, 49
Fastow, Andrew, 11
Fear of reprisal, 266
Federal legislature, 79
File transfer protocol (FTP), 144
Final audit report, 53
Financial Instruments and Exchange (FIE), 15
Financial losses, vii
Financial process, 184
Financial reporting, 23
Financial statement audits, 3, 310
  accuracy, 74
  authorization, 74
  classification, 74
  completeness, 74
  cutoff, 74
  material misstatements in, 74
  occurrence, 74
  result
    A Disclaimer of Opinion, 75
    A Qualified Opinion, 75
    An Adverse Opinion, 75
    An Unqualified Opinion, 74
  SOX compliance, 74
Finding sheets, 49
Finished Goods Stores, 195

Firewalls, 143
First line manager, 21
Fraud, 9, 34
Fraudulent activity(ies), vii, 77, 80, 154

G
General Ledger, 186, 189
Golden rule, 182
Grant and remove access, 131
Granting access, 106
Guidelines for the mock audit preparation, 308

H
Hackers, 139
Header record, 213
Health Insurance Portability and Accountability Act (HIPAA), 124, 239
HealthSouth, 13
High level procedures, 252
High risk area, 167
HIPAA compliance, 78, 239
Human Resources, 40
Human Resources department, 192
Hypertext transfer protocol (HTTP), 144

I
Identify and authenticate users, 133
ImClone, 13
Incomplete data, 215, 224
Independent accounting firms, 10
Information protection, 234
Information System Audit, 3
Information system design, 75
Information Systems Audit and Control Association (ISACA), 24
Information systems controls, 75
Information Technology audits, 2
Initiating auditor, 76
Input, output and interface controls, 213
Integrated audit, 207
Integration testing, 295
Integrity of processing, 136
Internal Audit Director, 19
Internal audit (IA) organization, 31
Internal auditor, vi
Internal Audit Services (IAS), 15
Internal audit staff, 18
Internal controls, 21
Inventory ledger, 195
Inventory management, 195
Inventory of spreadsheets, 228
Inventory process, 195
Invoice processing, 189
Issuance of stock, 198
Issues log, 282
Issues management process, 162, 262, 281
IT department, 136
IT interview, 335
IT organization, 136
IT professionals, 2

J
Job control language, 157

K
Key control, 45
Key lock, 123
Key Performance Indicators (KPIs), 103
Keys to the kingdom, 132
Kickoff meeting, 31, 35
Kozlowski, Dennis, 14

L
Lay, Kenneth, 11

Lead auditor, vi, 33, 52
Legal and regulatory laws, 17
Librarian, 158
Library control, 156, 165
Log, 45
Logging, 44
Logical access, 131

M
Maintenance costs, 80
Malicious virus, 143
Malware, 79, 140
Manual controls, 79, 83, 97
Manufacturing, 195
Master keys, 120
Material misstatement, 174
Medical data, 124
Medical information, 124
Memorandum of Understanding (MOU), 98, 235
Metrics, 103, 211
Minimizing risk, viii
Mischievous virus, 143
Mission of the audit staff, 36
Mitigate risk, 177
Mitigating exposure, vii
Mock Audit, 2
Monitor access, 132
Multi-tenancy environment, 235

N
National Committee on Fraudulent Financial Reporting, 23
New managers, 265

O
Observations and Recommendations, 352
Omitted processing, 224
On-demand network access, 231
Order entry, 185
Organization chart, 36
Organizations
  accept risk, 284
  avoid risk, 284
  reduce risk, 284
  risk sharing, 284
  transfer risk - mitigate the risk, 284
Output control, 214
Outside accounting firms, 31
Outsourcing, 235
Outsourcing controls, 227
Outsourcing environment, 236
Overstatement of inventory, 196
Owner of the data, 178

P
Parallel testing, 296
Password controls, 106
Password Guidelines, 108
Password requirements, 113
Password rules, 110
Passwords, 110
Passwords revoked automatically, 108
Payment of dividends, 198
Payroll processing, 193
Peer managers, 274
Peer reviews, 269
Penetration testing, 235
Percentages and numbers relating to the issues, 49
Performance, 80
Performance level, 98
Personal and sensitive data, 124
Personal information physical control, 123
Physical inventory, 198
Physical security, 115
Physical tape inventory, 121
Pilot testing, 297
Plans for remediation, 67

Portable storage media, 121
Possibility of fraud, 136
Postponement in complying, 44
Potential duplicate data, 214
Pre-approval, 182
Pre-planning, 31, 32
Pre-planning session, 32
Presenting the audit report, 350
Previous audits, 270
Primary accountability for overall control, 81
Printer rooms, 119
Prior audit issues, 39
Privacy, 234
Privileged access, 132, 133
Privileged users, 133
Pro-active activities, 246
Pro-active measures, 33, 35
Procedures, vi, 47, 252
Process, vi, 32, 252
Process documentation, 252
Process flow, 257
Processing auditor, 76
Process issues management, 281
Process narratives, 255
 business rules, 256
 control points, 256
 dependencies and relationships, 256
 input, 256
 key events, 256
 output, 256
 process description, 255
 process improvement plans, 256
 process measurements, 256
 process name, 255
 process objective, 255
 process owner, 255
 process scope, 255
 roles and responsibilities, 255
Process owner, 107
Production data, 179
Production environment, 296
Production library(ies), 155, 158
Program change request (PCR), 154
Programmers, 131
Project management, 210
Project manager, 210
Promote code, 178
Promote code to production, 183
Promote code to UAT, 183
Promotion of code, 158
Property, plant, and equipment records, 198
Proprietary physical control, 123
Protected health information (PHI), 239
Protective barriers, 115
Protocol of the audit, 36
Provide access to production data, 182
Public clouds, 233
Public Company Accounting Oversight Board (PCAOB), 16
Purchasing department, 189
Purchasing process, 188

Q
Quality management, 211
Quality of processing, 80
Quantification of the exposure, 286

R
RACF (Resource Access Control Facility) administrator, 135
Ransomware, 140
Raw Materials Stores, 195
Reagan, Ronald, 22
Receivables, 186
Receiving department, 189
Recommendations, 52
Reconciliation report, 48
Record all requests, 45
Record count, 213

Recording auditor, 76
Recording transactions auditor, 76
Recoverability, disaster, 80
Recovery control, 222
Recovery procedure, 222
Red flag, 172
Regression testing, 296
Regulatory compliance, 171
Reliability, 98
Remediation, 38
Repurchase of stock, 198
Request access to production data, 181
Request for access, 107
Request form, 107
Request for proposal (RFP), 189
Request for quotation (RFQ), 189
Request log, 46, 57
Requests for documentation, 34
Requisitioning function, 188
Response time frame, 67, 99
Responsiveness, 98
Restart procedure, 222
Restore data, 222
Restricted areas, 119
Restricted physical access, 119
Revalidation, 133
Revalidation of access, 139
Revenue functions, 184
Reviewing audit reports, 17
Revoke access, 108
Revoke user IDs, 108
Rigas family, 12
Rigas, John, 12
Rigas, Timothy, 12
Risk acceptance, 288
Risk assessment, 4, 27, 38, 86, 225
Risk assessment form, 284, 285
Risk assessment owner, 285
Risk assessment process, 283
Risk management, 211, 280
Risk revalidation, 288
Risks, viii
Role-play, 2
Role playing as auditors, 309
Roles and responsibilities, 36
Run books, 102

S

Safeguarding of assets, 312
Sarbanes Oxley control requirements, 28
Sarbanes Oxley (SOX), 9, 10
SAS70 report, 238
Scope creep, 57
Scope of the audit, 34
Screen shot, 159
Scrushy, Richard, 13
Secondary control process, 158
Secondary controls, 54
Section 302, 18
Section 404, 18
Securities and investments, 198
Securities ledger, 199
Security guards, 115, 116
Security threats, 142
Self-assessment(s), 162, 264
Senior executives, 18
Senior management, 18
Separate libraries, 167
Separate responsibilities, 83
Separation of duties, 83, 162, 172, 175
Sequence number, 213
Service company, 124
Service level agreement (SLA), 97
Service level objectives, 98
Service Level Priorities, 103
Service organization, 72
Service Organization Control Report (SOC), 236
Service Provider Responsibilities, 103
Shared pool of computing resources, 231

Shipping, 185
Show-stopper, 172
Sidgmore, John, 15
Sign in desk, 128
Sign off on a fact sheet, 53
Simulated audits, 2
Skilling, Jeff, 11
Small coding changes, 297
SoD matrix, 181
Software bug, 140
Special access, 132
Specifications and requirements, 294
Spreadsheet applications, 228
Spreadsheet controls, 227
Staff member, 53
Status meetings, 34, 51
Status meeting schedule, 36
Stockholders' equity, 197, 198
Successful audits, vi
Surprise audit, 33
Suspicious activity, 215
Swim lanes, 257
SYSADM authority, 134
SYSCTRL authority, 134
SYSMAINT authority, 134
System access, 108
System access controls, 131
System administrators, 132
System request (SR), 154
Systems administrators, 134
System security, 139
Systems testing, 296
System support personnel, 132, 134

T

Tailgating into buildings, 116
Tape inventory control system, 121
Task management, 211
Task responsibilities, 262
Temporary access, 180, 183
Temporary ID, 180
Temporary libraries, 155
Termination of agreement, 99
Test cases, 298
Test data, 294
Test environment, 296
Testing activities, 4, 211
Test plans, 297
Test results, 298
The Illusion of control, 3
Third party access, 233
Timeliness, 80
Timeliness of processing, 136, 213, 215
Transmission dates, 214
Transmission number, 213
Treadway Commission, 23
Treadway, James, 23
Trojan horse, 141
Tyco, 14
Types of audits, 73

U

Unauthorized access to data in the cloud, 234
Unauthorized access to facilities, 115
Unauthorized shipments, 196
Uncorrected errors and rejects, 215
Understatement of inventory, 196
Unintentional erroneous processing, 86
Unit testing, 294
Unreasonable data, 224
Unsatisfactory audit, 61
Unsatisfactory audit reports, 47
Update access, 179
Update production data, 182
User acceptance testing (UAT), 183, 296
User ID Administration, 106

V

Version control, 157

Virus detection, 141, 142

Visitor's log, 120

Visitors to be escorted, 120

W

Waksal, Sam, 13
Work effort(s), 154
Work management, 211
WorldCom, 14
Worm, 140
Writing Announcement Letters, 309

The manufacturer's authorised representative in the EU is Springer
Nature Customer Service Centre GmbH, Europaplatz 3, 69115 Heidelberg,
Germany. If you have any concerns regarding our products, please
contact ProductSafety@springernature.com

Printed and bound by CPI Group (UK) Ltd, Croydon, CR0 4YY
30/09/2026
02225286-0014